MW00651025

To our readers:

Anne Clayton, with other contributors have provided you with this excellent resource for marketing yourself and building a career in the pharmaceutical industry. Please feel free to contact us through pharmaceuticalsales.com or RxSales@aol.com. All questions via email will receive a response, within 72 hours.

Pharmaceuticalsales.com would like to cite The Pharmaceutical Research and Manufacturers Association of America (PhRMA), for their annual industry publications and reference material for this publication.

International Standard Book number (ISBN)
ISBN 978-0-9665121-8-2
10th Anniversary Edition, Published 2008
15001008-7669

Previous Editions

ISBN 0-9665121-7-0	Seventh Edition, Published	2005
ISBN 0-9665121-4-6	Sixth Edition, Published	2004
ISBN 0-9665121-6-2	Fifth Edition, Published	2003
ISBN, 0-9665121-5-4	Fourth Edition, Published	2002
ISBN, 0-9665121-6-X	Third Edition, Published	2001
ISBN, 0-9665121-1-1	Second Edition, Published	1999
ISBN, 0-9665121-0-3	First Edition, Published	1998

Library of Congress Cataloging-in Publication
Insight into a Career in Pharmaceutical Sales by Anne Clayton
Previous Registration 1998-2008 TXu 870-129, TX 5-899-946
Audio Compact Disc, Insight into a Career in Pharmaceutical Sales©
Contributions by Helen Elizabeth Ellie, J.G. Reichard
Mary Hammer, Dee DeBoyd, Peggy Swanson. Cover art by Nancy Young.
Professional Audio narration by John Ulett
Audio CD's by Lambert Imaging and Production

pharmaceuticalsales.com
1734 Clarkson Road
Town and Country, Missouri 63017

Published in the United States of America
Printed in the United States of America

Table of Contents

Introduction

Congratulations! You have chosen the leading book for advice, direction and career guidance to enter the pharmaceutical industry. You have taken the first step towards a vital and challenging profession and are about to embark on a step-by-step journey to your career. Pharmaceutical industry representative positions are one of the most sought after careers and will continue to show exceptional opportunities as it has over the past 125 years. The industry will continue to provide the dedicated individual with the professional, business and personal satisfaction desired in one's career.

It has been a common misinterpretation that mass layoffs are affecting pharmaceutical representatives industry wide and to a small degree this is correct, with very large pharmaceutical companies having reductions. Recently the terms such as "Big Pharma", "Biotech", "Specialty Pharma" and "Medium and Small Pharma", came into the mainstream language to describe the general size and often culture of a company, but overall, the number of pharmaceutical representative positions in the United States has not changed of any great significance.

Growth/Decline	Big Pharma	Biotech	Specialty Pharma	Small/Medium Pharma
+ > 15%	0%	20%	20%	30%
+ 6 to 15%	35%	60%	0%	25%
+/- 5%	47%	20%	60%	45%
- 6 to 15%	18%	0%	0%	0%
- > 15%	0%	0%	20%	0%

Source: On file at pharmaceuticalsales.com inc.

One can see the reduction in "Big Pharma" and when these press releases are made, a 10% cut in an organization of over 120,000 employees makes quite an impact in the press and those employed in the industry. Then again, another company with 66,000 employees announces a 20% reduction, more bad news. But when a foreign owned smaller organization of 15,000 employees' doubles their salesforce in the United States, not much is published. In reality, there has been outstanding growth in the Biotech, Specialty and Small and Medium Size pharmaceutical/Biotech company segments in the last few years. This has not totally off set the decreases of the larger pharmaceutical concerns, but, don't be discouraged by a comment or headline (recently as one stated, "When will the bleeding stop on pharmaceutical representative sales job cuts"). In reality, the overall reduction has been approximately 2-3% in the United States. Take into account we are discussing over 100,000 positions nationwide, the reduction is nominal. Further enter that normal turnover in the positions of a pharmaceutical sales representative is 12-14% annually, you can understand the reality of some of these headlines. Of course this is not to minimize the complexity of emotions that one goes through when a reduction happens to you, for any loss of work is difficult and most pharmaceutical representatives will possibly face this occurrence over a 30 year career.

Now, it's time to think of you as starting on an exciting mission. You can see the end point quite clearly, you see yourself enjoying and excelling in a challenging, respected career. You are the consummate sales professional in one of the most thriving industries in America. You are making a great salary versus any comparable careers, which includes a benefit package that rivals any Fortune 100 company. However, you are not exactly sure how to obtain your job "offer" to join the pharmaceutical industry, from where you are today. Purchasing Insight into a Career in Pharmaceutical Sales (*Insight* for short) has placed you on the correct path.

Insight is going to lead you every step of the way. The mission of the book is simple: provide job candidates seeking employment as pharmaceutical representatives in the industry with the tools and tactics by which to succeed. Reading, learning, and applying the lessons in this book will provide you with the greatest course of action for success. By practicing and following the detailed plan that is contained here, you will obtain your offer and gain entry into the pharmaceutical industry and save months. Yes, it is going to challenge you in many ways, as it has for thousands since 1998. *Insight* was the first book written in 1998, to address this topic of gaining entry to the pharmaceutical industry as a pharmaceutical sales representative. Numerous candidates will continue to revert back to the traditional methods of a job search, sending out cover letters and paying for professionally written résumés, primarily using recruiters and attending job fairs. Often candidates will hear a pessimistic comment and conclude this as a fact. Please, implement the tactics of this book, learn the pharmaceutical industry, read and study the book, listen to the two Audio Compact Disk and commit to learning the total process.

Insight provides you with pertinent knowledge that only one can obtain by spending 30 years in the pharmaceutical industry in a variety of positions. Not just a few years as a field representative. Along with that, an additional 10 years with my past co-workers, now friends and contributors which have held and are currently employed in positions across the industry, including Field Sales, Specialty Sales, Biotech Sales, Hospital Sales, District Manager and Regional Director positions. In addition, positions as National Account Directors, Regional Account Managers, Directors of Managed Care, Sales Training Directors, Brand Managers and countless other personnel, of which a few, whose career paths have taken them to the Executive Vice President and CEO level (from the field sales position). Even all this personal experience and contacts is not enough though, so countless hours have been spent on researching trends, both the internal and external forces on the pharmaceutical environment, products and companies pipelines.

Insight includes information on approximately 50 pharmaceutical/biotech companies, saving you hours of research time and setting a template for you to research a company as I have done. Annual Reports, 10-K filings with the Security and Exchange Commission, numerous press releases, countless phone calls and industry publications have been diligently scoured for you on a weekly basis, constantly updating files.

As always, before any actual interview, remember that change happens every business day, so every interview or networking contact requires you to visit that organizations website and research all recent press releases, in addition, visit some investment websites.

Reading *Insight* will have you confident and ready. There is always additional information and educational publications that can also assist you, the more knowledge you compile, the better prepared you are.

Numerous books have followed since I published and released my first edition in 1998; some have great advice, much similar advice, and some have the same advice since it has been copied word for word. Use caution with many *associations* or so called *certification* programs that require you to pay substantial amount for being a *member*. You are asked to take a small test after reading their book. As stated, one entity copied word-by-word chapters of Insight, and then asked you take a test (as if you earned a degree), then sent you your certificate. I would suggest making a few calls to the pharmaceutical companies Human Resource's department to verify this is organization is endorsed or even known, let alone given permission of the use of their logo. Their answer will be non-biased and you will know the truth, which seems to be fair to all. You may save a few hundred dollars and more importantly, hours of your time.

Chapter 1, The Industry, gives you a current status of the industry, including some of the most important issues that are having influence today.

Chapter 2, The Pharmaceutical Sales Representative, *Insight* gives you an in-depth view of today's pharmaceutical representative. You will see what typical compensation packages are today, career advancement opportunities and positive and negative aspects of the position of a pharmaceutical representative. One must realize, this position is not an "easy" job and is often misunderstood by many.

Chapter 3, Résumés Although no resume will win you employment, many common mistakes will quickly eliminate you from the interview process. You will learn some simple rules for the pharmaceutical sales résumé's and how their role is diminished in this industry.

Preparation is the backbone of your job hunting endeavor. Understanding your target market is perhaps the most important step in securing your "offer". This industry is quite different than most in gaining interviews, this can not be stressed enough. How to gather and compile **Research** is outlined in **Chapter 4**. Some companies are privately held, requiring some extra effort when researching their history, products and pipelines.

Chapter 5, "It's *not who you know*; it's *who you learn to know*"
With the first edition in 1998, **networking** is what I wanted to describe as the number one priority for candidates. Still, many candidates will email me and complain that their "resume" is not getting any responses and "job fairs" seem like a waste of time. Candidates have the toughest time keeping **networking** as their number one priority, reverting back to sending those résumé's, mass mailings to Human Resource departments and using recruiters. Why? Because it is easy. If there were not so many previous editions out there of *Insight* over the past ten years, this would be the new title of the book (It's *not who you know*, it's *who you learn to know)*. This is the foundation of what I am trying to describe to you in step-by-step detail. The process is inverted, not starting with senior management, (but if your uncle is a CEO, use him) or a top executive, but your local pharmaceutical representative calling on physicians, right in your local area. This Chapter, when put into action, will be your test of your dedication and tenacity for this career. These two competencies are absolutely mandatory for pharmaceutical sales.

You're going to get feedback on your performance here, before you're in the position of pharmaceutical sales. It is your key to obtaining "the offer" and in detail it is explained, with even a script written for you to utilize, when networking. **Chapter 5** needs implementation consistently, on a daily basis. Surely utilize every avenue to secure a position, for individuals have obtained positions using search firms, someone they know, an advertisement, but networking, doing the work yourself, is what 97% of us must do, as I had to 40 years ago. This is number action to getting the "offer".

Now it is time to advance your career with some *Insight* methodology. **Chapter 6, The Interview**, puts you in the actual interview, with a variation of every question that you're going to encounter. One hundred and six questions and a suggested answer for each. It suggests ways to tailor your individual responses in order to maximize your impact with the interviewer. You will learn to present yourself admirably, which will have you progressing to the first, second and final "face to face" interviews. Though the pharmaceutical industry has changed dramatically over the past 40 years, the interview questions have not, as always, District Managers are seeking to learn and uncover "behavior characteristics" or "competencies" that predict your chances of success in this industry. In addition, a list of guidelines for professional attire, which is imperative to follow during every formal and informal meeting you have. In addition, two Audio CD's are included to compliment this chapter for one cannot just read it once and believe you are prepared. Upload to you Ipod, MP3, play in your car, and know them by heart, how you are going to respond.

Chapter 7, Questions provides another 22 questions for you to ask in the interview, which will compliment you as a candidate and distinguish you from over 97% of the other candidates. These questions will stimulate further questions from the District Manager, which will secure that your competencies have been revealed in the interview. Interviewing 7-10 candidates in a day is strenuous and interview recollection of each candidate starts to blend no matter how well your notes are from the day, so this is where you must differentiate yourself and stand out. Every District Manager is not an excellent interviewer, there is little training on how to interview, District Managers are as nervous as the candidate, for their success rate in the process nationally is about 63%.

There are three outcomes from every interview process. **Chapter 8, Decisions** reveals how to handle each situation, even "the offer", with the required composure that insures your best possible outcome.

Chapter 9, Profiles contains over fifty pharmaceutical company profiles, that offer an overview of each company, some with numerous subsidiaries or divisions. A sampling from large, medium, small and biotech companies is included, plus the segment of Contract Sales Organizations (CSO's).

Finally, **Chapter 10, Commitment**, is a lesson that is taught to any sales professional, which is asking for a particular action. Here, I am going to do what I was taught and ask you for a commitment and action, as your enter you pharmaceutical career.

Chapter One
The Industry

Not so many years ago discussions concerning national price controls weighed heavily on the pharmaceutical industry and its investors. It was an election year (early 90's) with strong talk of universal healthcare. Now, here we are, an election year, with promises again of lower health care cost and coverage for every American. In addition, increased utilization of generic drugs is becoming more prevalent. Numerous patent expirations of major blockbuster brand name drugs have decreased the need for vast salesforces. The industry has failed to launch or gain FDA approval of new novel drugs at the rate of prior years. These factors coupled with increasing constraints from payors, such as managed care, government and employers. Finally, financial markets have also tightened up funds for investments; venture capitol for start-ups and emerging companies, which in conclusion, creates concerns for the industry's growth rate.

The Pharmaceutical Industry on Wall Street has held its own versus other stocks; though few have been stellar in most industries as of late, the pharmaceutical segment has been stable in comparison. Regardless, the Pharmaceutical Industry is among the largest and remains one of the fastest growing segments in the world. Global sales of pharmaceutical industry according to The Pharmaceutical Research and Manufactures of America (PhRMA) are approximately $750 billion in 2008.

Below are 10 reasons the pharmaceutical industry has remained strong over the past few decades of rapid change in the environment and why it will continue to remain stable for years to come. Each one is then discussed in detail.

1) **AGING POPULATION, LIFE EXPECTANCIES, UNHEALTHY HABITS**
2) **INCREASED INVESTMENTS IN RESEARCH AND DEVELOPMENT**
3) **INNOVATION AND ADVANCES IN TECHNOLOGY**
4) **NEW MARKETS FOR PHARMACEUTICALS**
5) **DEMAND FOR COST-EFFECTIVE HEALTH CARE**
6) **MEDICARE D, DRUG COVERAGE**
7) **TREATING OVERLOOKED PATIENT POPULATIONS**
8) **DEMAND FOR "LIFESTYLE" OR "QUALITY OF LIFE" PHARMACEUTICALS**
9) **FDA APPROVAL TIMES AND MARKETING REGULATIONS**
10) **EXPANDING PROMOTIONAL SPENDING**

Within the fifty company profiles in Chapter Nine, there are numerous drugs that are in the later stages of development. If FDA approval is gained, several of these drugs will not only improve the quality of life; will not just be life saving, but astonishingly, some of these agents may be society altering. Imagine if you will, a new vaccine, which is as usual as the many received today, but this vaccine will eliminate your chance of ever acquiring Alzheimer's disease. This will occur in the not so distant future. Scientist, researching diligently for over the past 15 years are getting very close. These individuals may work their whole career without an agent that actually comes to market, but their work is truly remarkable and needs for more recognition.

Now, within that same neurological therapeutic segment, imagine again, an agent that reverses the affects of Alzheimer's disease. Close your eyes and visualize millions of people checking out of long-term health care facilities and returning to their homes and loved ones.

Rising cost of research and development, pressures of Managed Care, Medicare D, Medicaid and increased generic utilization will continue to rise. These pressures are absolutely necessary, but there is a balance that must be reached, one that makes healthcare reasonable for our country, yet allows organizations to invest in agents that will continue to produce treatments that are needed across the world as we have done in the past, extending lives, curing patients, removing certain diseases from our society.

Regardless of all these challenges, the pharmaceutical industry has remained among the largest and most stable. Traditional pharmaceutical companies, along with those with genetic research and emerging biotech concerns continue to break clinical barriers. Traditional pharmaceutical companies' have either merged, or funded to work in a partnership with various biotech concerns. This is bringing solutions to diseases at a rate probably never before in history. What will the average life expectancy be in 20 years?

AGING POPULATION, LIFE EXPECTANCIES, UNHEALTHY HABITS

The two most powerful demographic trends are the aging population and increased life expectancies. These two factors are generating growth demands for pharmaceuticals, dramatically increasing the number of elderly persons. The over-65 population in the United States is expected to expand by about 31 percent by 2015, according to the United States Census Bureau. Every day more than 6,000 Americans celebrate their 65th birthdays. This phenomenon is a reflection of the baby boomer generation. Aging will provide a tremendous need and opportunity for the pharmaceutical industry. A *global* study by the World Health Organization shows that this older population will increase from the current level of nearly 400 million to over 800 million by 2025.

At the turn of the 19th century, the average life expectancy was only 47 years. Sorry, but I would probably be gone for a while now. A child born today can expect to live to be 80. These longer life spans are due to advances in medical care, improved standards of living, and the development of innovative medications and vaccines to treat deadly diseases such as polio, diphtheria, heart disease, and various forms of cancer.

As more people live longer, they will naturally experience an increase in health problems simply due to aging. Additionally, the long-term effects of unhealthy habits such as smoking, excess alcohol drinking, obesity, poor diet, and lack of exercise will result in increased incidence of diseases. Thus, this over-65 population becomes candidates for various treatments including prescription drugs. On average, the elderly populations consume four to six times more prescription medications per month, than individuals under the age of 65. With record numbers of patients with conditions, such as heart disease, stroke, arthritis, cancers, depression, osteoporosis, Parkinson's and Alzheimer's disease. Pharmaceutical and biotech agents that target these diseases will be in greater demand. The industry will dedicate the majority of its massive $43 billion annual research and development spending over the coming years toward these disease states. In addition to these diseases that will increase as a result of aging, the World

Health Organization reports that many chronic diseases will increase in the years ahead due largely to unhealthy habits and conditions mentioned above. These habits coupled with the lack of exercise and stress management brings our high speed, stressful lifestyle that is feeding this frenzy. These unhealthy habits are well-known risk factors for many common diseases such as ulcers, depression, obesity, and impotence. The four largest therapy classes in the world can be linked to unhealthy lifestyles-they are, in order of global pharmaceutical sales: Anti-ulcer agents, Cholesterol Reducers, Antidepressants, and Antihypertensives. These drug categories treat conditions that have been described as "diseases of civilization" because they are largely a phenomenon of Western culture.

INCREASED INVESTMENTS IN REASEARCH AND DEVELOPMENT

Today's top agents that reach the market are surely Research and Development driven over an average of 10 years. New products are the lifeblood of the industry. Research-based pharmaceutical companies invested $43.2 billion in R&D in 2006, with all but approximately $7.3 billion being invested from companies outside the United States. Meanwhile, the average Research and Development to Sales Ratio for all other United States Industries is less than 4 percent. Based on corporate tax data compiled by Standard & Poor's Compustat, pharmaceutical manufacturers invest a higher percentage of sales in R&D than any other industry, including high-tech electronics, aerospace, automobile, and office equipment such as computers, printers, and peripheral devices. The nature of the drug industry requires the most intensive R&D structures in the U.S. economy. R&D spending is rising sharply, both in dollar terms and as a percentage of total sales; it has doubled every five years since 1970. Many mid size pharmaceutical or biotech companies may employ 300-400 scientists.

The United States *industry* is the world leader, recently inventing and bringing to market over 71% of the world's new medical therapies. Of the 100 most widely prescribed drugs, 83 were discovered with private funds without any government support. However, the United States Government, with publicly funded health research, administered by the National Institutes of Health (NIH) has also increased their contribution substantially in recent years. The NIH investment contribution is approximately 22% of the total cost of Research and Development. Most press releases and negative articles will highly inflate this figure, stating that the government funds the bulk of all research. Government and academic scientists lead the way in research about diseases. According to PhRMA, the partnership that exists in the United States between private industry and the government is one reason why this country has surpassed all others in the world as the leader in pharmaceutical R&D.

The most significant result of the industry's continued investment in R&D is the constant flow of new drugs to treat disease, extend life and increase the quality of life. The Pharmaceutical Industry Profile published by PhRMA reports there are over 400 biotechnology products in the pipeline addressing some 200 diseases. In addition to the biotechnology advances, there are close to 700 traditional pharmaceutical compounds in development: This proliferation should keep both the industry and the public healthy for many years to come.

Besides drug development, there are other major results of pharmaceutical R&D. First is its contribution to the advancement of scientific knowledge, technology and new manufacturing processes. Second is its contribution to the American economy. Since 1990, the pharmaceutical industry has grown twice as fast as the overall economy. According to a report by the American Enterprise Institute, the key factor is the heavy investment in R&D, and the fact that effective medicines increase the productivity and growth for every sector in the economy, producing social returns much greater than private returns made by the companies themselves. The industry has been a significant source of new, highly skilled jobs, and is one of the nation's largest employers with approximately 235,000 employees nationwide, including an estimated 50,000 scientists and 99,000 pharmaceutical sales representatives!

INNOVATION AND ADVANCES IN TECHNOLOGY

There is also a constant demand from the consumer for quality health care. Americans have come to expect the best and latest in health care technology. In the past, many valuable discoveries were often made by accident. The twenty-first century, however, brings sweeping changes in biomedical and pharmaceutical industries. The U.S. Human Genome Project unlocked the mystery of DNA. By completing the map of the human genome, researchers are designing medicines for specific patient populations. This will result in medications tailored to an individual's genetic makeup. Physicians will be able to treat and prevent the root causes of cancer, heart, arthritic conditions, and Alzheimer disease. New products will combat illnesses that were once considered the inevitable consequences of old age: frailty, vision failure and loss of mental acuity. Just 20 years ago, mentioning the names of companies such as Genentech, Amgen and Gilead to a cross section of physicians, most would hardly be recognized. Most of the top corporations, traditional large pharmaceutical corporations are also aligned with genomic companies or have established genomic research facilities of their own.

The biotechnology industry is having an impact on medicine right now. It is on the forefront of innovation and high technology resulting in new discoveries every day. These "biotech" companies, specializing in genetically altered drugs, gene research, and molecular biology will provide new therapies and also improved therapies over existing problems.

Corporate marriages between biotechnology companies and pharmaceutical concerns are common. Sometimes by choice, sometimes by take-over, this practice provides small, innovative biotech companies with the financial backing for research, plus management and marketing efforts to successfully launch new products into the marketplace.

NEW MARKETS FOR PHARMACEUTICALS

Recent events in major markets around the world are opening tremendous growth opportunities for today's global pharmaceutical corporations. The "Third World" is becoming more developed economically. Rising standards of living in Latin America, Asia, Africa, and Eastern Europe are also good news for U.S. companies. As emerging nations raise the economic standing of the population, one of their top priorities is to improve healthcare. An increased demand for medications to provide better healthcare in many countries equates to a longer life expectancy for their residents.

The forecast calls for an explosion of growth in developing countries over the next five years, and in specific pharmaceuticals to aid the global aging population. The North American, European, Japanese, and Latin American markets will continue to dominate, accounting for 92% of all global sales during that time. Globally, the Middle East, Australia, Southeast Asia, and China are expected to grow most quickly. In Europe, Poland has the fastest growth rate, followed by Sweden, the Czech Republic, and Ireland.

China, with over one billion people, is a major potential market. According to S & P's Industry Surveys, major U.S. companies doing business in both Russia and China include Johnson & Johnson, Merck, Bristol-Myers Squibb, Eli Lilly, and Schering-Plough.

Figure #2: SALES BY GEOGRAPHIC AREA, *PhRMA MEMBER COMPANIES 2005

(dollar figures in millions)

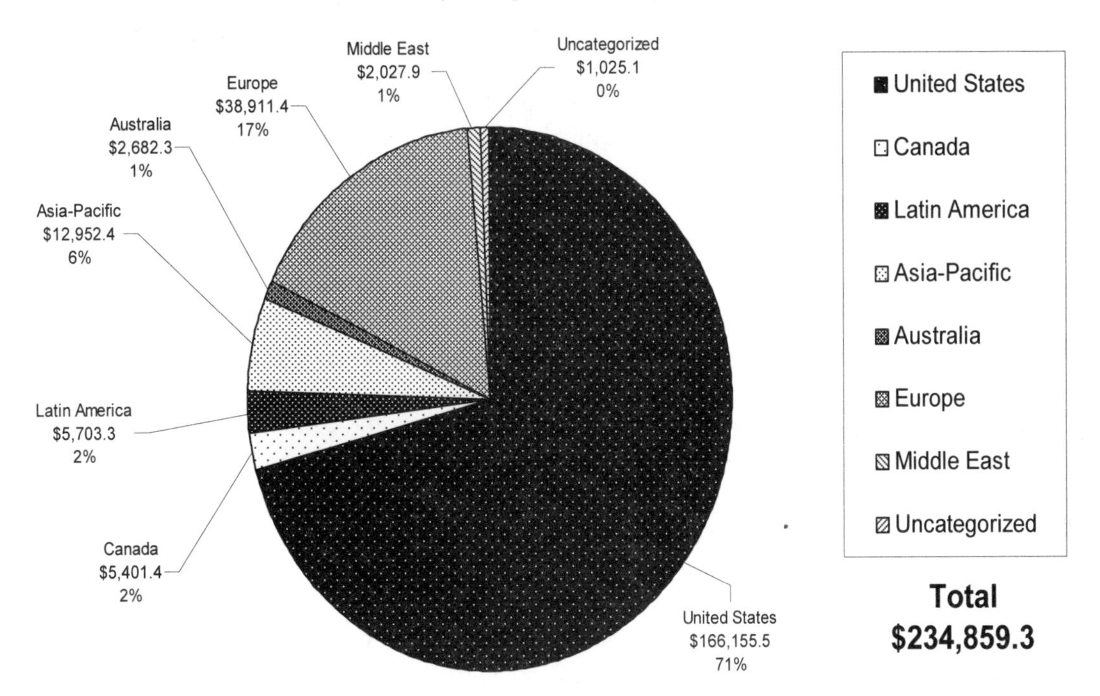

Source: Health Care Financing Administration

The pharmaceutical industry provides excellent opportunities for career advancement in sales and marketing to various global markets. Adding to the potential for global pharmaceutical sales and marketing careers is the fact that many of the major U.S. companies are divisions or subsidiaries of large parent companies based primarily in Europe or Japan.

There is an inherent risk in global markets. Economies can be unstable, shaped by politics and world events. Recent problems in Afghanistan, Iraq, Iran, Russia, North Korea and other countries may cause more U.S. drug companies to lose money in their total global portfolios. However, health is always going to be a growing global concern.

DEMAND FOR COST-EFFECTIVE HEALTH CARE

Prescription drug therapy is cost-effective. This means that a treatment or medication meets a specified goal at an acceptable cost compared to surgery, hospitalization, physician visits, and nursing care. Pharmaceuticals often eliminate the need for these more expensive interventions. However, this is a fact that is not widely recognized or acknowledged which can have negative fallout for the industry. The pharmaceutical industry is fighting a public relations battle. Columbia University economist Frank Lichtenberg found that every additional dollar spent on newer drugs reduces other medical costs by three dollars or more! For example, admitting an AIDS patient to the hospital costs approximately $3,500 a day. A protease-inhibitor cocktail at $16,000 a year is a comparative bargain, avoiding numerous hospital admissions. Prescription drug therapy for ulcers can costs less than $500 per year, but replaces the need for ulcer surgery costing nearly $30,000. Nearly $400 billion would be saved by taking advantage of more cost effective medicinal treatments and cures for the seven major uncured diseases (Cardiovascular, Cancer, Alzheimer's, Diabetes, Arthritis, Depression, Stroke, and Osteoporosis). Nearly 300 medicines are in development for these diseases. Costs include health care, lost time at work, lost wages, etc. Using an example of a migraine headache, one study showed that drug therapy saved an employer $435 per month per employee due to a reduction in lost productivity on the job. Cost to the employee was approximately $15.00.

However, healthcare delivery can be inefficient, and this has given rise to Managed Care Organizations (MCO's). Eliminating inefficiencies in the system is the goal of MCOs, which include what many refer to as Health Maintenance Organizations (HMOs). These MCO's manage and administer the overall healthcare benefit for employers at relatively lower cost than traditional "fee for service" insurance plans. Some national examples in the United States are Aetna, Cigna, United Healthcare and Humana. It is just mandatory that these cost are controlled by these organizations, for when General Motors is spending more for healthcare than steel, Starbucks is paying more for healthcare than for coffee beans, cost control is mandatory. The goal of Managed Care is to lower cost, while keeping the level of healthcare high, which may result in decreasing the access to specialists, or limiting patient's choice of healthcare provider to a specific list of doctors, hospitals, etc.

Another area where choice may be limited is in the pharmaceutical benefit (what drugs are available to the patient and the cost assigned to each). Pharmaceutical Benefit Management companies (PBMs) function as intermediaries between MCO's and/or employers and pharmaceutical companies. In 2008, about 93 percent of MCO's use PBMs to manage their drug benefits. PBMs must try to utilize lower cost generics if possible and have established formularies, or lists of preferred drugs approved for reimbursement for the patient. Prescriptions account for only 10 percent of the healthcare cost, but they are often the fastest growing expense for the PBM or MCO and ultimately the employer, with the emerging pharmaceutical agents, biotech therapies, some of which may cost in excess of $30,000 a year (i.e. Multiple Sclerosis monthly injections of a newly released best in class medication).

This is just an issue that must be recognized and dealt with effectively if United States corporations are going to be able to compete on a global scale and the employer can operate a business without healthcare being their highest cost.

MCO's and PBM's also provide services such as mail order pharmacy, utilization management, and physician prescription monitoring and education. PBM's can represent millions of members, or "covered lives" and have broad decision-making power over which drugs their members can buy. These members give PBM's a powerful influence with pharmaceutical manufacturers. Currently, the "big three" PBM's in the pharmaceutical industry are CaremarkCVS, Medco and Express Scripts Inc. They are able to negotiate discounts or rebates from a pharmaceutical manufacturer, taking into account first the efficacy of a drug, the safety and then the pricing. In return for selecting a particular product within a given class, the pharmaceutical company is rewarded with much higher utilization of their product, for other agents are often blocked or only obtained at a much higher cost that the patient must provide. The rebates from the pharmaceutical manufacturer are passed along to the MCO or the employer who then can pass lower premiums to the employee and lower co-payments for the patient or increase their profit as an employer (which could turn into more jobs, expansion, vacation time and other benefits). The PBM receives an administrative fee for all their services. Many patients, physicians and pharmaceutical representatives feel that it is the PBM or MCO that is blocking access to a particular product, when in reality; it is always the payor, the employer, or possibly the state in the case if Medicaid. Imagine yourself operating a business, you have to select a level of healthcare for your employee's, each selection has certain cost associated with them, sometimes one will choose one option (at a particular cost per employee), or one will select several options that can be offered to the employee at various levels of contribution from them financially via their paycheck. The number of options of various plans offered is endless. One employee within a company may have one choice of drugs due to their election and choice of benefit and contribution, where another employee from the same company, may have less choices, due to their choice.

The discussion here of course, has focused on managed care and the pharmaceutical segment but as a whole, managed care organizations have favored drug therapies because of their cost-effectiveness compared to the various other options they manage such as surgery and hospitalization.

One tool for managing drug costs by managed care that needs to be mentioned is the "Tiered Co-Pay" pricing system. Under this system, generic drugs have the lowest co-payments at the Tier One position. Next, the Preferred Brand Name Drugs have the lowest "brand drug" (no generic is available) at the Second Tier, and finally the Non-Preferred Brands require the highest co-payment at the Third Tier. An example may be a cost of $15.00 for a Tier One drug to the patient. A Tier Two drug which is a Preferred Brand cost the patient $37 and finally a Non-Preferred Brand at the Third Tier cost the patient $75.00. One can see that as a patient, with a savings of $60.00, you may ask for a generic that may suffice when appropriate.

	Tier One:	$15.00	generic agent. four times a day
Asthma therapy:	Tier Two:	$37.00	newer brand, once a day dose
	Tier Three:	$75.00	new brand once weekly dose

Numerous evolutions of above, including 5 tier plans, percents of the actual drug cost, etc., have evolved over the years. But PBM's and MCO's by direction of the employers have had to become more involved to reduce rising cost. The most successful way they have done this is by shifting cost to the patient, where deductibles and co-pays have had dramatic increases. Again, not one plan fits all, with countless offerings by each provider where levels of co-pays and coverage can differ from two employees of the same employer. A PBM may have over 200 formularies that they administer across the United States to meet the needs of their clients.

As an employee, patient, or individual, one has to take more responsibility for their health decisions, though it is understood that sometimes conditions, disease states and accidents are not avoidable. But by shifting more cost to the patient, living a healthier lifestyle is rewarded.

Total health care spending in the United States increased 7.7 percent in 2006 and 6.1% in 2007 according to the Kaiser Family Foundation Health Research and Educational Trust, the first consistent slowdown since 1999. Despite the slowdown in growth, healthcare spending still grew nearly twice the rate of the overall economy, which increased 3.6% in 2007. With the focus on containing healthcare costs, there has been a popular notion that hospitals, physicians, and pharmaceutical companies have benefited from increased pricing. It is also a popular notion that the main culprit in the high cost of healthcare is the high cost of medicines, and that Americans are spending more on prescription drugs than on other health care items or services. This is a false assumption due to the cost shifting noted above and the increased out-of-pocket expense.

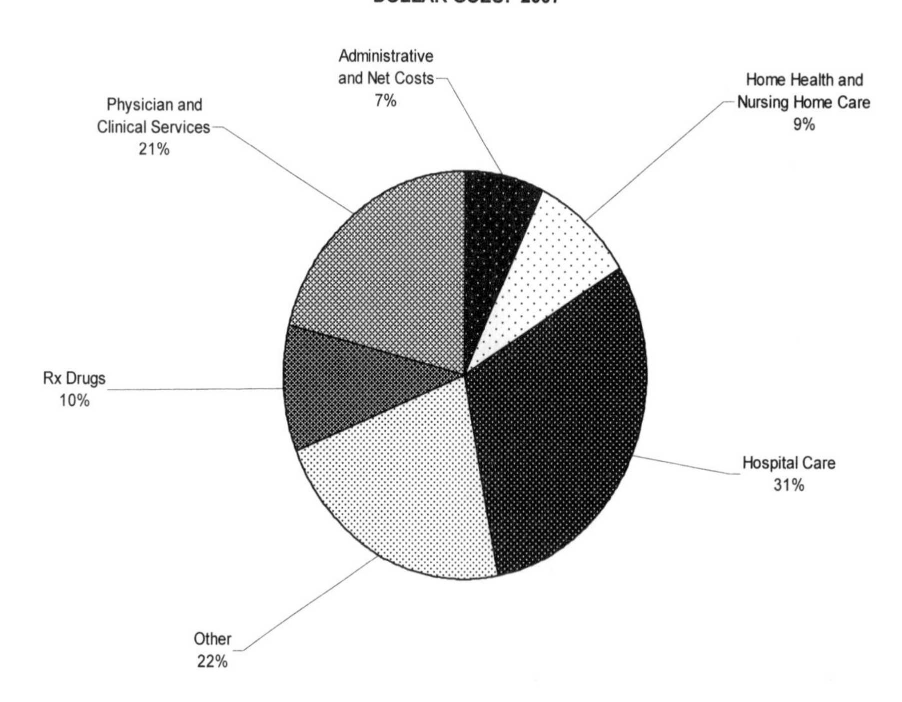

Source: Centers of Medicaid and Medicare

However, the percentage of healthcare cost attributed to pharmaceuticals is projected to increase over the next several years reaching approximately 13.9 percent in 2012. That is due to an increase in pharmaceutical spending of 16-17 percent annually over the next two years and then slowing to 9 percent annually through 2012 by increased cost management by MCO's health plans and by PBM's becoming even more restrictive, and health premiums increasing, shifting more cost to the patient. Even with the projected lower rate of increase, total healthcare expenditures for prescriptions drugs will double again by 2014.

UNITED STATES EXPENDITURE FOR PRESCRIPTION DRUGS

Year	Sales	Percentage Change over previous year
2006	$174,667.40	5.1%
2005	$166,155.50	3.4%
2004	$160,751.00	8.6%
2003	$148,038.60	6.4%
2002	$139,136.40	6.4%
2001	$130,715.90	12.8%
2000	$115,881.80	14.2%

Source: Healthcare Financing Administration

Money spent on prescriptions, questions of pricing, and coverage of prescriptions will continue to draw the critical attention of politicians and the media. Most discussions on the role of pharmaceuticals in the health care system focus, not on their long-term value, but on their short-term cost. One reason for this is that drug purchases are one of the few expenses that until recently have been paid directly out of pocket, especially for the elderly over 65, who did not have drug coverage until 2006 with Medicare D. Despite all the measures implemented by government and MCO's, prices for prescription drugs have continued to increase, wider than inflation. There are more people filling prescriptions now than ever in history. To illustrate, U.S. total health-care spending rose 7.4 percent in 2006. In the same year, U.S. prescription drug spending increased 12.9 percent. This is again, a combination of an increased demand for prescription drugs and higher prices that are fueling growth. Historically and still today the use of pharmaceutical products has been scowled upon, rather than applauded regardless of the reduction they bring to the total financial cost of healthcare within the United States.

Substantial evidence supports the assertion that increased use of innovative medications can help people avoid more expensive and invasive treatments. Many MCO's and employers have initiated "care management" or "disease management" programs for patients with chronic diseases, many of which rely heavily on prescription medications and *increased* drug utilization where the patient is monitored to be compliant with their medication. The development of innovative pharmaceuticals is the most promising and cost-effective method to keep Americans out of hospitals, out of operating rooms, and out of nursing homes. In short, pharmaceuticals can and will help keep people healthy and productive.

MEDICARE D, DRUG COVERAGE

One of the most sweeping healthcare changes for the United States was July 15, 1965 when President Lyndon B. Johnson signed the Security Act of 1965, which two critical parts were Medicaid and Medicare introduced. Medicaid is for families with low incomes and is managed and funded 50% by each State, but also funded 50% by the Federal Government. Medicare is funded by the Federal Government alone and was introduced with several parts. For all individuals over the age of 65, Medicare Part A, covered hospitalization and limited stays at skilled nursing facility periods. Medicare B, covered physician visits and outpatient hospital services and laboratory cost. That was it though, no pharmaceutical coverage was included, and so all expenses were paid by those patients over 65 while expenses related to hospital and physician coverage were completely covered. One can easily see why the pharmaceutical industry "image" became quite unpopular over the last 30 years. Individuals actually never really saw the cost associated with hospitalization or physicians, but every prescription, every month was paid for, either fully by cash, or if fortunate enough, an employer's retirement benefit design.

Thirty-Six years later, Medicare D was passed for all senior citizens under the Medicare Prescription Drug, Improvement, and Modernization Act, signed into law by President George W. Bush in 2003 and began on January1, 2006. MCO's had to compete for Medicare beneficiaries (patients) in 2005 with various benefit designs at different price points when patients began the process in 2006. This was preferred over having the Government administer the entire benefit in order to help keep prices competitive. Among these organizations, there is competition for patients (who may switch plans during the year), competition for offering the best product at the best price by keeping their cost down and negotiating pricing with providers. These Medicare D providers negotiate with all the pharmaceutical companies for discounts and rebates to have their drugs listed on the plans formulary, giving access to that medication to the patient. Much rhetoric one hears is that there is no discount given to this population, that the government has no power to negotiate drug prices with pharmaceutical companies, which is preposterous.

The Prescription Drug Benefit also includes a more comprehensive coverage for people with low income and limited assets. Most significantly, people with incomes below 100% of the federal poverty level will pay no premiums, no deductibles, and minimal co-pays.

This has created a large learning curve over the past several years within the pharmaceutical industry, the sales volume and channels have shifted quickly. Often within companies there are separate divisions established in sales and marketing to address Medicare D, versus the commercial segment of the industry.

A typical state may have 25-75 Medicare D plans to offer their patients, which has created a vast amount of clients that must be called on by the industry and pharmaceutical representatives with knowledge of numerous plans in their area and their patient formularies to inform physicians.

TREATING OVERLOOKED PATIENT POPULATIONS

We are in an age of ever expanding knowledge, technological advances, and new scientific and medical discoveries. Our knowledge of the human body, the processes of disease, and our genetic makeup will be translated into new capabilities to study, diagnose, and treat a variety of illnesses. Even in a time of recession, we are also in an age of an expanding access to the healthcare system.

The methods and extent to which common diseases can be detected is improving. More sophisticated, sensitive, and less expensive diagnostic technologies are leading to widespread use of screening programs, which lead to better analysis. Thus, diagnosis and treatment for common diseases such as elevated cholesterol, osteoporosis, and prostate cancer can be addressed before or at the early part of onset of the disease.

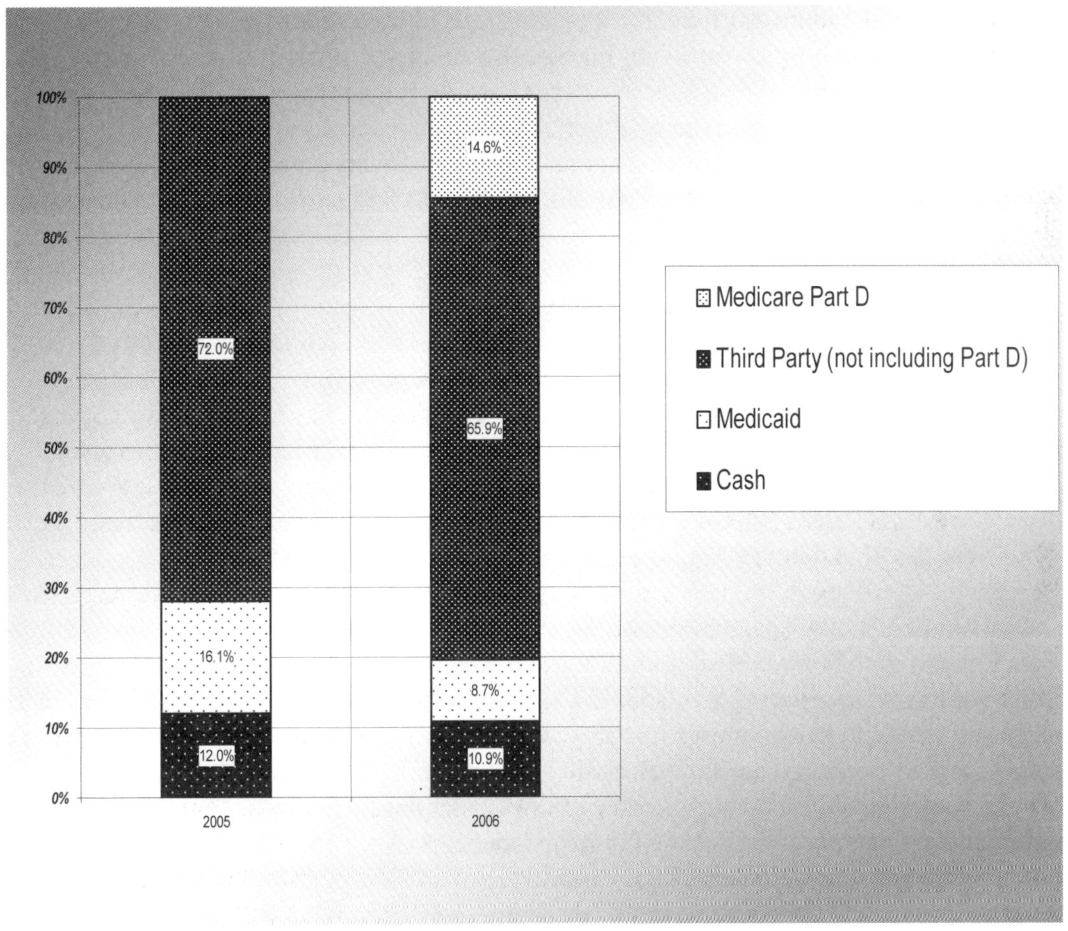

Source: IMS

DEMAND FOR "LIFESTYLE" OR "QUALITY OF LIFE" PHARMACEUTICALS

More than ever, people want pharmaceuticals to enhance their lives, not simply treat illnesses. Generally, the baby boomer generation is not staying healthy by exercising, eating well and getting enough sleep, but rather by aggressively pursuing medical care when--and even before--health problems arise. Their expectations are that modern healthcare should fix their medical problems. This led to the "new drug culture"--the concept of drug products that will improve a person's functional capacity and overall well being. Baby boomers are attracted to "better-for-you" products, which has created greater demand for new pharmaceuticals.

An example is the treatment of erectile dysfunction for men, for which there are now various competing products on the market (as if you have not seen a commercial). Attention is turning to medications for women's sexual function as well. Weight management is also a rapidly growing therapeutic category, as is cosmetic surgery and procedures such as the use of Botox injections for removing wrinkles. These therapies give rise to questions about what should or should not be considered a medical problem or a disease, and more importantly raise the questions of who should pay for their treatment. That definition may be expanding to include problems that can be treated with "quality of life" and "lifestyle" medications. Examples of such problems include the appearance of wrinkles and loss of hair.

FDA APPROVAL TIMES AND MARKETING REGULATIONS

As the principal federal agency responsible for enforcing U.S. drug laws, the Food and Drug Administration (FDA) regulates the introduction of new drugs. Pharmaceutical companies must submit extensive data to the FDA demonstrating both the safety and the effectiveness of new drugs before receiving approval for sale in the United States.
In addition, the FDA requires that drugs be produced according to specified "Good Manufacturing Practices" (GMP) guidelines. Manufacturing plants are subject to FDA approval and must be inspected periodically. If manufacturing plants are not up to specific codes, substantial fines can be bestowed to companies not in full compliance. Once a product is approved, the manufacturer must also receive FDA authorization for all its marketing practices and pieces. In other words, the FDA must approve exactly what a pharmaceutical company can state or claim about their products, as well as how they go about publicizing and promoting them. Again substantial fines can be levied to those who do not stay within what is stated in the products package insert. The information that a Pharmaceutical Representative may deliver must always fall into the information that is approved by the FDA.

Pharmaceutical companies until recently were benefiting from a friendlier regulatory environment for new drugs. To help bring down the high cost of drug development, the FDA began streamlining the review process in 1992 and adding an administration fee to new drug applications. Current approvals since 2005 have been timely yet the FDA has become more vigilant in reviewing any possible side effect that may appear when an agent is exposed to a larger population, often asking pharmaceutical companies for additional information, delaying releases of products by several years or in some cases, the decision not to seek approval for the agent.

Another role of the FDA, in addition to approving new products, is to monitor marketing guidelines which regulate how pharmaceutical companies promote their products. Marketing guidelines have become less restrictive in regards to direct-to consumer (DTC) advertising. This contributed to an increase in DTC advertising by pharmaceutical companies, leading more patients to make specific requests for products to their physicians. On the other hand, "off-label" restrictions have increased by the FDA and pharmaceutical companies with any discussions by pharmaceutical sales representatives concerning any "off-label" or unapproved uses of a product.

In short, a physician may use a drug for any use that they feel is appropriate in the best interest of the patient. The drug may not have an indication for this particular usage though by the FDA, therefore a Pharmaceutical Representative is strictly forbidden to address any such topic and only those indications that are contained in the Package Insert (that accompanies each drug) which is submitted and approved by the FDA are allowed to be addressed. Significant fines for any "off label" promotion have been handed down by the FDA over the past several years included the loss of employment by any Pharmaceutical Representative that has used off label promotion in their position.

EXPANDING PROMOTIONAL SPENDING

Pharmaceutical companies have stepped up marketing efforts on all fronts to take advantage of favorable conditions in the market. Money spent by pharmaceutical companies for research and development was $43 billion in 2006; in contrast, the industry spent $12 billion in 2006 marketing and direct to consumer advertising. Typically, sales and marketing of prescription drugs fall into two main categories--Professional Promotions and Direct to Consumer Advertising (DTC). Professional Promotion includes: sales presentations in doctors' offices, hospitals, pharmacies; medical journal advertising; drug samples; meetings and events including continuing medical education; direct mail; Internet-based programs; and promotional items (pens, pads, and any office trinkets). The various strategies in the promotional mix are changing as DTC and Internet-based promotions expand. However, the overall strategy continues to be professional Pharmaceutical Representatives. In January 2009, the Pharmaceutical Research and Manufacturer's Association adopted a code by which are even more stringent guidelines that have the goal of interacting with the medial community with the highest ethical standards and is for stricter then the 2002 code. The code focuses on informing physicians about the benefits and risk of the promoted products, giving scientific and educational information and support medical research and education.

The principle behind the code is that the patients need paramount to any interaction. This has been implemented by PhRMA, (not the FDA) and placed limits on entertainment and non-educational items, with withdrawing any excess spending in entertainment, dinners and tickets to theater and sporting events.

This is a great move by the PhRMA association and one that I believe due to the large amount of mergers and acquisitions over the past 40 years (which have created large disparities in size of companies), sets a benchmark for all to follow and levels the playing field for the industry to follow.

On the other hand, note-pads and pens are a tad over restrictive if anyone has worked in a physicians office, these little items sometimes provide very critical communication methods within the physicians office regarding "the patient". As stated, overall, this is positive high code of ethics that few industries would impose on themselves. It would be interesting if other industries in the United States would adopt such principles, such as the alcohol industry with Direct to Consumer Advertising (which advertising, quite frankly, is entertaining).

More interesting, comments by a Senator stated that consumers will benefit from this move, saving $19 billion dollars a year (a figure hard to arrive at from any data source that I can research). Yet a few clicks of the mouse to the Center for Responsible Politics, shows that this same Senator has accepted slightly over $198,000 in political contributions over the past ten years, which may be high also?

Most importantly, you need to know that the pharmaceutical industry political contribution or donors for the last ten years only have 4 companies in the top 100 companies in the United States for the high dollar amount of funds being donated to politicians and the first one comes in at number 59, the largest pharmaceutical company in the United States, which is half of the American Medical Association at number 13. The other three companies in the top 100 all rank below Walt Disney which is at number 71, and are in positions 77, 86, and 97, all who's revenue is quite more robust in relation. Those are the facts that the industry should be more vocal about, for high standards are the norm and something that we have to be proud about. Yet, this is not what is conveyed to the public during any election cycle seen over the last 30 years, most importantly is the ratio and spending on research and development

PHARMACEUTICAL RESEARCH COMPANIES' R&D SPENDING EXCEEDS TOTAL PROFESSIONAL SPENDING & DTC PROMOTION

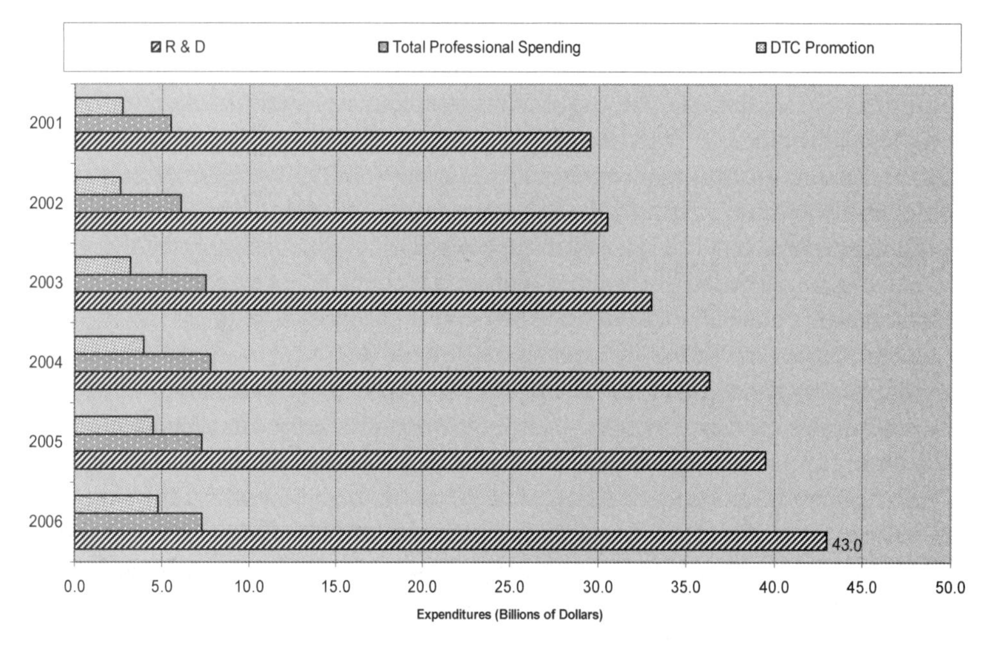

Source: Pharmaceutical Research and Manufactures Association of America

Increased DTC advertising has led to greater consumer recognition of the benefits of pharmaceutical therapies, and created brand recognition and loyalty. This strategy is not always popular among physicians, but such advertising makes more patients aware of ailments and encourages them to see their doctors to learn more. One poll of 1,200 people showed 74 percent believe these ads help them be more involved in their own health care; 67 percent say the ads teach them about risks and benefits of drugs. Of patients who talked to their doctors about a drug that they saw advertised, 50 percent asked for a prescription by name and 70 percent of them received a prescription for the brand they wanted. According to Scott-Levin, a pharmaceutical industry market research firm, there is a direct correlation between the spending on DTC and product sales; those products that are heavily advertised are the ones most often requested by patients. DTC is expected to continue at a steady pace in the years ahead. Though television is the dominant medium, companies are increasing their annual budgets for more varied types of DTC advertising.

Although the pharmaceutical industry was slow to embrace the Internet as a marketing tool, today virtually every company has a product information web site and some have e-business divisions. According to Cyber Dialogue, a New York-based Internet market research firm, companies spent close to about 9.65 percent of the total DTC budget on Internet marketing.

Pharmaceutical Sales Representatives are the industry's most critical tools for promoting its innovative product offering. During the early 1990's, the industry began to cut back on its sales force size. The assumption was that once managed care dominated the healthcare system the physician would no longer be the decision-maker and there would be little need for large forces in the physician offices. However, experience in recent years has shown that even under managed care physicians remained the ultimate decision-makers in choosing prescription medications. Successful companies have returned to traditional sales and sampling strategies for "face to face" selling is always number one. The return on investment is obvious for the physician office-based sales force.

During the past 5 years, the size of sales forces has been relatively stable. In the last several years there has been several reasons for sales force declines, whether anticipation of FDA approval of major agents or the unexpected removal from the market of several blockbuster agents that side effects appeared that were not identified in smaller population clinical trails. 2008 has not shown any dramatic changes, but with nearly 100,000 pharmaceutical representatives, variances of 10-15 percent depending on the developments of R&D and approvals by the FDA will become more common in the future within these cycle's of limited drug introductions.

Will the industry be able to sustain the 100,000 number of pharmaceutical representatives? It is a question that quite frankly there are far too many factors to take even an educated guess, the political climate, Research and Development, FDA regulations, both federal and state laws, and sampling policies will all have a say. Having 3 and 4 representatives calling on the same physician by the same company entity every week, are diminishing, for the good of all. Large product portfolios need large salesforces, but the physician access issue, will persist.

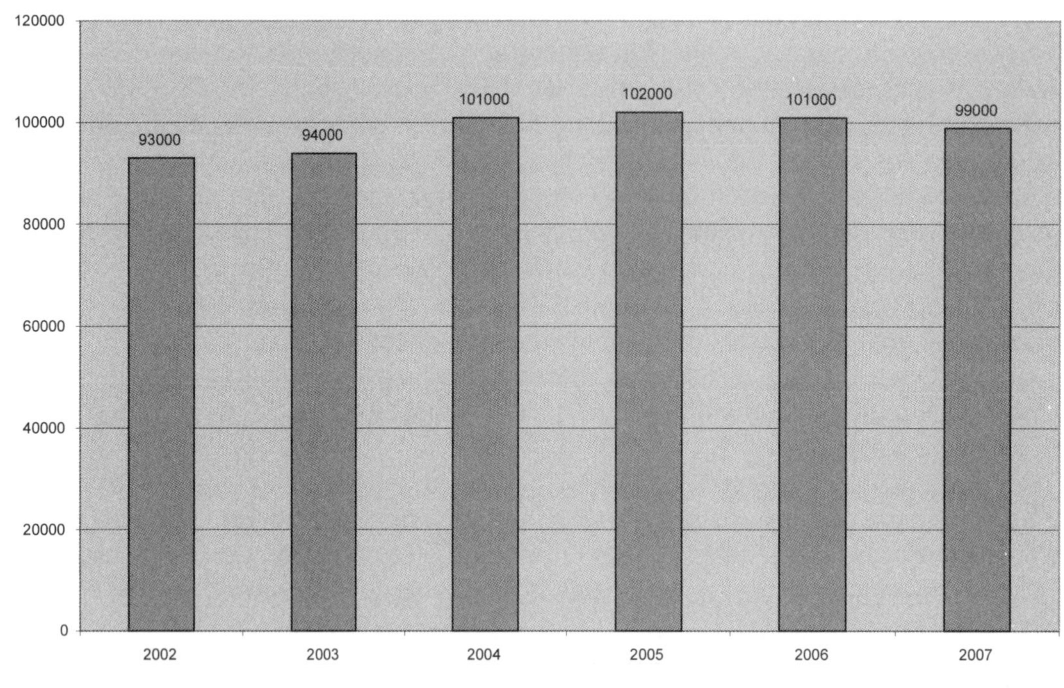

SOURCE: Verispan

The above figures are based on traditional pharmaceutical and biotech companies. It does not take into account the tremendous growth of Contract Sales Organizations (CSO's). When adding this segment into the equation, there has actually been growth in the total name of pharmaceutical representatives. This segment will actually become a more significant resource with the recent attention to extremely efficient sizing of salesforces, allowing for almost instant increases (with product or company acquisitions), or rapid decreases due to an older product loosing patent protection, or sale of a therapeutic category to another organization. Today's CSO salesforces are well trained and many individuals have between 5-10 years experience in the industry.

Finally, with new biotech and pharmaceutical companies continuously emerging in the United Sates with their sales forces and several foreign entities, whose size rivals our current largest companies, this number may even increase.

Chapter 2
The Pharmaceutical Sales Representative

In this chapter of *Insight*, you will learn about the actual job of the Pharmaceutical Representative. You will see that both a challenging and rewarding career and an excellent work life are yours for the taking. After discussion of a typical workday, this chapter focuses on some of the normal challenges faced by the Representative. Upon completion of this chapter, you will have a basic understanding of the entry-level position, and be able to answer the following questions:

- **What is a Pharmaceutical Representative?**
- **What competencies are companies looking for in job candidates?**
- **What does the Representative need to know?**
- **How are they trained?**
- **What does a typical day look like?**
- **What does it take to be successful?**
- **What are some positive and negative aspects of the job?**
- **How are Representatives compensated, and what are the financial incentives?**
- **What are the career advancement opportunities?**

In later chapters, you will learn how to dig deeper into the job and uncover potential opportunities in your area. For now, take some time to review this chapter. It will give you the solid base of knowledge you will need to begin the networking process, described in Chapters 4 and 5.

What is a Pharmaceutical Representative?

For a perspective on this exciting position, begin with a look at some of the various titles used across the industry to designate the Pharmaceutical Sales Representative. Behind these titles are individuals who provide the first line of contact for many large, medium, biotech and smaller sized pharmaceutical manufactures and marketers across the industry. Each individual possesses a high degree of technical expertise, selling skills, and professionalism.

- Pharmaceutical Sales Representative
- Senior Pharmaceutical Sales Representative
- Territory Manager
- Hospital Representative
- Hospital Specialty Representative
- Professional Medical Representative
- Professional Sales Representative
- Specialty Representative
- Senior Specialty Pharmaceutical Sales Representative
- Manager, Account Executive

For the Pharmaceutical Sales Representative, the primary target audiences are physicians and pharmacists. Obviously, you will be selling to highly trained and technically oriented professionals.
Such an audience demands that you also have a high level of expertise. You must know your customers' business, your products, your competitors' products, and the diseases and health conditions for which your products are prescribed.

Does this mean you have to be educated in a medical or health –related field in order to relate to your customer? Absolutely not! The goal of the Pharmaceutical Representative is no different than that of any sales professional promoting virtually any product or service. Pharmaceutical salespeople are professionals selling the goods and services of an organization. The key to success lies in thorough preparation to guide you in making effective sales calls and following up on your commitments. Success requires determination, attention to customer service, and hard work. It does not need a specialized degree in any one area. It is no different than selling in any other industry. That is why people from all sorts of backgrounds, educational levels, previous sales experiences, and even non –sales backgrounds are successful in the pharmaceutical sales industry. Successful sales abilities in other product or service areas will transfer well to the pharmaceutical industry. Success is success!

Now let's drill down a bit in terms of what, and who, a Pharmaceutical Representative is and does. To begin as a Pharmaceutical Sales Representative, SALES is your middle name! Your responsibility is to increase market share and total volume of prescriptions written for your pharmaceutical products by the prescribers in your territory. Thus, what you are is a Sales Professional. Simple enough! That said, as a sales professional, your job entails everything that goes along with the sales territory: customer profiling, data analysis, tough gatekeepers, entertaining, relationship building, generating reports, product training, selling skills training, sampling regulations, planning, itineraries, scheduling and routing, communication, meetings, travel, reports, and finally, becoming ever so important in today's marketplace, is a knowledge of the payor and coverage of you and your competitive products. This is something that will be a must in the future of the industry, knowing which Managed Care Organization (MCO), which Health Maintenance Organization (HMO) or what Pharmaceutical Benefit Manager (PBM) has established your product in their benefit system. This is truly where value is going to be given to the client. A Pharmaceutical Sales Representative must keep all the balls in the air at once, and achieve a high level of performance and professionalism. You must do what's expected in terms of meeting quotas, and your communication, administrative work and follow through must be impeccable.

Your objective is achieved when the needs of your physician is met in regards to knowledge of your product. As a Pharmaceutical Sales Representative can take ownership of this knowledge, because obviously that is where you will spend your time and effort. The quick answer to this question is that any pharmaceutical sales representative can change the physicians' prescribing habits with frequency and a consistent message. But this will only be short term, for the pharmaceutical representative that can provide value with their goals, while being proactive in today's marketplace will excel. A physician may treat a patient that has a medical benefit (this is the benefit that pays the physician), that is completely different from the pharmaceutical benefit.

The pharmaceutical benefit may be one of nearly two hundred (that is two hundred different formularies with different cost for each drug) which comes from a choice's of the patient's employer, the state, or the federal government, whoever is the end payor with the patient.

The term Prescribers refers not only to the physician, but also the Physician Assistants and Nurse Practitioners who also prescribe many medications (which varies based on individual state's laws). That being stated, I usually use the term Physician or Doctor from here on to indicate all prescribers. Physician "habits" merely refers to what medications the physician uses. By and large, this becomes a habit over time, in what actually is prescribed and this can be your challenge to overcome. Your goal is to have them accepting you as a valuable resource, not only about your products, but disease states, and the multiple payors that operate in today's environment.

It takes selling at different levels to change physician prescribing habits. Since not much happens unless you get access to the physician, that is a good place to start. There are ways other than face to face selling that change physician habits, but many have been on a swift decline, such as speaker programs, continuing education, written notes and information left behind or dropped off for the doctor, entertainment events; selling to partners, nurses and office staff on your side and so on. But for now let's look at access.

Access is the number one challenge you will face because it is through access to the physician you will maximize the opportunities you have to sell to that customer. Your prospective employer will be interested in what you think about gaining precious minutes with your customer. The best approach to this is to be relationship and service oriented- always think in terms of the value you are bringing to the doctor, and the relationship you have with the gatekeepers and entire office staff. If there is relationship, service and value, you will get and maintain time with them. If not, you will find yourself shut out. High rapport and high customer service are essential. Read on for more access and other key skills and responsibilities. To summarize what the Pharmaceutical Rep is, he or she is the consummate sales professional, attentive to every detail of the sales call including pre-planning and careful follow up; is customer focused, creative, flexible, positive, and technically oriented and an expert in the disease states, products and competitor products. Finally, the representative is also a goal-setter, aggressive, and determined to get the results they desire.

What Competencies are Companies Looking For In Job Candidates?

The essential qualities desired by a pharmaceutical company are generally the same as those of other sales organizations. Of course, you must demonstrate to prospective employers that you have the competencies that they are looking for in a new employee. You have to convince the first interviewer that you have the qualities that fit the profile his or her company has in mind. You can create the opportunity so do so by following the strategies outlined in this book.

There are hundreds of well-meaning individuals who have the basic qualifications and abilities to get interviews with pharmaceutical companies. However, as a District Manager for many years myself and in discussions with other District Managers today, there is a frustration that sometimes surfaces during the process of interviewing and selecting the best candidate.

This frustration stems from a lack, not an abundance of candidates that rise to the top and set themselves apart from the average. Even after looking at recommendations from other members of the district, running classified ads, eliminating hundreds of resumes, receiving referrals from search firms etc., there can often will not be a single candidate that goes the extra mile to stand apart. By this I mean the candidate who knows the company, knows the job, is prepared for the interview, and follows up afterwards. Make the effort to demonstrate your excellence. Position yourself to win by dedicating high effort and energy to this process. Follow the steps, be confident, demonstrate high energy, be devoted to the details, and you will be the one who stands out among the many.

Now, I know there are many who feel they are doing this and are still not succeeding. To them I say you must keep trying. Learn something from every contact, phone call, interview and each time you are turned-down. It can take many months or on a rare case, a year, to get the job you want. I have often told candidates over these past ten years, who email me and state, they are losing their confidence, maybe this career is not for them; they are just not getting "the offer" after numerous interviews. They have even gone through months of interviews, with one company and being down to one of two candidates left and being told no, we are going with the other candidate.

My reply is what happened to me, over 40 years ago, which quite frankly is why I told myself I would write this book from my "learning" experience. I am no author, but wanted to teach others of a process that could help hundreds. I received enough rejection letters (that is how you were notified in those days) that I could literally have taken the stack of them and wallpapered my bathroom, covering every square inch. But I learned a little something from each interview (one, was I had to ask for the job in every interview, which I thought was silly, for why would I be there) and as the months passed, I became more confident in the interview process. Some, who did not hire me, gave me a tip or two, which now isn't allowed. I was a Registered Nurse without one day of sales experience. Finally after about six months I received two offers on the same day (a Friday in August) and took the weekend to decide what organization to go with. Then after doing the interviewing for twenty of my thirty years on the other side of the desk, I often saw so many young candidates making the same errors. Again I knew I had to write this book. So, hang in there, you have a great resource to guide you to your objective.

You will discover that these attributes described in this section can be demonstrated clearly in the way you approach and progress through the networking and interviewing method. Central to the strategy is the concept that the job search itself is an ideal opportunity to clearly demonstrate your own potential in a powerful way. You must sell yourself as the right candidate on order to get the job. This is the first opportunity that the interviewer has to assess your talents in sales. You are talking about your skills and at the same time demonstrating them. The employer is the buyer. It is similar to the selling situations you will face as an employee of your new company. Thus, be at your best in all your contacts with prospective employers from the very start.

Most companies have a definitive profile, and interviewers will tailor their questions to identify whether you fit this profile. Each company will have identified certain traits, skill sets, and abilities that they will attempt to evaluate in each candidate through the interview process.

These areas are also called "job competencies". Some competencies are considered "core" which means they are inherent in an individual and can not be trained or developed. In other words, the candidate either has them or not. Core competencies are in the areas of positive attitude, motivation, drive for results (goal orientated), and work ethic. Other competencies can be obtained or developed in an individual by training and practice. These are in areas of selling skills and knowledge. Please note- for those of you without prior sales experience you can learn to sell. Good sales people are the result of training, self-learning, and practice. In addition there are many jobs that though not titled or typically thought of as sales are actually utilizing and developing the competencies required being in sales. Teaching, working on teams, gaining approval for budgets or projects, making presentations, purchasing functions, and many other roles provide this experience. In addition, a successful track record, progression in responsibility and salary level, setting and accomplishment of specific goals, use of persuasion and presentation to convince others to take action, etc., all show your ability to sell. Therefore, you need a plan for your interview—be prepared to illustrate, with examples, each of the qualities you possess. Familiarize yourself with the following attributes. As you prepare for your interview with the questions in Chapter 6, develop your answers to demonstrate these competencies. Whether you have had previous experience in sales, you will need to describe and use examples, those activities that reflect that you have demonstrated these competencies. Examples include:

Results Oriented or Goal Oriented: Your activities are directed towards an identifiable, stated or written goal.
Motivation: Show what makes you get up in the morning, and what excites you about the job and company you are pursuing.
High Energy: The ability to stay focused and enthused in all aspects of the job over time. May include the ability to stay persistent, produce high quantity and quality of work, and put in long hours when necessary (and long hours will be necessary from time to time).
Flexibility: Able to perform well under changing conditions and demands.
Communication: Simply put, communications are everything you do and say, and how you do it. As a sales representative you are in the business of constantly communicating to your customers and your company. This includes listening, speaking, presentation skills, business writing skills, and telephone skills. Presenting yourself well from the start will go far in demonstrating that you have this talent.
Determination: You have the intention to get what you want both personally and in business. You succeed in the face of adversity. You do not become discouraged, are not afraid to take risks, and you learn from your own mistakes.
Drive: You have the zeal to achieve goals, and make a sense of urgency to complete large and small tasks. You are not complacent or easily satisfied.
Confidence: You are calm and attentive; you are not arrogant, but very sure of yourself in front of people. You have straight, relaxed posture, good eye contact, and voice projection. The best way to be confident is to be prepared!
Reliability and Integrity: This is trustworthiness. It is being responsible for your promises and commitments to the customer. Follow-up is extremely important in pharmaceutical sales. For example, you may be asked a question for which you do not know the answer.

How long will it take you to find out and communicate it to the customer? Pharmaceutical selling is an ongoing consultative process. Your follow-up is what establishes your relationship as the customer comes to trust that you will always keep your commitments. If your customers trust you they will also trust your company and your product.

Listening Skills: It is a fact that salespersons talk too much instead of listening. Good listening is essential to strong relationships; it involves understanding and clarifying with questions what the customer is saying. With good listening skills, a customer feels heard and will be more receptive. These skills allow you to uncover customer needs so you can direct your product presentation to meet those needs.

Creativity and Innovation: Create strategies, develop solutions to problems, and take advantage of opportunities. In pharmaceutical sales, for example, creative representatives think of unique attention getting ways of opening a sales presentation.

Teamwork: As sales in the pharmaceutical sales industry changes to meet the challenges of the health care system, such as managed care, selling in a team approach is becoming important. A sales team could include a sales representative, hospital specialty representative, managed care account manager, and district manager to achieve a common goal of increasing sales in a given managed care organization or physician group practice.

Achievement: This can be shown by a history of success in other sales and career areas, in school, and community or extra-curricular activities.

These attributes provide an excellent framework to help you prepare for interviewing. Individual companies or District Managers may look for additional traits or certain "hot buttons". Hot buttons are specific attributes that a manager feels are especially critical, and they weigh most heavily in his or her selection of candidates. You can finish out about these ahead of time through your contacts with a sales representative in that company (described in Chapter 5). During your networking, a good strategy is to ask for the desired requirements for the job as early as possible in the process. By uncovering these early on, you will be able to effectively match your skills and abilities to fit the needs of the company. You will perform this skill for product presentations once you are hired. During your preparation for the interview determine specific examples from your past experience that you can present to illustrate each attribute you possess. This practice is critical to successfully interviewing.

What Does The Representative Need To Know?

Simply put, the Pharmaceutical Representative needs to be an expert in the medical specialty area in which his or her products will be used. This may seem daunting at first. How can you know as much as a physician or pharmacist who has all of those years of training? There are several reasons you can accomplish this. First, you will be dealing with a relatively small area of medicine compared to all of medicine. The physician or pharmacist has an extensive background involving hundreds of medications, many different disease states, and multitudes of treatment options. Your knowledge, on the other hand, will be highly specialized, focusing exclusively on a few medications you represent, only one or two diseases and a limited number of treatment options. You will become an expert in your given areas.

Secondly, as a newly hired representative, you will embark upon an elaborate company training program. The pharmaceutical industry, as a rule, provides training and development that is unparalleled in any other industry. Most companies are proud of the extensive and demanding nature of their training programs. It is helpful in your research of each company to investigate its training program. You will learn when and how to approach this topic in later chapters.

Training is conducted in two broad areas: 1) Knowledge, which is the information you need about your products and your customers and 2) Skills, which are the learned behaviors and habits that you need to perform your job.

Examples of Knowledge building can be found in the following:

- Anatomy and physiology
- Diseases for which your products are used, such as asthma, diabetes, cancer and depression
- Diagnosis and appropriate treatments
- Your pharmaceutical products and competing products are referred to as product knowledge
- Customer types and suggested selling approaches for each type
- The health care system, physicians, pharmacist, managed care, benefit designs of local employer's, retail pharmacy, hospitals, long term care, patients, etc.

Specific product knowledge on a medication that you promote is highly emphasized. For example, you will be required to know the following details about your products and their competition:

- Mechanism of action (how it works in the body)
- Indications of the medicine (what it is used for)
- Contraindications (when it may not be used)
- Dosage regimens
- Side effects
- Warnings and precautions (under what circumstance is caution advised)
- Current scientific medical studies
- Cost of therapies

Examples of skill building are:

- Call planning and preparation
- Business planning and customer targeting, referred to as territory management
- Listening and selling skills
- Group presentation skills
- Negotiation skills
- Call reporting
- Computer skills
- Analytical skills, sales data interpretation
- Strategic and creative processes
- Teamwork, leadership, and managing your career

- Setting up and managing a home office

Thirdly, many training sessions are company specific. These include policies and procedures for working day to day within the corporate environment. Examples are reporting procedures for sales call activity, travel and entertainment expenses, and use of your company car. Why do companies place so much emphasis and investment in training? The goal of each company is to represent itself in the best possible light. When you represent a company, you are the company to that customer. A physician must feel very confident on prescribing a pharmaceutical product. They are placing the health of their patient and reputation on the line with each treatment decision. Therefore it is imperative that you project the utmost professionalism, confidence, and knowledge to that decision-maker.

It would be a liability for a pharmaceutical company if a representative were ill prepared and therefore misinformed its customer physicians. All statements made by a representative are considered "promotional claims" and must comply with FDA guidelines. Pharmaceutical companies must monitor this closely to ensure that their sales force is performing to this high standard.

How Is The Representative Trained?

Training programs for all of the top pharmaceutical companies are similar. These programs usually begin with extensive at-home reading assignments over a period of two weeks or more. During the home study period you will need to absorb a large amount of information from product training manuals including anatomy and physiology, disease states, diagnosis, testing, and treatments including your medications and the competition.

Representatives are not required to take any certification program to learn basic medical terminology, or be tested by some group of individuals that have developed an association. Pharmaceutical companies prefer to train their representatives to their own standards, which includes numerous competencies that one can not obtain by way of reading a book and taking a quiz. Save your money on these programs (that seem to have sprung up within only the last eight years) and either place it towards a Dale Carnegie Sales Training Course (if lacking sales experience), or your first course towards a solid MBA program. Both of these will be better received and add more value to you whatever course your career path may take you. This will also appear great on your resume. Just list the program and state, now enrolled with an anticipated graduation date.

In addition many companies recognize one Certified Medical Representative Program, CMR. In this a program, which the company pays for in full, consist of taking courses to enhance your knowledge at a graduate school level. The Certified Medical Representative Program (CMR) has been in existence for near 50's years and is well recognized in the industry as the "Gold Standard" but this is something one would never undertake before gaining employment in the industry.

A pharmaceutical company's home-study is followed by two to four weeks of classroom sessions under qualified instructors including numerous role playing of sales calls. In addition, Medicaid, Medicare D and Managed Care Organizations business acumen is taught. The role-play situations are used to practice what you are learning. A trainer will play the role of a customer so the trainee can become familiar with questions and objections you will encounter during sales presentations. After this initial period, your training will move into the field. A trainer, manager, or experienced representative will work with you in your territory. You will also observe other representatives working in other territories. Your District Manager will work with you frequently at first, then perhaps every four to six weeks. Their role is to provide observation, insight, motivation, and coaching to your performance. You will need to be able to accept positive criticism well and have a desire to learn and grow. Many companies will use the training program as an ongoing evaluation of the candidate. You will discover challenges that are unlike those of any college program you have ever experienced. Be prepared to take it very seriously.

Training in the pharmaceutical industry never ends. You need to know about the new drugs that have been approved by the FDA. This is an ongoing process. Medical science will continue to provide new advances and scientific breakthroughs for new products, new clinical research studies, recalled agents, and uncovering new disease states. As in any sales industry you will continually face the threat of new competitors and the advent of new market opportunities. Nowhere is this more the case than in today's ever-changing healthcare environment. This profession rewards the individual who builds their knowledge and skill levels.

What Does A Typical Day Look Like?

As with many other sales professions, Pharmaceutical Representatives work from their homes. There is no one to look over your shoulder every day. Your self-determination is the key to your success. You should emphasize your independent drive and self motivation as you interview.

First of all, many Pharmaceutical Sales Representatives are working in a Primary Care office setting. Primary Care physicians make up the majority of offices out there. They are generalists as opposed to specialists. Types of Primary Care Physicians include Internal Medicine, Family Practice, and General Practitioners. They can be MD's (Medical Doctor) and DO's (Osteopathic Physicians). Pediatricians are also considered Primary Care, as are some Obstetrician/Gynecologists. A typical day consists of presenting your products to Primary Care Physicians, and their Nurses and office staff. Your Manager and your company usually determine the specific number of calls you make, which physicians you will call on, and which of your products you will promote to a physician. Most companies require a minimum number of calls, usually in the range or 8-10 physicians per day. In addition to physician calls, you may also call on retail pharmacies and hospital clinic pharmacies. Your "call plan" is a list of targeted physicians in your geography. Armed with your call plan, sales data, sales support materials, product samples and literature, you will prepare for the day's calls. This is usually done the night before as you organize yourself for the following day. Only then are you ready to venture out to make your calls on the customers.

Your company's "Plan of Action" (POA) or similar term helps you set your overall goals, objectives, strategies, and individual tactics. The POA includes what products and promotional messages you will emphasize. The plan of action is based on the priorities of the company as determined by the sales management and marketing teams. To illustrate, imagine that your employer, XYZ Pharmaceuticals, Inc., has decided to promote their antibiotic for the next twelve weeks. Thus, for that period, the activities of the organization will be geared towards this goal. Representatives' presentations will shift to increase market share in this product category. Specific tools such as visual aids (product information), speaking programs, DTC advertisements and journal ads may be geared towards the same goal. After this twelve- week period, selling focus may shift to promote a different product, perhaps a new line of oral contraceptives or anti-inflammatory. Promotional plans often are based on financials or calendar periods, such as quarters or trimesters.

As your day begins, you will make sure everything is planned and ready for the day. This includes all the visual aids, product literature, samples, computer/PDA, sales reports and data, and even having your cell phone charged and ready to go. Either the night before, or in the morning the Representative will conduct a thorough pre-call plan. This is a vital part of your day and prepares you to make the most impact possible with a given customer. To adequately pre-call plan, you will review your post-call notes from the previous call to that doctor. In addition, you will review sales data to see if that doctor has increased or decreased in the number of prescriptions, or share prescriptions written for your product and competitive products. Armed with such data, you can determine your objective for the call and how you are going to accomplish your objective. A good Sales Representative will plan the entire call from the initial questions to the material being presented, material left behind, and specific closes to be used. Each call is tailored to the individual physician in order to have the most impact. Begin your pre-call planning by asking yourself this question: "What do I want the physician to do differently as a result of my call?" From there, the initial questions, product messages, materials and closes should all support the objective. After the call, recording what transpired and planning the next steps right away will ensure you have a smooth follow through and transition into the next call.

Close communication is also a part of a typical day. Normally, you will start your day by checking voice and email to see if there are any communications from your manager and/or counterparts that require immediate action or response. "Counterpart" Representatives are those Representatives from your own company with whom you "overlap" or share territory, but promote different products (you may or may not have counterparts based on how your sales force is structured). Coordination of effort is important among counterparts, as is the concept of team selling- taking a team approach to an individual physician or physician office. You may meet on a weekly basis, perhaps more frequently, or at the least touch base by phone or voicemail. Your day in the field will begin around 8:00 a.m. or as soon as physician offices and pharmacies are open and available to make calls. During your day, you will enter physicians' offices to make your presentations. This is the major focus of your day of course. You will be challenged to overcome obstacles between you and this all-important customer. Obstacles include the constraints on the doctor's time, working with (or through) the office staff, answering questions about reimbursement of your products and perhaps being bumped by one of your competitors! Your knowledge of the doctor's preferences and schedule, your rapport with office staff, and other tricks-of-the-trade will help you meet this challenge.

Once you are in front of the physician, you may have a few seconds or several minutes to perform the skills and communicate the knowledge necessary to gain the doctor's confidence and commitment to prescribe your product. During this time, your preparation is the key to your success. You are a resource of information, providing unique services to the physician and ultimately the patient. Thus, you must understand the physicians' needs and attitudes in order to position your product to satisfy those requirements. Your final goal is to gain the physician's commitment to prescribe your product.

Part of the typical day is, on occasion, a breakfast or lunch meeting with the physician office. This may mean feeding the entire staff, or just the doctor. It is becoming more rare, do to constraints, but it may require additional time and planning to physically pick up the lunch, or you may have it catered, which saves time. Regardless, it is a great opportunity to get expanded time with both the doctor and the entire office. Many Reps, depending on the company, will have one to even three lunches per week. The frequency of lunch depends on how many you can schedule and how much money has been budgeted for this purpose. You may also share a lunch meeting with one of your counterparts. During this sit-down meeting, you will both have the time to fully present your products.

Though not always, it can be part of the typical day to be planning and conducting a speaker program (an expert speaker giving a lecture), a promotional or educational event. First of all, as we discussed in Chapter 1, there are limits to what Pharmaceutical Representatives can do regarding entertainment. Due to PhRMA Guidelines, most companies are no longer providing entertainment other than meals, with set budgets. However, educational programs are a staple of your promotional strategy. In a typical day, you may be including oral and written invitations to your customers during sales calls. You may be attending speaker programs in the evenings or on weekends. These are a good opportunity to have your customers hear your product message, and learn from outside experts in the field, rather than from company representatives.

You may also be involved in exhibits or displays at larger symposia which may be local such as at a hotel or may be out of town and require you to travel. Regardless of the location, working and exhibit is part of the job, offering you a venue in which the physician comes for continuing education and in the process will stop by your booth for information and discussion on your products. You may also have a display at a local hospital where you have made arrangements to set up a table in the hallway or physician lounge in order to meet and call on doctors as they go through their hospital rounds. Again, these are opportunities outside of the typical physician office call for you to affect the physician prescribing behavior.

There are aspects of every industry that make it unique, such as product lines, customer audiences, decision-makers, the purchasing environment, sales-cycles, call frequency, the various payors, and others. The goal of selling pharmaceuticals is the same as for any product. However, this industry has some characteristics that are inherently different from other businesses. For example, the Pharmaceutical Representative does not sell directly to the end user of the product, or the patient. In other words, the "decision maker" does not actually buy or take the medication. In fact, the decision maker (physician), the consumer (patient), and the payor (insurer) are all different individuals or organizations. The Pharmaceutical Representative presents their products to the prescribing physician, dispensing pharmacist, or other purchaser such as a hospital.

The decision-maker is generally the prescriber. The pharmacist can also decide, in some situations, to dispense a product other than the one prescribed by the physician. This can happen in two ways. The first is generic substitution, whereby the pharmacist dispenses a generic form of the same medication that is prescribed. Secondly, the pharmacist may call the doctor and request permission to dispense a completely different medication, but one that has the same overall effect on the patient. This is a process called therapeutic substitution. Thus, both the pharmacist and the physician influence which medication the patient ultimately gets.

Further complicating the scenario is as previously discussed, another very important decision-maker referred to as the "payor", or the "third party". Think of the patient as the first party, the health care provider (doctor, pharmacist, etc.) as the second party, and the person paying the bill the third party.

Because the prescribing physician and the dispensing pharmacist are the primary audience of the Pharmaceutical Sales Representative, I will limit the focus of discussion to office based physicians and retail based pharmacists.

Another characteristic of pharmaceutical sales is the unique selling process. First, the process of selling to a physician would not be characterized as a hard sell. There is no push to get the customer to "sign the bottom line" by using aggressive sales techniques and power negotiations. Rather, pharmaceutical selling is characterized as consultative. You are a consultant to the doctor providing educational and informational data to support his or her decision to use your products. This is not to say that you do not gain a commitment from the doctor. You must close the sale firmly (does not mean aggressively) if you are to change the doctors behavior. You must ask the physician for a commitment to prescribe your products, and continually reinforce that commitment. However, you must earn the right to ask by winning the trust of the physician. This is accomplished by consistently providing accurate product information, published literature, clinical studies, reimbursement information and answers to any questions that come up regarding patient examples in studies, education materials, samples and whatever additional information the physician requires.

The physician is in search of the most medically appropriate product that will achieve optimal results for the varied needs they have. The biggest need, of course, is to provide benefits for the patient. A physician is basing his or her decision on years of extensive education and experience. They also possess unique characteristics, strong attitudes, or hot buttons, which drive their prescribing habits. For example, a given doctor may be more likely to use one medicine over another because it is new or perceived to be more scientifically advanced. This type of physician is an early adopter of new products. Another physician will do the opposite, preferring older and more proven therapies. This type of physician is a late adopter.

Other requirements affect the physician's decision to prescribe a particular medication. These are the professional and personal necessities of the individual physician. Many needs also arise from the physician's consideration regarding third party influences. Such third parties include the group practice in which the doctor is a member, a hospital system where the doctor is on staff, managed care organizations that provide a flow of patients to the doctor, governmental and other health plans, employers, and insurance companies. Your challenge is to uncover all the various needs and attitudes of a given doctor. You can then position the features and benefits of your products to best meet those needs and gain the commitment to prescribe. Physicians are creatures of habit like anyone else. They typically have a small group of medications they have become comfortable with and prescribe repeatedly. Changing their prescribing habits is your challenge.

It may take several sales calls on an individual physician before you successfully close the sale and the doctor prescribes your product. The selling cycle may be longer or shorter for some doctors, depending on the needs and attitudes previously described. A contrast is the retail sales environment, where a sale must be made on a single encounter with the customer. This is not always the case with a physician- it means that you may not ask for the business, or close the sale, on the very first call. Always ask the client for a commitment to try your product; so many well experienced representatives will fail this on every call.

Another challenge awaiting you on a typical day is differentiating yourself from your competitors, as well as their products. As you now know, selling pharmaceuticals requires a technical and consultative approach. However, this fact does not obviate the benefits of relationship selling. People buy from people, as the saying goes, and physicians are no different. Developing good rapport with your customers is essential to gaining their time and attention. Physicians' offices have 75 to 100 individual sales representatives from different companies and industries calling on them. Sometimes the office staff will have five Pharmaceutical Representatives that call on them in a single day. They are busy and have limited time, so it is your job to obtain the doctor's time and attention. Your excellent rapport, product knowledge, communication skills, and professional demeanor can set you apart form representatives of competing pharmaceutical companies.

Physicians differ in their overall attitude towards Pharmaceutical Representatives. These decisions span from complete refusal to speak with pharmaceutical salespeople to an open door policy. This range of mannerisms is one aspect of the job that offers a challenge to the representative. For example, you need to be innovative to create opportunities to get in front of the "hard-to-see" doctor.

Product samples and patient information may be a part of your total offering. If so, this provides the physician with an excellent service for his practice. Most physicians applaud the practice of free samples. These are used to start therapy or sometimes treat a particular patient with that medication. Often the doctor can evaluate the response to the drug without having the patient incur the full cost of the prescription at the pharmacy. Sometimes physicians will provide a patient with two different medications (such as treatments for allergies), and have the patient try each one at home. The patient will decide which one works best. Physicians will also use samples to assist a patient who cannot afford the cost of the prescription. Product samples are an excellent service that can be offered to the physician who in turn can provide a better service to the patient. I should mention a word here about sampling because sampling is taking a larger piece of the Rep's administrative work through the week. Sampling is a highly regulated area of your job. The federal government regulates how companies handle samples in order to minimize sample misuse and diversion (selling samples). Individual companies must comply, which results in very strict procedures and reporting for how Sales Reps utilize their samples. Suffice is to say that the result is more time spent counting and recording sample inventories and disbursements. This could be a computerized or paper process.

A large part of the typical day is spent planning, organizing, and reporting. You will manage your time by planning your calls for the day and routing yourself in the most efficient way, based on appointment times and customer locations. You will assemble all the necessary materials- sales information, visual aids, clinical studies, and product samples. It is important to stock and organize the supplies you need in your company vehicle. This will ensure that you have what you need and your day runs smoothly. Recording and reporting each call is also critical to your success. The method you employ will vary slightly by company. The advantages of recording call activity are that you can retrieve the information later, use it to evaluate your efforts and what you accomplished, and remember what the customer commitment was, and importantly, what commitments you made and what you need to do next. Most companies now use laptop computers to enable you to instantly record your calls "in the field". Computers also offer you instant access to customer records and are excellent tool for sales tracking.

What Does It Take To Be Successful?

Many personal characteristics and traits are essential to your success. These requirements were described in this chapter and will be revisited in later chapters- they are the qualities you will want to demonstrate during your sales interview process. The following keys to success are practical applications of your individual talents. This discussion will give examples of successful goals and strategies.

First, excellent product knowledge forms the basis of your sales presentations. Secondly, successful sales representatives consistently maximize their selling opportunities. Simply, this means that they make the most calls at the right times, to the right physicians, with the right messages. Thus, they see the highest number of valuable physicians within their territory, and deliver the best marketing message. By doing so, successful reps create the best chance of success in every call. Not to say that every call must or will be a success- there are many obstacles and challenges to most every call; but good sales people know the secret is in the numbers- the more calls you make, the better your odds of having physicians utilize your medication. Perhaps you will not be friends with every physician you call on, but always be your best on every call. However, you need only have a relatively few high writing doctors to understand the merits and contributions of your products to be successful. A good Representative lives by the old 80-20 rule. That is 80 percent of the prescriptions are written by 20 percent of the doctors.

What is good, professional rapport? It means learning the physician's needs, schedule, patient types; reimbursement concerns current prescribing habits, and hot buttons. Is he clinically or technically focused? Does he prefer a product because it is convenient, inexpensive, or new? Does he pay attention to all those managed care formularies, or does he focus on just one or two that has influence on his practice? Now, you must know your products and where they are placed on every MCO formulary, Medicare D and Medicaid Preferred Drug List in your area. You have to give value to every physician and their office on every call. Rapport also means trust. It is imperative that what you say is accurate and that you are dependable. It takes time to develop a sales relationship before an actual sale or commitment to prescribe can take place. There are no short cuts, and if you are to learn the intricacies of the industry, you will still need to give yourself a minimum of 18 months, with two or three years in a given territory to really get up to speed and see high productivity. This concentrated time at the outset of your career will be invaluable as you progress, whether you remain in sales, pursue management, or even the office of the Chief Executive Officer.

As you begin in your new territory, you will be assigned a selected audience of physicians, pharmacists and hospitals. You will be on a schedule that puts you in front of the same customer every two, four, or six weeks, depending on your company's size and direction. This schedule is your call cycle and determines your call frequency. The sale can sometimes require several contacts, which you will accomplish as you repeat your call cycle over time. Success is dependent on a consistent selling message, frequency of contacts, and professional relationships.

What Are Some Positive and Negative Aspects of the Job?

As with any career choice, there are positive and negative aspects of a career in pharmaceutical sales. In summarizing the most common job aspects we use information that we acquired from numerous interviews and focus groups with pharmaceutical representatives.

The job requires autonomy in your daily activities. Some people enjoy this aspect and the freedom to be creative in their sales effort. Others complain that such autonomy leaves them feeling isolated from co-workers and without direction. Individuals who are not disciplined and self-motivated will find themselves struggling with distractions. The cell phone (with lower rates) has helped in this manner, for representatives are in far more frequent contact with other members of their district, team, or pod. Determination and a drive for success are essential attributes for this reason.

Job burnout can be a problem with Pharmaceutical Representatives just as it is with other demanding professions. One of your biggest challenges is to keep yourself motivated daily. Even I, writing this book can tell you, that spending eight years as a Pharmaceutical Sales Representative, there were ups and downs. Times were you felt you could not face another crabby receptionist. I knew when it was time for another challenge and integrated that approach the rest of my career. It is not always possible, depending on your individual situation (family, children, schools, spouses career), but it is what worked the best for myself.

The best way to do so is to set short-term, realistic goals. Look for new challenges and be creative. Most of all, advice I received from an older representative that has since has passed, over thirty years ago, when I took the position a bit too serious, he stated, your taking this much too serious, "HAVE SOME FUN WITH IT"! Your District Manager has experienced the same job stresses that you have, and they are responsible for helping you stay motivated. He or she may be a good resource, some will be open, admit their challenges during their career, mostly others will not, so learn to take care of yourself. Some of my representatives I encouraged to obtain their MBA (which I did myself during one low period), of course the company paid for it, it was quite expensive then and even more now and is an accomplishment that stays with you for the rest of your life.

There is a twelve percent turnover rate in the industry during a good year, which indicates that this job is not for everyone. Research suggests that some Pharmaceutical Representatives become complacent in their positions over time and no longer experience the job satisfaction that was present in the beginning of their careers. The day-to-day work can become tedious, and it requires your own creativity and motivation to make it exciting. Having supportive management and a team spirit among your peers is also helpful. Calling on six to nine physicians per day, spending time in waiting rooms, idling in traffic, and going to pharmacies and hospitals is a hard day's work. Sometimes the heat of summer or freezing winter snowstorms challenges your resolve. Will physicians complain if you don't make a sales call? Hardly! Will your manager know if you ended your day early every now and then? Probably not, something that is possible but will show in due time. Your determination and persistence will be the key to the success of your career.

I have spoken with many representatives with ten to thirty seven years on the job. On the positive side many experienced veterans reported that job satisfaction increased over the years. The continual learning associated with new products and technologies offers unlimited challenge. The rapport and long-term relationships they have developed with their physicians and pharmacists are personally valuable and one of the most highly rated reasons for satisfaction. Many have become life-long friends, doing things on a social basis, almost as a co-worker in the earlier years, nearly a family member in the later years. These representatives started with many physicians starting their practice and called on them until their retirement. These long-term customers also appreciate the experienced representative and recognize solid pharmaceutical representatives are a tremendous resource. Career sales representatives find satisfaction in the recognition they receive. Multiple sales awards, generous raises, and commission payments come with hard work and experience. The number one reason given for long-term success is practicing a strong work ethic and receiving the rewards and recognition that is deserved from that practice.

To summarize, individuals in this field are as unique as in any profession. You will discover whether this career is a good fit for you only through investigation and research- a process you have already started! Before you decide for or against this career choice, gain the broadest perspective you can from individuals within the profession.

How Are Representatives Compensated And What Are The Incentives?

Compensation packages in the pharmaceutical industry vary from company to company. Typically, you will receive a combination of base salary plus a bonus or commission on sales achievement. Recent research shows that the median base salary for **all** pharmaceutical representatives was approximately $68,000 in 2007. Primary care representatives averaged around $60,000 in base salary, specialty representatives earned an average of $73,000, and finally hospital pharmaceutical representatives had an average of $82,000. Bonuses and commissions are generally paid out by quarter, trimester, and semester or yearly based on your sales performance. Industry norms show a wide variance in bonus structure, with annual earnings ranging from $10,000 to $35,000 and higher in rare instances. Obviously, you should look at both salary and bonus potential but have some concern if the majority of compensation is on commission with a company in the pharmaceutical industry.

With many companies, you may be offered additional compensation. Virtually all pharmaceutical companies provide a company car. This should be considered part of the entire package, and is said to be worth more than $15,000-$17,000 per year in base pay (take into consideration this includes insurance, license, taxes, all maintenance and fuel). Some companies offer stock options, though these may be reserved for Director level positions and above. Profit sharing is less common, but may be part of the mix for some companies, often start-ups.

To illustrate, consider a Pharmaceutical Representative who works for a company that pays a low base combined with a high bonus structure. Let us say this individual earns a base salary of $60,000, and is eligible to earn between $20,000-$30,000 on bonuses and/or commissions. The total package is worth around $85,000 per year. In another company, that same representative may earn a larger base salary say $70,000, but only be eligible for a commission and a bonus of around $15,000. The total package is the same as in the first example. Again, this always varies from company to company and more importantly, one must recognize that within the same company there is often a new plan at least annually. I have seen Pharmaceutical Representatives actually change companies due to a bonus plan, not only to have the same plan instituted at the new company a few years later. With tenure, you will experience great bonus plans and then, a year later, a terrible one; this is a part of any sales position and not exclusive to pharmaceutical sales. A first-year Pharmaceutical Representative can usually expect earnings of $60,000-$90,000. In addition, there is compensation for business and small entertainment expenses, a company car or car allowance, vacation policy, medical and dental plans, 401K, flex care plans and savings plans, full reimbursement for your MBA. You can expect your base salary to increase yearly if you stay with the same corporation. Many companies have different pay levels associated with certain criteria of performance and length of service within the organization.

How Is Sales Performance Measured?

It is important for any representative to know how sales performance is measured. This is another topic for you to explore during your research into the industry and contacts with prospective employers. It is not advisable to inquire about the amount of compensation in any stage of the interview process, except when you have an "offer in your hands". However, you should inquire about the basics. For example, what methods of evaluation are used to measure job performance? What percentage of total compensation comes from base salary versus bonus and commission? This information will provide insight into the management style of the company. For example, if a company places emphasis on representatives' autonomy and creativity, then they will reward this behavior by placing a larger percentage of total compensation into bonus or commission. Bonus and commission payments are at risk- they are yours to earn, yours to loose.

Sales tracking and measurement in pharmaceutical sales is historically problematic. As noted with interviews of well seasoned representatives, this is something that will never be totally accurate within the industry, yet is something that is accepted. In recent years, it has become more of a science, but there is always a variance, either plus or minus, from the actual numbers. In brief, there are vendors, or specialized companies, who make it their business to accumulate distribution and prescription data from the various points along the supply chain. Then they process it into usable data runs and sales reports, and make it available to pharmaceutical companies for purchase. Thus, your company can provide you with specific sales by market share, number of prescriptions written, and tablets sold by territory, zip code, and even by specific doctor. In addition, data regarding reimbursement issues is available, what plans does the physicians practice include, their ranking, percentage of patients, etc. All of this data is extremely expensive. As mentioned earlier in this chapter, physician level prescription data is an indispensable tool in planning and evaluating your own efforts on any individual physician. Imagine knowing exactly what and how many prescriptions your customer has written over the past two months, for example, of not only your product but the competitor's product as well. It is powerful information, but not to be shared with the physician, of course, or even let on that you have the information. It is strictly confidential company data. Some doctors are aware that the industry has this information. Physicians even participate in giving additional information for a charge to various organizations seeking trends within the customer. As recently as of 2007, some states are offering physicians the ability to "opt out" of disclosing any prescribing patterns.

It is now possible to track sales by individual prescription, which is a much more accurate way to measure sales performance. Once a doctor writes a prescription and the patient has it filled, the representative responsible for calling on that particular physician is credited with the sale. In this system, it does not matter in which pharmacy or zip code the prescription is filled. It also gives you specific data on the prescribing habits of each one of your customers- an obvious benefit when it comes to evaluating and planning sales strategies for that doctor. This detailed level of data is very expensive for pharmaceutical companies to purchase. However, it is worth it because of its value in evaluating and targeting customers. Your time is also expensive for pharmaceutical companies, and you are more productive when you target doctors that respond well to your selling efforts or have high potential for prescribing your products.

What Are The Career Advancement Opportunities?

Advancement opportunities are available within the pharmaceutical industry. Directions in which to advance are many and can offer most individuals to seek out their particular field of interest within the industry. Opportunities may be categorized into basically three different areas of career specialization, to keep this a reasonable size, they are as follows:

- Career Field Sales/Corporate Accounts
- Field Sales Management
- Corporate Office Functions

Advancements in these three categories are accessible to representatives from the entry-level sales position. Each area offers unique experiences, builds additional competencies, and opens more doors for increased responsibility and compensation. Companies have various policies and programs for advancement, so this varies from company to company.

First, field sales opportunities are positions available within different divisions or segments of the sales force. They offer increased responsibility, experience with new customer types, different products, and new career challenges and growth. As the health care system changes, organizations rather than individual practitioners may make decisions about treatment. Such organizations are physician groups, hospital systems, MCOs, PBM's and governmental agencies. This shift has created opportunities in the pharmaceutical industry as companies expand and adapt sales forces to service these newer segments of the marketplace. Examples include:

Senior Sales Representative: A life-long career in sales can be rewarding and provide an excellent work-life. This promotion does not significantly change what you are doing,

but acknowledges your experience and advancing sales acumen. It is offered to reward those with long-term success as a pharmaceutical representative as a valued member of any organization.
Hospital Sales Representative: This position offers new customer types, professional settings, and selling situations. The environment is in community based and teaching hospitals and/or universities, including schools of medicine and colleges of pharmacy.
National Accounts Executive: This is the fastest growing position today requiring extreme business acumen and knowledge of commercial, Medicaid and Medicare segments, including product distribution. Accounts include managed care organizations, pharmaceutical benefit managers, specialty product distributors, wholesalers and retail pharmacy chains.
Regional Account Executive: Another growth position, this is an advanced field position, targeting HMOs, smaller PBMs, and Physician Groups on a local or regional basis. It requires advance knowledge of the payer environment and overall health systems and usually advancement from District Management.
Government Affairs Representative: Legislation and policy changes will influence the pharmaceutical industry no matter what happens in the White House. Again, a position that will continue to grow and require a high level of intelligence to reach the physicians needs. Pharmaceutical companies are involved at all levels of government. Customers include state Medicaid programs, regulatory and licensing boards, professional societies, associations, state public health departments, and formulary committees.

The Second category of career options is sales management, examples include:
District Manager (DM): Responsibilities include hiring, coaching, and managing an entire district of currently ten or more representatives. This is an area on a personal note of mine that the industry has really spread to thin in it's expansion over the last 15 years, with representatives obtaining coaching, reinforcement, and feedback only 3-4 times a year at any high degree.
Regional Director (RD): One who has responsibility for seven to twelve District Manager's and their subordinates? At the top of the sales force is the Director of Sales, who may be a Vice President (VP), and may report to a Senior Vice President, most often consisting of sales and marketing, or directly to the CEO.
This structure varies from company to company of course.

The Third category includes opportunities in the corporate headquarters.
Sales Trainer: Designs, develops, and delivers all types of training.
Marketing manager, Product Manager: Develops sales strategies, forecasts, interact with advertising agencies and develop promotional programs for the sales force to implement.
Communications Manager: Develops sales and corporate communications materials and programs in support of marketing and sales strategies.
Professional Education Manager: Developing educational programs for physicians and pharmacists.
Sales Administration or Sales Operations Manager: Logistical areas of the sales force, such as computer systems, call planning and reporting, supplies, and bonus compensation.

Each of these advancements will require a successful background as a Pharmaceutical Representative for a minimum of two to three years. Progression to Director-level appointments requires experience in the corporate headquarters or "home office". Regardless of your long-term aspirations, your short-term goal is to achieve an entry-level position. Once you are working in the industry, develop your knowledge and skills to the best of your ability.

Use all resources available to you through the training department, your manager, experienced representatives, and corporate headquarters contact. Identify your strengths and weaknesses. Evaluate where you can make the best contribution to the company, how you can maximize your strengths, and what interests you the most. Communicate to your manager that you are interested in development and advancement and do this on a consistent basis. Evaluate your situation and develop your goals for the future.

One never knows the management style of a District Manager they will encounter. Some managers consistently ask their field representatives, what your goals are, what do you want to accomplish by when. A solid manager will attempt to assist a representative writing out this plan, with various measurement points with each performance review.

It is important that this be a vital part of your career. It is something that will keep one motivated throughout the year. Remember how motivation is such a key component of the position. If your manager does not recognize or forgets to incorporate these into your position (which is not uncommon when an individual is managing ten to twelve representatives) make sure that you take several additional steps to make it known to the regional manager within your organization and incorporate this consistently into your comments on every performance review.

In addition, at meetings, make your career objectives known to others within the company in those roles, whether marketing, training, managed care, etc. Yes, again, "it's *who you learn to know*". Ask what you can do within the organization to assist you reach these goals. Many times, District Managers will assign various projects to correlate with these career goals, whether making presentations regarding reimbursement issue's or breaking down clinical trails related to one of your top promoted products, by which you explain the intricacy of the study design, who the study is authored by, medical journal that study was published in, results, conclusion, etc.. Another way a District Manager may incorporate your career goals within your current role is have you act as the district liaison with that particular department, giving you additional exposure within the organization. Always remember though, sales achievement must remain solid in your current position and a minimum of two or three years (my opinion) is something that will be very vital to you having a solid foundation in this industry.

Chapter 3
Resumes

Resumes should be meticulously crafted. Their main purpose is to prevent you from being quickly and immediately being eliminated as a potential interview candidate. This is an important fact about resumes. They constitute that all-important "first impression" that can either land you an interview, or land you in the wastebasket. Eight to twenty seconds is all the time the average manager takes to look over a resume and decide whether the applicant should be granted the opportunity to move ahead in the process.

Picture this scenario: XYZ pharmaceuticals need to fill several new positions. Human Resources places the jobs on various employment and company websites. In addition, the local District Manager alerts her Sales Representatives to "keep an eye open" for potential candidates. Companies offer their Representatives incentives for referrals of competent candidates. I have had a representatives earn 8K in referral bonuses in a year. Combining these multiple recruiting strategies produces hundreds of resumes. It used to be typical for a single advertisement in a large metropolitan newspaper to generate more than two-three hundred resumes. Of course the internet, job sites, referrals (networking), searchfirms have diminished the amount of ads even placed in newspapers today.

So, what happens next to all those resumes? Picture them being screened according to basic criteria by an individual, perhaps a HR (Human Resources) specialist, an administrative assistant, or even a temporary employee assisting the company for the project. After some résumé's are eliminated (examples may be, hand written, no degree, no employment for years), the remaining are reviewed again using higher standards, the stack grows smaller. Eventually, by the process, there are twenty-five to fifty remaining. The resume stack has been sufficiently narrowed for the next step.

Wait a minute! What did those remaining twenty-five to fifty applicants do that was so special? The answer may surprise you-it is what they did not do that made the difference. They did not make simple mistakes that resulted in rejection for others. Certain mistakes make you unappealing to the prospective employer. In other words, employers are initially screening out, not in, their applicants from the stack of resumes.

Employers are looking for reasons to extract particular applicants based strictly on their resumes. This is an easier and less time consuming process than determining which applicants should be interviewed. As the stack grows smaller, either someone in HR or the District Manager can now focus on specific criteria such as the career history, education, and recommendations from current Sales Representatives from that smaller selection of resumes. Then possibly the phone interview starts or more screening down to a selection of a dozen, it depends on the company, the individuals.

So how do you get over the first hurdle? What were the basic criteria and higher standards being used in the XYZ Pharmaceuticals example above?

Keep in mind that when it comes to resumes, pharmaceutical companies are somewhat old fashion, they are not using computers seeking out "key words" very often, in fact, I have not heard of it being used to date. Your resume has to have some key words, but they are for the human eyes to see. Those key words are pharmaceutical, pharmaceutical sales and most likely, a four year college or university degree.

Resumes should be well-written as possible according to the following guidelines, and be part of the overall networking strategy that I recommend (described in Chapter 5). However, online application forms are sometimes required, and are used for screening purposes. Even as you network with a representative and soon your resume is before that District Manager who is doing the hiring, you may be asked to fill out an on line application at the companies website, which is a policy of the corporation. As you fill out this type of application, treat it like a resume. Just be aware that automated resume management (not automatic scanning as mentioned above) programs exist out there, and may be used whenever resumes are collected in an electronic form. Your resume will remain on file for a period of time.

You can prepare your resume for uploading, electronic sending and scanning by not using formatting features such as bolding, italics, underlining, and shading. Using Microsoft Word will make it acceptable for attaching to emails. Rich text format (RTF) is also a good option. Use of a standard font and size (Times New Roman or Arial 12pt for example) is important. Regarding "keywords", you will already have many of these in your resume if you include an **Objective: Entry level Pharmaceutical Sales**, a **Pharmaceutical Preceptorship**, job history, achievements, and that all so important four year college degree. This is really want you need to have, nothing excessive.

Those résumé's now all collected by the home office and those current employee referrals (which always get more time and attention) are in front of a hiring manager. What can you do with your resume to give it the best advantage of surviving the initial cuts? Considering that the average time spent reading a resume is not more than a few seconds, it must be concise and easy to read. The Manager will be looking first at the header for the name and location, then objective, then current position, and then education. After that, if she likes what she sees so far, she will look at your previous positions and other information. Common problems that will eliminate your resume are perceived lack of experience, lack of four-year degree, geography in terms of where you live versus location of the territory, gaps in employment, with no explanation, if you took time to raise your family, state that. Perceived job instability or frequent job changes, poor format, or too wordy/lengthy, poor grammar and misspellings, and typos. If you have found a few in this book I apologize.

Twenty Simple Rules for Resumes and Cover Letters

After 40 years, phone calls with managers who have made numerous hiring decisions recently and conferences with some Human Resource personal, I have derived the following guidelines. These twenty rules should keep you from being disqualified by your target company and being dropped from consideration before the interview. Again, that is our objective with your resume.

Do not focus on mass mailings or blindly sending resumes to pharmaceutical companies. In the rapidly changing business environment of today, this approach is too passive. Unsolicited resumes rarely, if ever, get a response. I can tell you, that they are often not even opened and read.

Once you make direct contact with a potential employer and they agree to see you, only then, if possible, use your resume. Send it directly to the hiring manager and all your networking contacts, not to the corporate Human Resources Department. If this is against what you're told to do, include Human Resources and still mail your resume to all the others mentioned.

1) Outward appearances count heavily. Regardless of how good your handwriting is, always and without exception type everything. This includes the mailing address and your return address on the envelopes. Print directly onto the envelope if possible. If not, type the information onto a white label, and then affix it to the envelope. Many managers state they will not even open a handwritten envelope, and will discard immediately a handwritten cover letter or resume. Use a large, full-sized envelope. Use an envelope that is strong and large enough so you do not have to fold your resume, this will keep it neat and professional. It will also make it easier to scan, which is what employers will do to make it easier to store and send by email. For the same reason, do not staple your resume to your cover letter.

2) Do not be tempted to use colored paper to differentiate your resume from the mass. No manager with whom we spoke ever gave favor or "extra points" for this. Instead use 100% white cotton paper with the largest weight you can obtain. No other color is more professional than white, period! Have your resume printed using a high quality laser printer.

3) How should you send your resume? First, avoid the temptation to fax your resume. Even if you mail the original hard copy after faxing it, your faxed copy ends up being seen first, and probably most often. The best approach is to mail or email your resume. First, emailing your resume as an attachment is quite acceptable, and may be preferred by many managers because it's ease in storage, transporting, and forwarding to others. Recruiters prefer email and it is a very acceptable means to use. Include your cover letter in the same email as a separate attachment. Next, mailing is an excellent means to distribute your resume. Again, whenever possible, even when timing is not crucial, use an overnight mailing service or U.S. Priority Mail at the least. Express Mail from the U.S. Postal Service delivers overnight for an extra charge. In addition, the U.S. Postal service can deliver mail to a post office (P.O.) box. Other overnight services do not have that capability. Finally, because it is mailed in a sturdy 8.5 X 11 inch cardboard envelope, it will be protected from damage and you can avoid folding it. It will stand out in any collection of resumes and always was one of the first I would pick up.

4) When you are sending a resume in response to a classified advertisement from the newspaper, you will find that the "want ads" do not list the District Manager's or the Human Resources Representative's name. In this case, you have to rely on the strategies described in Chapters 4 and 5. Use these tactics to discover the appropriate names. Ideally, through your networking efforts, you will find the District Manager's name which you can add on your cover letter; they are more likely to pay attention to your resume. Many times, however, classified advertisements are blinded and do not even mention the company name. You should still respond with your resume and cover letter to these ads. You want every opportunity to interview and gain offers. If you have been following the method of networking, before the advertisement was ever placed you will know which companies are hiring.

5) Past performance is the best indicator of future success! Accomplishments are critical because they support your claim that you will be successful in pharmaceutical sales. Whether your previous accomplishments are in sales or any other field, they must be stated concisely in measurable or quantitative terms as much as possible. Show the numbers (sales, profits, quotas, calls made) and other measurable achievements such as recognition (awards, promotions, projects completed). Use short statements that begin with an action word such as "achieved", "earned", "increased", etc. Such statements build confidence that you are able to do the job, and are easier to understand then long accolades in paragraph form. Use of bullet points is great, for you want this to be an easy read.

6) The format or style of your resume helps organize the content and makes it attractive and easy to read. The chronological format is the one to use. List your job history by dates of employment, beginning with your present position and moving in reverse chronological order. Briefly describe the major responsibilities and your most important achievements. Include specific results! Please note: Do not take a list of competencies from Chapter Two and have them listed one after another under a summary. I can not tell you how many thousands of these are sent. The competencies can be cut and pasted to any resume. If you can do that with yours, you are not giving specific results. Begin each phrase with action verbs. In a functional format, group your work accomplishments, responsibilities, and duties according to functional skill such as "Sales" or: Organizational Skills". Choose specific skill headings or use a general heading such as "Key Skills". Sometimes, a combination of the two formats is useful. You would begin your career objective, followed by a "Featured Skills" section from the functional format, and then add your job history as in the chronological format. See the examples of each at the end of this chapter.

7) Here is a brief description of the components. Again, see the resumes at the end of this chapter for specific examples of these components. Heading (contact information), next list you're **Objective** with a concise statement of the job you want. Then, mandatory is a Pharmaceutical **Preceptorship**: as noted in the examples for every candidate without experience. Next list **Sales Experience or Professional Experience**: Also called the "job history", here you provide your current and previous positions, with all results and achievements that give further support to the objective and summary.
Always have numbers and percents in the first few bullet points if you have had any type of sale experience. Round up or down to an odd number, they always have more weight. If you have sales experience, be sure to list the word SALES first. List your employers with city and state, the position held, and the dates of each position. If it is a position that is not going to be understood by the average 10th grader, than give a short explanation of what the position is. Next list your **Education**: List your education after your work experience. There is one exception to this rule, if you are a new graduate, then list your education first, followed by your brief job history if appropriate. List your educational background beginning with the highest degree first (Master's, Bachelor's,) followed by major concentration, name and location of school. If you attended several schools, no need to list all them, just the one where you obtained your degree from. Finally optional

is **Professional Development**: Under this heading, if applicable to the position you're applying for, Pharmaceutical Sales, include any special training or credentials earned outside of your degree. This could include courses in sales, public speaking, computers, and technical areas. Avoid casual sports and hobbies on the resume. Things to include are any foreign languages, military service, major sports accomplishments and ending with Excellent References upon Request.

8) Regardless of how much information you may desire to communicate, you can always get it down to one page if you focus on the truly critical information. Do yourself and the reader a favor by keeping it to one page! See the sample resumes at the end of this chapter for examples of good formats. Keep one-inch margins, so not to crowd the page with long sentences. Leave blank space between short items of information. Include your name, address, telephone number, and email at the very top of your resume. This will allow the hiring person to contact you even if your cover letter is discarded or otherwise separated from the resume.

9) Provide a clear short objective. Entry level Pharmaceutical Sales, only five percent of job applicants do this. Managers want people who want a job in this industry and the one that is open. State your objective clearly and simply, not wordy, vague, or say anything about your long-term career goals. Avoid overused expressions about a "challenging opportunity" or a "progressive organization". Such verbiage communicates nothing and is just taking up space. Again, state your immediate job objective only. You can include more detail in your cover letter, if desired.

10) If you have completed one, and you should, include the "Pharmaceutical Sales Preceptorships" or "Pharmaceutical Sales Field Research" as a separate heading on your resume. Include a brief statement describing key job components that you observed. See example resumes at the end of this chapter and read more on the Preceptorship.

11) Do not list your salary history, current salary, or desired salary.

12) Do not list personal information such as age, date of birth, marital status, children, religious affiliations, or political affiliations.

13) Leave out explanations or "reasons for leaving" previous positions.

14) List the time spent in each job, indicating the first and last calendar year in which you were employed. Avoid any gaps in time; describe what you did in that period.

15) Do not list personal or professional references on the resume. Type your references on a separate sheet of paper. List three personal references and three professional references and bring it with you to present at the interview.

16) Triple check for errors on your resume and cover letter. Make certain that you have used proper grammar, punctuation, and spelling. Typographical errors send the message

that you are not serious about the job, or you simply lack the skills to produce a proper letter and resume.

17) Make extra copies of your resume and put them in your interviewing file. Bring them with you to all of your interviews. Offer your resume to the hiring person as you begin the meeting. They should have one already, but do not assume that they will have it in front of them. Additionally, this proactive measure communicates that you are attentive and that you anticipate the needs of the interviewer and the customer. A nice touch is to bring your resume in a file folder with your name labeled on the file tab.

18) Cover letters: The cover letter is essentially your way of thanking the employer for reviewing your resume and setting the stage for the interview. Always send a cover letter with your resume, and address it to an individual by name if at all possible. Keep the body of your cover letter under 100 words in length. Your cover letter should be direct and to the point. State clearly that you have researched the position being offered, that you want the opportunity being offered, and you have essential skills that will make you successful. Get the reader's attention by making it specific to them and their organization, including how you heard about the opportunity for example in response to an advertisement. Give contacts by name, such as, Representative Joe Gerard suggested I contact you." Use a formal business format for your cover letter and sign it neatly and legibly. Your cover letter should match your resume in format, font, and paper stock.

19) Regarding Grade Point Averages (GPAs) include it if you have graduated in the past year or two, but only if it is favorable, over 3.0. Once you are in the work force for a couple of years and have a documented professional track record, the GPA becomes less important. Some managers may place value on it more than others. My view is that academic achievement is one piece of the puzzle, one data point, but is not a reliable indicator of success in the position of pharmaceutical sales.

20) Finally, have a current resume prepared at all times throughout your career.

For additional help with writing your resume, there are thousands of resources available as from professional resume writers. It is not the objective of this publication to create the "perfect resume". The résumé's weight is diminished in the pharmaceutical representative hiring process. Remember, networking is always your primary objective. This is a position where you will be face to face with your customer in an interactive dialogue. It is very hard to read a resume and judge those competencies that are reflected in that scenario. This is why the resume will not get you a position. Your competencies have to be demonstrated, and if they are to a pharmaceutical representative in that company and they inform their District Manager that "this person" has those competencies, you are going to get the interview. That is the objective of the resume, achieve it by networking and having a resume that is professional and backs up the pharmaceutical representatives' recommendation.

Helen Lee-Murphy
1994 West 4th Ave, Suite G, Denver, CO 80015
303.847.6311
helenlmurphy@gmail.com

Objective: Entry-level position in Pharmaceutical Sales

Pharmaceutical Preceptorship: Accompanied several well experienced Pharmaceutical Representatives in the field to observe daily selling activity and confirm this career.

Sales Experience:
Brant Publishing, Aurora, CO January 2008 to Present
Account Executive, promoted advertising and communications products in 4 state areas

- Increased sales revenue from $15K to $75K by securing thirteen new accounts, increasing frequency of reach and follow-up with large client.
- Increased sales revenue from $75K to $203K including 21 accounts in the second year by targeting accounts based on prior needs assessment analysis.
- Ranked #4 nationally out of 81 Sales Representatives by differentiating approach and more consistent communication and frequency.
- Initiated, developed, and maintained accounts' expanded customer loyalty through excellent customer service relationships and efficient resolution of disputes, including follow up calls to every major order received.

Newtones Instruments, Kansas City, KS April 2006 to January 2008
Account Manager, marketed structural systems to the telecommunications industry

- Successfully attained sales growth of 21% with 39% increase in profit margin in year 2006 by targeting well identified accounts.
- Penetrated and established successful relationships with key accounts TTI, SSC, and NetWorks, knowing their specific needs and that Newtones could meet them rapidly.
- Achieved "Winners Club of Excellence" award in second year, 2006-2007

Office Projects, Inc, Overland Park, KS June 2004 to March 2006
Territory Manager

- Ranked top Territory Manager for three consecutive months, January through March 2006 by focusing on the banking segment.
- Consistently surpassed quarterly sales and gross profit, exceeding budget by 33% in second year. Analyzed all previous books of business and ranked accounts according to those who the most profitable of the past 4 years within the company.

Education: BA, Marketing Communications, 3.7 GPA University of Kansas, May 2004
University of Kansas Division One Track and Field Team, Scholarship
Proficient in Microsoft Office

Excellent references upon request

Janet Lynn Jones
1234 Summer Boulevard
Winter, PA 19123
215.555.3456
jljones@mac.com

Career Objective: Entry level position in Pharmaceutical Sales

Pharmaceutical Preceptorship: Accompanied several well experienced Pharmaceutical Representatives in the field to observe daily selling activity and confirm this career.

Education:
UNIVERSITY OF DAYTON, DAYTON, OHIO May 2008
Bachelor of Science in Business Administration
Minor in Spanish

Major Accomplishments:
GPA of 3.8 with coursework including marketing, chemistry, statistics and semester exchange program to Mexico City
Dean's Lists all semesters, while working full-time earning 90% of all tuition and expenses
Alumni Scholarship awarded in 2006
Student Council President 2007-2008

Sales Experience:
EAST DAYTON COMPUTER, DAYTON, OHIO 2008-Present
Salesperson, retail computer store, advised clients on hardware and software purchases. Interviewed clients to do a needs assessment for which product would be best and offered free trails for weekend.
Performed cashier and quality control functions.
Promoted to Assistant Manager

EARL'S DRUGSTORE, WINTER, OHIO 2007-2008
Pharmacy Technician, Consistent with daily communication to Physicians and office staff.

UNIVERSITY OF DAYTON, DAYTON, OHIO 2007-2008
Laboratory Assistant, Computer Lab. Assisted students during laboratory hours.

Skills:
Fluent in Spanish, Microsoft Office

Excellent references upon requests

Brian K. Shelton
3728 N Harvard
Chicago, IL 60613
847.846.7668
bkshelton1@yahoo.com

Career Objective: Entry level pharmaceutical sales position

Pharmaceutical Preceptorship: Accompanied several well experienced Pharmaceutical Representatives in the field to observe daily selling activity and confirm this career.

Sales Experience:
Account Manager, AT&T Business Chicago, IL July 2009-Present
Responsibilities include proposing and closing new businesses, selling the customers up AT&T's value chain of products, and managing the care, billing, and maintenance.

- Achieved 109% of year-to-date quota as of the end of April by increasing call frequency.
- Breakfast of Champions participant in October 2008, December 2008, and January 2009, ranked in top 3% nationally in sales achievement.
- Successfully completed AT&T Rolling Thunder Training Program

Data Network Account Executive, AT&T Chicago, IL February 2007- July 2008
Responsibilities included prospecting and calling on non AT&T businesses, proposing value-added services, negotiating contract terms, and closing new business.

- Brought four new clients into AT&T Chicago office increasing sales 51% in first quarter by up selling added features that clients would become more efficient.
- Created customer leave behind document that was adopted by my entire sales team which focused on the productivity of our offerings.
- Successfully completed AT&T Voice Essentials Training

Education
MBA University of Chicago (Graduation May 2010)
BA Business Administration Mendoza College of Business December 2006
Deans List Senior Year, Major GPA: 3.75
Minor: Management- Consulting
Division II Basketball Team Championship 2003

Excellent References upon Request

August 15, 2008

Ms. Nancy Young
District Manager
34 Corporate Drive North
Plaza Park, CT 03201

Dear Ms. Young:

I am applying to the position of Pharmaceutical Sales with CM Pharmaceuticals. I believe that my background and experience match the responsibilities and requirements that you are seeking.

I have a B.S. degree in Business Administration and three years of sales experience. I am a results oriented person with strong relational skills. The following points are highlights of my professional career that have prepared me for the position:

A versatile professional with direct sales experience and proven sales record.
Strengths include client need assessment, and consultative selling techniques with results documented in my attached resume. Strong ability to establish and maintain long term client relationships

Thank you for taking the time to review my attached resume, I would like to meet with you to discuss the opportunity further, I will contact you in the next week to follow up.

Sincerely,

Mark Craig

August 24, 2009

Michael Buckley
1234 Summer Boulevard
Winter, PA 23005

Ms. Ruth Boardman
District Sales Manager
XYZ Pharmaceutical Company
240 West Argonne Drive
King of Prussia, PA 19414

Dear Ms. Boardman:

Mr. Ernie Brown recently informed me of an open sales territory in the Philadelphia district due to a promotion. He suggested I contact you.

I am excited about a career with XYZ Pharmaceuticals with your current product portfolio and pipeline of new novel products, such as Aspirin XL, I know I will excel in such a challenging work environment. From my own research and conversations with Mr. Brown, I know I can make significant contributions to your sales team.

I would like the opportunity to interview with you. I will contact you by telephone early next week to discuss it. My resume is enclosed for your review. Thank you for your time and consideration.

Sincerely,

Michael Buckley

October 27, 2010

Mark Kirchoff
1234 Summer Boulevard
Winter, PA 20035

William Betts
District Sales Manager
XYZ Pharmaceutical Company
240 West Argonne Drive
King of Prussia, PA 19414

Dear Mr. Betts:

I am interested in the position of Pharmaceutical Representative (Philadelphia Inquirer, May 13). My resume is attached for your review.

I have focused my education towards a career in the pharmaceutical industry. During the last semester break, I spent three days with various well experienced Pharmaceutical Representatives to learn more about this career choice and confirm this is absolutely my goal.

From your current product portfolio and exciting new drugs in the pipeline, such as Aspiril XL, I know I will excel in such a challenging environment. I am confident that I would make a successful addition to your sales team.

I want the opportunity to prove myself in your interviewing process and as a successful sales representative for the XYZ Pharmaceutical Company. I look forward to your reply.

Sincerely,

Mark Kirchoff

Chapter Four
Research

Market yourself to others who work in the industry. This process is known as "networking", which simply means getting to know people and letting them get to know you. All it entails is presenting your professional skills and abilities effectively, to a specific audience, for a business purpose.

What do networking and research have to do with each other? Networking is the "people" preparation that goes in hand with the "paper" preparation. There is a cardinal rule at the core of the system, one that you have heard many times, especially if you have been a Girl or Boy Scout. That rule is BE PREPARED. You will find all the tools you need for success in this chapter and the next two. Chapter Five takes you into people preparation, but let us start here with the paper preparation. Upon completion of this chapter you will:

- Understand helpful techniques for research and finding resources of information
- Develop a system to keep any vital information readily accessible, including the use of company profiles provided in Chapter 9.
- Be able to set yourself apart from the candidate field by demonstrating to a potential employer that you are well prepared for the interview, as you would prepare for the sales calls in your territory.

Why Do You Need To Prepare Yourself?

The first major pay-off for being adequately prepared is that you are relaxed and confident. Your performance in networking and interviewing situations improves considerably when you are poised and thinking clearly on your feet. The candidate who is unprepared will never be at ease in the situation and will be afraid of what might come next in the interview. This distraction can cause you to stumble over easy questions, and will result in poor listening skills and ineffective communication.

Secondly, good district managers are looking for adequate preparation. They know that the individual who prepares well for an interview is demonstrating a key aspect found in the successful sales professional. The manager will correctly assume that, because you are well prepared for your interview, you are the kind of person who will be motivated to prepare well for a sales presentation. The reverse is also true. In other words, why should a manager hire a person who does not take the time and effort to excel in an interview? Will something happen to motivate that person when he or she is hired? No! The manager wants to see you demonstrate now; those things you say you will do for the company later. Thus, the under-prepared candidate has already missed the opportunity to show that he or she is capable of self–directed research and education, a habit that directly relates to success in pharmaceutical sales. Show your motivation!

Next, a manager will be more likely to hire the candidate who knows what is expected in their career rather than someone who is blindly seeking any type of employment. By having an understanding of the pharmaceutical sales industry and the specific company with whom you are interviewing you differentiate yourself. You can show excitement for specific products, new product launches, therapeutic discoveries, or a recent increase in sales, for example. You can emphasize aspects of your background and personal attributes that relate to the company or product. You can say with confidence that you want to work for this company because you have done the research and know the business and professional commitments of the organization. You will shine when asked the inevitable question, "Why do you want to work for XYZ Pharmaceuticals, Inc.?"

What Does It Mean To Be Adequately Prepared?

Being prepared means that you know what to expect, are ready, and will not only participate in, but control your interview. You should be prepared with your answers to typical questions. Also be ready to ask smart ones of your own. You should be able to demonstrate a basic understanding of a sales representative's job in the pharmaceutical industry, and of the specific company with which you are interviewing. These aspects are presented in the following chapters of *Insight*. The central point of this chapter though, is to teach you how to conduct industry research, which is an integral part of the preparation you will need for successful networking and interviewing. Where do you get the information? Industry information is accessible from these general areas:

- Consumer media sources
- Company published information
- Business publications
- Industry publications
- Internet sites
- Consumer media sources

The most readily available source is the everyday consumer media. The news media frequently and fervently reports on health issues, and consumers are listening. Public awareness is high due to health issues, which attracts attention and raises viewer ratings. These easily accessible sources of information include the following:

- Local newspapers
- National newspapers such as the Wall Street Journal and USA
- News magazines, such as Time and Newsweek
- Business periodicals, such as Forbes, Fortune, and Crain's
- Television news magazine broadcasts such as Dateline and 20/20

You can start building your own awareness by reading these reports as part of your normal routine. Read thoroughly the daily newspaper for health and medical related stories. Look for any headlines on healthcare, managed care, insurance companies, medical breakthroughs, new prescription drugs, and pharmaceutical manufactures. Read each article with a questioning eye. What are the issues? What is the main message? Who wrote this and what is the author's perspective? You will not need to buy many subscriptions if you make a habit of stopping by the public library to browse and read. You can also obtain copies of pertinent articles for later reference.

Consumer media sources are also good for information on specific medicines. Look for advertisements of prescription drugs in magazines and television commercials. In the ad, the manufacturer is communicating the features and benefits of their product. This will give you insight into how they are positioning the product in the marketplace. Who is the manufacturer? What features and benefits are being offered to the patient? These features and benefits are often the same promotional messages being used by the pharmaceutical representative. Some print advertisements include an abbreviated version of the package insert, which is also called "drug labeling". This is in the fine print section, and it lists indications (under what circumstances) the drug is to be used, side effects, dosages, patient instructions, and a brief explanation of how the drug works.

Excellent baseline information is available through multiple media sources. Educating yourself on healthcare and the pharmaceutical industry is a way to develop life-long learning habits. However, for more specific and in-depth information, locate a medical library, where you can have access to numerous medical journals. The best resources are medical school libraries, large "teaching" hospitals, and other university settings.

Besides accessing general healthcare and pharmaceutical industry information, what can you do to get the business and marketing information you want before interviewing? Where can you find the details about a specific company's financial performance, sales force size, product line, and products currently in research or awaiting Food and Drug Administration (FDA) approval? There are two main sources for detailed company-specific information:

- Company published sources, annual reports, website communications tabs, recent press releases and webcast
- Sales representatives working for that company

Chapter 5, "Networking", will discuss interacting with Sales Representatives. Let's look now at company-published sources of information. Examples of these are annual reports, 10K filings, current marketing initiatives, and marketing material. Annual reports are available by just about all companies via their web sites with the option that allows you to download them immediately. View reports for the last several years when interviewing, Is the company on track with its own agenda? Are forecasters' goals being met? Are new products making it to the marketplace as promised in previous years' reports? What is the corporate direction? See if plans for the organization come to reality and get a solid history of the organization.

Next, directories such as Standard & Poor's and Dunn & Bradstreet are good sources of recent information. All public companies must file a "10K, 10Q Reports" every quarter with the Securities and Exchange Commission (SEC). These are abbreviated annual reports; they are available to you also online.

Visit the investor's site on every pharmaceutical company's website. Sign up for stock alerts, emails of press releases (new product introductions), earnings calls, webcast, etc. The information today is endless via most company's investor relations. Your research should also include a review of the business newspapers and periodicals. These include The Wall Street Journal, Crain's Business, Business Weekly, Forbes, and Fortune. You can use the business index to search for all published articles on a specific company by name. You can then request back issues from the reference desk at your library and read the articles. Call around to different libraries until you find one with a business index and access to previously published articles. Of course these are also available on line, but can get quite costly, usually requiring a subscription to gain full access to the site.

Company specific research should also include a thorough review of the company's web site other than just the investor tab. These sites are an excellent source for company overviews, product summaries, drug labeling, stock trends, employment opportunities, and even more employee benefits. They can be quite time consuming, so until you have an interview or networking session, the profiles in Chapter Nine will have you well prepared.

Your research may also include trade journals of the pharmaceutical industry if you would like to increase your depth of knowledge. These publications often discuss prevailing and emerging business trends, profile organizations, review products, and highlight key individuals. Some examples are *Pharmaceutical Executive* and *FDC Reports*. Thousands of libraries subscribe to electronic –retrieval services, that will speed your research. A lönger listing of references is available with the "Suggested Resources" at the end of this chapter.

How Do You Keep And Readily Access Vital Research Information?

You may be collecting articles and doing research over the course of a job search that could last for weeks, months, or longer. It may be quite awhile before you need to access that information for networking and interviewing. How will you keep track of everything you want to remember or save for future reference? You need to have a storage method for important research and networking information that is easy to use. I suggest that you create an electronic and hard file on each company for which you have collected information or with whom you have made contact. Save general industry information that does not pertain to any single company in a separate file. As you find articles on companies of interest, print them out from the internet, clip them from newspapers or magazines, or photocopy them. Take notes during your research and add these to the appropriate file. You can also add product advertisements, computer printouts of web site information, and package inserts that you can collect from pharmacies. All of this will have you better prepared and set you apart for your interview.

Additionally, you need to document your networking contacts and track your telephone calls, meetings, and correspondence. Save your notes on all calls and interactions with sales representatives and managers, your meetings, and your interviews. Maintain your current resume as well as the original one that you sent to the company. Also, keep copies of your resumes, cover letters, thank you notes, and follow-up letters in another readily accessible file.

Company Profiles

Company Profiles in Chapter 9 contain company summaries, their history, annual healthcare revenue, sales force size, current products and their therapeutic area including those products nearest to the later stages of approval. Again, great sections by which to get you started with fifty companies and save you countless hours of time.

Networking

Networking is one of the most important sources of vital company information, and should be an integral part of your research. Your resources are the many current representatives of pharmaceutical companies. Interacting with these people is the way to find out what is important to their respective organizations right now. An example is that I just read a major pharmaceutical company released a new product within the last 12 weeks, when discussing this information with a Regional Director of the company position with the company, she stated that this was a product, though approved, will not be promoted by the salesforce due to the limited utilization. Networking with Pharmaceutical Representatives can give you routines of the business within that specific organization's culture. Through these individuals, you will discover up-to-date information about the company as I describe above. You will learn their sales region/district/ territory goals and performance within the organization. You will discover what is happening in your region of the country and in specific districts and sales territories that may be very different to the company nationally.

Always refrain from any unprofessional websites that are full of gossip, with the mention individuals names or actual proprietary company information. Professional networking allows you to uncover success stories and identify challenges via Pharmaceutical Representatives, from the area where you will be working. This is something you are not going to find in an annual report. You can learn how you can possibly contribute to the organization right there in your area. Discovering this information first hand from sales representatives will round out your "paper" research. This is a critical part of your interview preparation.

The advantage of performing all this research is realized only if you successfully demonstrate your expertise in the interview. There are several approaches and you may want to use all of them. Now that you have done the preparatory work, how can you best leverage all your efforts?

- How do you demonstrate to a potential employer that you are prepared?
- Can you be differentiated from other candidates?
- What is the benefit of hiring you?

As mentioned above, an important benefit to you is the confidence that comes from knowing you are ready. Your confidence will show in your voice, eye contact, and posture. Stand and sit straight, look the interviewer in the eyes and project your voice loudly by breathing deeply from the diaphragm.

A second benefit, of course, is your ability to discuss specific company information. Make a point of presenting it. Take advantage of the natural flow of the dialogue to interject what you know. Show that you have done your research. You will appear energetic and attentive to detail. It will show you went the extra mile to learn something about the company.

Here is an example:

Interviewer: "The Company will launch a new wide spectrum antibiotic this fall"
Candidate: "Yes, I read about the exclusive once-a-day dosage of your new drug. It appears to offer some exceptional benefits to patients and physicians treating pneumonia."

Be sure to include names of company individuals you have met with or talked with on the telephone. Here is an example:

Candidate: "When I met with Helen Ellies, I learned that the sales force is currently undergoing product training for your new anti-ulcer medication. I understand that there are several other new products under development as well in your pipeline."

As you are presenting your professional strengths, a brief description of your research and networking method makes a great example of your self-motivation, determination, and other attributes. Bring along your company file and lay it on the table as you talk. If the interviewer shows interest in this, which he surely will, go into more detail and show off what you have.

Begin your interview by making a point that you are prepared. State in your opening remarks, "I have researched XYZ Pharmaceutical Company and the sales representative position. I know that I can be an excellent fit for your company." This opening statement will often get a curious response such as, "OK, tell me what you know about the company." The ball is in your court and you are doing just what you prepared to do. Your effort is paying off. You have taken control of the interview.

Next, you can demonstrate your preparation by providing specific company information. You can also do this by asking intelligent questions. Use specific company information as a lead-in to your questions to the interviewer. Add an initial statement that first gives information about the company. For example:

Candidate: [give information] "I understand that XYZ Pharmaceuticals is focusing on diabetes and hypertension currently [ask question]. Which therapeutic categories does your pipeline seem to focus on moving forward?"

Clip and save prescription drug advertisements from consumer magazines and medical journals. Publications such as the Journal of the American Medical Association or the New England Journal of Medicine, are excellent sources for this (remember the target of these advertisements is the physician, not a patient). Preferably, find an advertisement for a medication manufactured by the company with which you are interviewing. Bring it to the interview and have a short sales presentation to the interviewer on the product. The magazine advertisement can became your sales "visual aid", as you observed during the Preceptorship and you are demonstrating that you can make a presentation just as if you were presenting to a physician. You will place yourself in the top 1% with this tactic. Be sure, to ask for the commitment from "the customer", by stating, "Will you use this product in your next three to five patients when appropriate?"

A Final Word on Research

Surprisingly, less than about 5% of candidates will perform *any* research. Over 20 years of interviewing and I can not tell you the number of candidates who didn't bother to learn the company's products, their names, or the name of the CEO. This is very sad when the candidate is otherwise showing good potential. In contrast, when a candidate is well-versed in the industry, the position and the company itself (this will only be about 1-3% of the candidates) the District or Regional Manager knows that this individual is determined to succeed. Sure, every candidate is going to trip up with a product name pronunciation or disease state, which is common.

Demonstrating this type of interviewing skills, gives a District Manager confidence in their decision to hire an individual, a decision that will cost the company on an average nearly $180,000 to train, when a candidate does the research. The entire working relationship gets off to a great start. This will help you secure yourself a position at the top, which guarantees your success. Challenge yourself to execute the research and begin right now.

Resources, bookmark all for future reference:

www.coreynaham.com Outstanding site for over 10 years, daily updates with unlimited resources and links for the pharmaceutical industry, a benchmark site.
Fair Disclosure: Corey with numerous years experience in the pharmaceutical industry has endorsed my book over the past 10 years and is a good friend.
www.fiercehealthcare.com Site for candidate, current industry personal, seeking daily delivery of pharmaceutical breaking industry news.
www.clinicaltrials.gov fantastic to see the research trails that are actually taking place currently
www.pharmrep.com Pharmaceutical Representative Magazine published monthly, well worth the $50.00 per year to keep abreast of industry information.
www.pinksheet.com Pharmaceutical industry information, a standard in every home office in the industry, though subscription rates are too high for the candidate, great information is available at various areas on their site, an Elsevier Company
www.healthnewsdaily.com another excellent resource by Elsevier
www.pharmexec.com News features, for most positions in the industry, by Advanstar Communications Inc.
www.pharmweb.net Full website with directory, excellently done
www.biotechnologyheathcare.com Updates in the biotech segment, again a must in the growing channel of biotech, provided by MediMedia a leader in services to the pharmaceutical and biotech industry
www.healthleadersmedia.com A solid resource to check often for healthcare's marketplace, HealthLeadersMedia, HCPro, Inc.
www.ptcommunity.com Industry and product news, superior on information on today's marketplace, just a must by Medimedia
www.pharmaceutical-business-review.com Daily news updates, well done by Progressive Media Group.

www.pharma-mkting.com Industry news and networking site by VirSci Corporation.
www.pharmtech.com News from various facets of the industry
www.phrma.org Pharmaceutical Research and Manufacturers America, the industry's "voice". A must visit for every candidate, that is a great complimentary source of many references and information in this book. A "must read" for candidates.
www.eyeforpharma.com Global pharmaceutical industry insight for additional topics by First Conferences Ltd.
www.fcg.com Industry news, again on a global insight by Computer Sciences Corporation

Note: Neither pharmaceuticalsales.com nor the author has any contractual agreements with any of the above listed website's or resources. In addition there are no financial agreements with any pharmaceutical related business consultants, search firms, resume writing consultants, etc. in any manner.
Finally, there are no link exchanges provided on the pharmaceuticalsales.com website for any organization except coreynahman.com which has existed since 1998 and a friend of the First Edition. This site has an enormous amount of news and reference for not only the candidate, but the experienced representative,

Chapter Five
"It's *not who you know*; it's *who you learn to know*"

This chapter describes a unique way for self-marketing within the pharmaceutical industry. This method is the key to successful employment. Read this chapter and put the strategy into practice. Sending out the mass mailings of resumes and cover letters will yield little in the way of results.

You have probably heard the old adages, "You need to know someone to get into the pharmaceutical industry" or "It's not what you know, it's who you know." This expression refers to breaking into business and moving up the corporate ladder. Now, forget all about that old adage and learn **"It's *not who you know*; it's *who you learn to know*".**

This chapter will provide a sure-fire way for you to market yourself to the targeted environment and must be your primary strategy. Yes, you will still be checking the newspapers and responding to want ads, contacting recruiters and search firms, but these can not be your primary strategy. Remember you are going to differentiate yourself from the herd. What you need to do is simple, and it works. It helped me into the industry and has proven successful for thousands of candidates since I wrote the First Edition of "Insight" in the spring of 1998.

Your goal is so simple, become familiar with all the pharmaceutical representatives working in your geography, and more importantly, have them become familiar with you.

By following the strategy described in this chapter, you will accrue the following advantages:

- Obtain inside information about an opening before it is advertised (if advertised
- Be known (and well thought of) by the employer before an opening even exists
- Demonstrate your initiative and creativity to potential employers in your geography
- Establish important relationships with individuals in the pharmaceutical industry
- Possess detailed knowledge about the industry, the company, and the position
- Demonstrate your detailed knowledge of the industry to representatives in your area
- Learn the key individuals, Pharmaceutical Representatives and District Managers who recommend and do the actual hiring within your area

Okay, now you want to begin, so what do you do next? First, create your own database of current pharmaceutical industry professionals working in your desired geographic area. You can employ various means to accomplish this. Here are some suggestions:

Visit a physician's office: Typically, doctors' offices have from 25 to 75 sales representatives in the pharmaceutical industry calling on them on a consistent basis. Explain your desire to enter the pharmaceutical sales profession and ask if they will photocopy the business cards of all the Pharmaceutical Representatives who call on their office. Often, these business cards are filed together and can be easily addressed by an office secretary or nurse. Start with your own doctor, or the doctor of a family member (surely they should give a little assistance, if not, look for another physician for your care), or friend of a family member may be able to assist. Get the word out with friends and family, most times, someone knows a pharmaceutical representative. Finally, common for most candidates, do not be afraid to walk into a physician's office cold. Be sure to tell them what you are doing and ask for their assistance. You are going to experience rejection, probably more rejection than success, but that is just part of being a salesperson. SMILE! Keep trying different offices until you get what you want. I suggest trying large medical buildings and starting at the top floor and working your way down. During this process, you're actually going to run into Pharmaceutical Representatives face to face while they are working the building. This will give you an excellent opportunity to express your interest in the industry, and ask if you can call them sometime and obtain their business card. Dress your best, as though you were going to an actual interview.

During your office visits, speak directly to the physician or nurse if available, about recommending a specific Sales Representative for you to contact. Ask for a name that stands out as someone they respect and consider an excellent Pharmaceutical Representative. When you contact each Pharmaceutical Representative, make it a point to inform them that the doctor specifically mentioned them as being exceptional or outstanding in their field. If possible, state exactly what the doctor or any member of the staff has said. This is a positive way to break the ice when you introduce yourself.

Apply these same successful strategies when you visit a hospital or retail pharmacy. Always ask for copies of their representatives' business cards. If you explain what you want to accomplish, most pharmacists are willing to help you. If your current work environment is a hospital, the hospital pharmacy and emergency room are also goldmines for Pharmaceutical Representatives' business cards. Maybe you also know a nurse or pharmacist that can assist you with this networking. Independent pharmacists, rather than large pharmacies, may be more likely to keep a file of business cards or have some more "one on one" time. They may be familiar with local representatives and be willing to share information.

Another way to develop contacts is to call your State or Pharmacist Association. Explain your desire to enter the pharmaceutical sales profession and ask if they will recommend a few contacts so that you can learn more about the industry. Many of these associations are located in your state's capitol. They may have regular meetings which you may be allowed to attend if possible.

Once you have collected your business cards, add them to your database. Now you are ready to start making telephone contacts. I have some suggestions to help you ask questions during your initial contact that will produce your desired result. The goal of this phase is to gain job information, get to know pharmaceutical industry personnel, specifically develop rapport. Please read *Insight* entirely before you begin this networking phase. Once you have the business cards of 15-25 representatives (maybe less if you're more rural in location), make a few calls per day, perhaps two to three. Explain briefly who you are and the purpose of your call—that you are interested in pharmaceutical sales as a career, and you would like to briefly discuss it. Always ask the person if it is a convenient time for them, or if another time would be better.

Let them know that you are willing to fit their schedule. The evening is best because representatives are out making sales calls during the day. Do not by shy!

Here is an example of how you might begin the telephone conversation:

"Hello, Ms. Young, my name is Janet Jones and I am interested in learning about pharmaceutical sales. Is this a good time to call you? I was given your card by Dr. Wellborn who suggested you would be a valuable resource because of your professionalism. I would like to talk about your career. When is the best time for you? I will work my schedule around yours."

Remember to conduct yourself professionally. As the saying goes, "You never get a second chance to make a first impression." Put yourself in your "Interview Mode" because this helps you prepare to be the best candidate for the job. Treat all contacts in your networking process as potential interviewers and as potential co-workers! Be upbeat, positive, and professional. If your contact will talk with you, then you have achieved your first goal. It may take awhile, a week or two before you suggest a meeting, possibly your treat for a breakfast or lunch. A personal meeting is more memorable, gives you greater opportunity to sell yourself, establishes rapport, and builds relationships. If some representatives decline contact, hang in there, it is part of your process, don't take it personally, and keep networking. Some contacts may decide they would rather not meet with you, but would be willing to give you more time on the telephone, so be prepared for this situation. Ask when would be a good time to call back, and then during that follow-up call proceed with your discussion and questions as you would in a face-to-face meeting. Many representatives will gladly share their time and expertise while there are others who will not. Respect their wishes and remain professional as you thank them for their time. Remember that rejection is common in sales at all levels. Never forget that you are a salesperson who is marketing yourself in this situation. Many times, you will be turned down. Even a refusal adds to your knowledge base, which helps your career potential. Sales people know that there is a certain percentage of failure in their sales calls. Your persistence will pay off and you are going to get an offer!

Another situation you should prepare for is voice mail. You can use this to your advantage by being prepared ahead of time with a concise message. State your name, purpose of the call, and inform them that you will call again later. Here is an example of a voice mail message you might leave for a networking contact;

"Hello, Ms .Young, my name is Janet Jones. I am interested in a career in pharmaceutical sales. Dr. Wellborn suggested that you would be best to provide some insight into pharmaceutical sales, and gave me your card. The purpose of my call is to discuss this with you. My phone number is 847.768.4343. I will call again to speak directly with you. Thank you for your time."

Note that you do not ask the contact to call you back but leave your number. Take the initiative to make the connection yourself. You must attempt to reach the person, calling at various times of the day and evening, and leaving a concise message each time.

After you have tried to reach them two or three times (and left a brief message each time so they know you tried), it is appropriate to leave your number and ask for a return call.

Here is an example of such a message:

"Hello, Ms. Young. This is Janet Jones calling. I would like to speak with you about the pharmaceutical industry, and have been unable to reach you after several tries. Would you please return my call at a time most convenient for you? My telephone number is 847.768.4343. If you get my voicemail, please let me know the best time for me to call you back, and I will do so. Thank you."

Keep your messages brief and to the point. This helps you make a good impression. Your new network contact will sense that you are not likely to take up much time. If your contact wants to offer their time, he or she can certainly do so and will gladly call you back.

Use the same brevity and professionalism in recording your own outgoing message for your incoming calls. Avoid gimmicks, child greetings, your favorite rock/rap song or any background noise. Identify yourself by name, telephone number, and request that the callers leave a time for you to return their call.

Here is an example of an outgoing message:

"Hello, this is Janet Jones, at 525-5152. Please leave your name and number and when it is a good time for me to return your call and I will do so. Thank you."

Because you are asking people to call you back, always be prepared for their call. The value of using a database and Profiles in Chapter 9 is that you can find needed information quickly. You should have made notes of your previous contacts. It is perfectly fine to ask the caller to hold for just one moment while you locate your information. This also gives you a little time to take a deep breath and gather your thoughts for the call. Remember to smile when you speak. Sure they can not see you, but though it sounds silly, you will sound better on the telephone. Now that you are speaking to your contacts by telephone, you want to make an appointment to see them in person. Offer to meet at their most convenient time. Invite them to a breakfast or lunch meeting where you can talk one-on-one. Sales professionals are often too familiar with providing meals for their customers, and it can be a refreshing change to have someone buy them breakfast (less expensive) or lunch. If they do not have time for a meal, perhaps a coffee/coke break would work better. Have them choose the restaurant or coffee shop that would be convenient for them. Have several locations in mind in case they want you to pick the place.

You have made your appointment! You are on course and networking the way that is required. Remember, this is your first interview with someone who can boost your career, so be prepared. At this stage of the game, you will be controlling most of the dialogue. Review all of the information you have learned about the company and show your contact that you are familiar with their company. Your preparation will demonstrate that you are serious and committed.

Your contact will not feel that you have wasted their time. On the contrary, they will be more likely to provide you with the information you want, and help you reach your goal (rapport with the representative) and even in the future connection with a District or Regional Manager. When you meet, bring your resume (though don't offer it to your contact right away) and other information you have collected about their company to show your dedication. Leave a copy near the end of the meeting and there is never any need to mention reading this book, *Insight*. Write down various notes from the Company Profiles regarding what you want to say and ask. Be friendly and enthusiastic. Remember this individual will be a critical part of your job search. They will be evaluating you, wondering if you would be a good candidate to work with, and one that they can recommend to their company. Most pharmaceutical companies pay a finder's fee or recruitment bonus to their own employees when a candidate they recommend is hired. This bonus can be between two and ten thousand dollars (with the average more toward the lower side), which is far less costly for the company than retaining a professional recruiter. Pharmaceutical Sales Representatives are often on the lookout for good people! Sometimes there is even contest for them to see who can secure the most candidates when there are openings during an expansion for a new product.

The contact person with whom you are networking is representing their pharmaceutical organization. You are representing yourself. If you show up in attire that is inappropriate, your contact will probably conclude that you are not likely to demonstrate good judgment in their organization or to their District Manager.

Now, what kind of information do you want from your meetings and telephone calls with industry contacts? First, thank the person for meeting with you. State that you are excited about the career opportunities available in pharmaceutical sales and you would like to learn as much as possible about his or her job experience. This is one of the most important things; learn more about the individual, their history, their entry into the industry, their education. In short, you have three goals for this meeting. First, learn more about the individual by focusing the meeting on them. Develop a relationship that you are able to continue the process in a few weeks. Second, gain an understanding of their company and their view of the industry. Third, refrain from presenting your resume to fast, which will change the agenda to you and loose your ability to accomplish the first two goals.

Twenty networking questions you might use are listed below. Write these down on a legal pad and enter a few of your own. You will not ask all these questions at one meeting, of course, but tailor them to your interests with this particular organization. Be sensitive to the other person; do not bombard them with closed-ended questions. Instead, include open-ended questions that will encourage them to discuss freely. Begin with questions that are more personal and show interest in the person. This will invite them to speak and builds rapport.

QUESTIONS FOR YOUR PHARMACEUTICAL INDUSTRY CONTACTS

(Remember the great Dale Carnegie, "everyone's favorite topic is themselves")

1) Why did you decide to enter a career in pharmaceutical sales?
2) How did you get your position in pharmaceutical sales?
3) What educational background do you have, where did you attend school?

4) How did you obtain your current position with XYZ?
5) What is your current area or territory?
6) What do you enjoy about your company?
7) What, if anything, about the position, has surprised you?
8) What is a somewhat typical day like in your territory?
9) How many physicians do you call on?
10) How do your products rank in their therapeutic category?
11) How does your company measure sales performance?
12) What kind of training did you attend with your company?
13) How is your company's salesforce structured (districts, regions business units)?
14) What new products does your company have in development?
15) What are some career options that you have within your organization that may be of interest to you?
16) Do you know of other Pharmaceutical Representatives with other organizations?
17) Do you have any of their contact information, business cards, email or physical addresses?
18) Is there a local professional association of pharmaceutical sales representatives in this area?
19) I am very interested in a career in the pharmaceutical industry;
20) Can you notify me if you hear of something regarding open territories?

Conclude by thanking the individual for taking the time to meet with you. Ask if you may follow up with a telephone call to see if there are any positions open or possible opportunities in the future. Ask if they would contact you in the future if a territory even looks as if it might become available in any area. It is to your advantage to know about it as soon as possible so you can respond quickly. Be absolutely sure to send a follow-up letter or card to personally thank the individual for the meeting. See the example thank-you letter provided at the end of this chapter. Now, what do you do? Complete your notes, adding information you learned to your files and database. It is well known that Pharmaceutical Representatives and Managers state that if a candidate does not show this simple courtesy (sending a note) they will likely be eliminated from future meetings. If your contact has provided you with additional names, make those connections as soon as possible.

When you hear of an available position, move quickly and make contact with your network! Express great interest in the position and ask for an interview. Get your resume to your contact person, and to the District Manager (if known), immediately. Again, use an overnight delivery service.

If you do not hear of any open positions right away, be patient. Your networking process will expand over time. Continue to make new contacts and meet more people each week, which will lead to a growing number of appointments each week. Be confident that you are building your own success and that over time you will gain the interviews and the "job offer" you are seeking. It may take several months or more of networking with your contacts. Some opportunities may come up even a year later. To maintain your relationship with your network, follow-up with telephone calls every four to six weeks. They will remember you and call you when there is an opportunity.

With this strategy, you are placing yourself in front of other candidates. Only you can make it work. Stay focused and persistent. You will close the sale!

Observe several Pharmaceutical Representative's performing their job in real situations with real customers. I refer to this strategy as the "Pharmaceutical Preceptorship" (described below). Please, don't send emails with all your excuses why you can not accomplish this, I have heard most, for nearly 20 years, whether car insurance, company policies, HIPPA (Health Insurance Personal Privacy Act). HIPPA is amusing, for the Pharmaceutical Representative believes that they are entitled to the patient's medical information, that's preposterous. They are passing you off, a bluff, you need to build better rapport with these individuals, then suggest meeting them in a large medical building lobby and accompany them on a few calls. Candidates still email me quite often stating that they accomplish this part of the process, so keep at it.

District Managers want to hire an individual who is knowledgeable about the position for which they are interviewing. In other words, they want to know that you have researched the job thoroughly, you know what is involved, and you are determined to get it. One way to demonstrate this is to show that experience on your resume. First, state clearly that you want to work in a pharmaceutical sales position. As covered earlier, your resume has, Objective: Entry level pharmaceuticals sales position. The next line list "Pharmaceutical Preceptorship". To achieve this, ask all of your networking contacts to allow you to accompany them for a day or even just a few hours as they go about their normal routine. Go on more than one Preceptorship so you can see different styles of how a representative works. Please, never assume you're seeing the best, or even the middle on the performance curve, but you are seeing a style that may be successful. If you are still in school, your holiday breaks and summers off are great times to accomplish this objective and add that you're researching this for career options.

Though a great addition for the resume, the **Preceptorship** is mandatory before any pharmaceutical sales interview. It will help you to see first hand what happens on a daily basis. As you go through the day, observe everything you can about what the representative is doing, and why. Actually, you can pretend you are a trainee or perhaps a District Manager for a day! The "ride-along" (shadowing for a day or Preceptorship) is very common, many companies make it a part of the interview processes, not only to be sure candidates know exactly what's involved in the position, but more importantly for feedback to the hiring manager from the Pharmaceutical Representative you are riding with. No matter what the situation of spending time in the field with a Pharmaceutical Representative, I want you to take note of the following (this comes from being a District and Regional Sales Manager for numerous years, by the end of the day, you will know if you rode with a true pro).

1) How does the representative plan his or her day?
2) Do they have an itinerary, call plan, or other means to plan their routing?
3) How they arrange their selling material before entering an office?
4) Do they mention a specific goal and history for this physician they're about to call on?
5) What is the Pharmaceutical Representative trying to accomplish on this call?
6) How they greet the office staff? Do they know their names?
7) If not, do they attempt to learn and make note of names for future calls?

8) If the Pharmaceutical Representative is asked to wait, what do they do with down time? Revisit their daily plan? Catch up on paperwork? Build rapport with the office staff, provide value? Or do they read the latest Sports Illustrated and People Magazine?
9) How do they open their presentation with the physician? Is it enthusiastic, engaging? Would it get your attention if you were a physician?
10) What material do they use to sell the product? The Sales Aid, Clinical Reprints?
11) If they do use clinical studies, observe how they introduce the study (author, journal name, date published, etc.) and draw out key points.
12) If this Pharmaceutical Representative does not use a visual sales aid, clinical reprint or other materials during the day, surely, look for another representative to ride with for a better learning experience.
13) How do they use the product samples to assist their selling efforts? Do they explain their value and usage to the customer? 92% Percent of representatives fail to do this in a recent study. A sample for a patient is valued conservatively at $15-$175.
14) What questions do they ask the physician to learn their prescribing habits?
15) Do they emphasize the features and benefits of their product? Describe the dosing, side effects, or drug interactions to watch out for?
16) Do they gain commitment of the physician to try the product on some patients if agreed upon? Do you feel the physician will use the product?
17) Do they make some notes after the call and immediately plan for the next call? This will quickly show you a difference between the amateur and professional.

Your responsibilities on the Pharmaceutical Preceptorship:

Be on time! Be well-dressed, as for any interview, remember, you are being interviewed at all times. Offer to purchase lunch. Importantly, do not let your guard down. Be conversational but not too casual or familiar. As a rule, do not tell anything to this representative that you would not print on the top of your resume! Be a top notch professional every minute; again, your interview best at all times. Take notes of what you observe during the day, at the end of day when you have departed. Use your notes during an interview process for a particular company. You can refer to them when you meet the manager. For example, "I really noticed how Henry closed the call to gain commitment from the doctor…" Sometimes, a field ride may be part of the interview process, recommended by the manager. If this is the case, you will definitely need to discuss in detail the events of the day and your observations and conclusions. Another candidate vying for the same position may also be doing field travel. So be at your best and make the most of it. Always as any good salesperson asks for action at the end of the day, ask the representative to put in a good word for you to the manager. State, that you believe you would be an excellent fit for this company and career opportunity with XYZ Pharmaceuticals. Follow up with a letter of thanks that evening to the Pharmaceutical Representative and send overnight. See example letter at the end of this chapter.

Now that you are actively networking and researching the industry, you are likely to get to your next step-the interview! Chapter 6 promises many more insights into this exciting stage of attaining your career goal.

SAMPLE LETTER FOLLOW-UP NETWORKING MEETING

December 16, 2008

Janet Lynn Jones
1234 Summer Boulevard
Winter, PA 19123

Ms. Nancy Young
XYZ Pharmaceutical Company Inc.
1134 W. Emma
Milentz, PA 19126

Dear Ms. Young:

It was a pleasure seeing you today. I value your making the time in your busy schedule to meet with me. It was great to learn how you have established yourself within your territory in such a short time with XYZ Pharmaceutical Company.

Your position sounds exciting, yet challenging. I will call the contacts you gave me, and I have scheduled myself to attend the Philadelphia Representative Association meeting next month.

XYZ Pharmaceutical Company seems like an excellent organization. I believe your new product for high cholesterol will be a huge success in an extremely competitive market. I would like to have the opportunity to interview with XYZ. I appreciate you informing your district manager of my desire to enter this industry with your company. Should any territories become available, please contact me.

As we discussed, I will call you in four to six weeks. In the meantime, please call me if any opportunities arise. My phone number is 847.522.1323. Again, thank you for your time and assistance. I am looking forward to keeping in touch with you in the future!

Sincerely,

Janet Lynn Jones

SAMPLE LETTER: FOLLOW-UP PHARMACEUTICAL PRECEPTORSHIP

December 13, 2008

Janet Lynn Jones
1234 Summer Boulevard
Winter PA 19123

Mr. William Betz
XYZ Pharmaceutical Company Inc.
1134 W. Argonne Avenue
Milentz, PA 19134

Dear Mr. Betz:

I appreciate the time you spent this afternoon showing me aspects of your job with XYZ Pharmaceutical Company. Your years of experience sure demonstrate your rapport with the physicians and office staff.

It was fascinating to see the consultative sales approach you use and how you schedule your day. Dr. Charles Wellborn was interested in your new product for cholesterol and was eager to hear the points you made from the medical journal article.

Again, I would like to express my interest in any territories that become available with XYZ Pharmaceutical Company. I appreciate you informing your district manager of my determination to enter this industry. With your recommendation, I will forward my resume to him.

Thank you so much for your assistance. As we agreed, I will call you in four to six weeks to check on the status of any opportunities in your company. In the meantime, please call me if an opportunity develops. My phone number is 847.512.3425.

Sincerely,

Janet Jones

CHAPTER SIX
The Interviews

As you successfully apply the networking strategies described, you will soon be reaping the desired result—Interviews. The chapter you are about to read describes what you should expect from the interview process and how you should prepare for it. This approach helps you to be at your best, with the greatest level of confidence. Included at the end of the chapter is a list of guidelines for professional attire that will have you looking and feeling your professional best as well. Follow these guidelines for dress for all your networking activities also.

Your first meeting is potentially the beginning of a long-term relationship; therefore, it is critical that you present a positive, winning image throughout the interview process. Initiate that relationship on your terms, and be the consummate professional.

Interviewing with pharmaceutical companies has its unique challenges. There are several different types of discussions you might experience with any given company. How you handle each of them is critical to your success. There will be a progression of meetings as you advance through the interviewing process. Be prepared for the various conversations you will have. Fortunately, your strategy will be essentially the same regardless of the type. However, there are some variations in how you must conduct yourself. The different types of interviews as follows:

- Screening Interview
- First Interview
- Final Interviews
- Job Fairs
- Second Interview

Companies and District Managers will vary in how they conduct each step. They will also differ in the type of questions they ask and the manner in which they ask them. This fact underscores your need to be prepared for anything since you may or may not be given prior advice regarding the types of questions you will be expected to answer. For example, some interviewers may ask questions consisting of situations that occur in the day-to-day work of the Pharmaceutical Representative. In some cases, you will be given the situations in order to prepare for either a telephone screening or a face-to-face interview. The situational questions could be customer-related or company-related. Customer related situations would be challenges that come up with doctors, office nurses, and receptionists or gatekeepers. They could also be objections to your product, such as having a higher cost than your competitor has. Company-related situations are about working on teams with other representatives.

Because some companies are asking job-specific questions, it is important for you to study the answers in this guide. Just as imperative is time in the field with several Pharmaceutical Sales Representative's to observe what their daily selling activities consist of, as discussed in Chapter Five. Perform the preceptorship's early in your job search. Create a list of scenarios that you want to observe and use the situations Insight provides. Ask the representatives you talk and meet with how they would handle each one. You may add excellent and creative answers to your knowledge base. Not every company will ask situational questions about selling pharmaceuticals.

However, regardless of the situation or exact wording of the question, the interviewer is looking for evidence of whether or not you would be the right candidate for the job. Obviously, you have not had previous experience selling pharmaceuticals and the interviewer is aware of that. Initially they are looking for the way you think, how you sell, and what your skills are in different job competencies. Your answers should always include specific examples about how you were successful in similar situations, either current or past positions. This is critical. The interviewer will be looking for explicit behavior patterns and will ask if you do not provide them. One suggestion is to use a simple format to describe your accomplishments: Situation-Task-Action-Results. This is sometimes referred to as the STAR format of interview questions, or "situational" format. Even if the question is about selling to doctors or other aspects of pharmaceutical sales, your answer should include a similar personal experience and detail how you handled it successfully. Your answer would be complete by starting with a brief description of the actual situation, the task or goal to be preformed, the action you took and the result of that action.

Regardless of the style of question or your answer, make every effort to demonstrate what you are saying. In other words, have proof of your success wherever possible, such as ranking reports, awards and recognition, sales data, etc. Also, be ready to show examples of your work, such as written memos, presentations, plans, and projects. This is important to do in the interview because it gives the manager confidence that you are telling the truth, and it demonstrates an important skill used by pharmaceutical representatives- that of backing up your product claims with proof sources: visual aids and clinical reprints. Skillfully using your own proof sources as you answer questions will be an outstanding way to show your job skills. Some refer to a Brag Book for this purpose, but be sure to use it throughout your interview where it relates to the answers you are giving. Avoid paging through the Brag Book all at once, let the interviewer speak.

Studying each question in this chapter will help you understand what the interviewer is trying to assess. Behind each question is an essential skill or behavior for successful performance on the job. The essential skills are "competencies", as listed and discussed in Chapter 2. To simplify the competencies, they can be condensed into three categories that you should keep in mind as you develop and rehearse your answers:

- **Achievement drive: Results oriented, creative, confident, history of sales success**

- **Strong work ethic: Motivation, reliability, communication**

- **Positive attitude: Flexibility, teamwork, high energy**

SCREENING INTERVIEW

Screening interviews are conducted, to put it bluntly, in order to reduce the number of candidates after the unacceptable resumes have been removed from the stack. They are designed to identify the general qualities, or profile, of the desired candidate. These dialogues are often conducted by telephone, but also face-to-face. Usually the first twelve questions numbered in this chapter are covered in this section.

Several characteristics distinguish the screening interviews from other types. First, it is usually brief and lasts about twenty to thirty minutes. Second, someone may conduct it other than the District Manager (such as a Human Relations Specialist at a Job Fair, Sales Trainer, or Hiring Agency). Finally, it is generally an identical set of questions for all candidates. A scoring system is used to determine who will advance to the first interview stage.

Screening interviews may not be scheduled ahead of time. You should be prepared for a call whenever you are actively networking. Keep your interview file close by and easily accessible at all times. Include your resume, job accomplishments, sales achievements, networking, and research notes that you have collected on each company.

TIP: *When the phone rings for a screening interview, feel free to ask the caller to wait just a moment , saying you would like to close the door, turn off the radio, get off the other line, let others know at home not to disturb you, or whatever. Take thirty seconds or so to gather your file and collect your thoughts. Then lift the receiver and thank the caller for waiting.*

If you have done your research and practiced your answers, you will sail past the screening step. Be sure to take notes. When you hear, "Send me your resume", remember this can be a gentle way of getting you off the phone or a sincere request by someone that is genuinely interested in moving you on in the interview process. Either way, try to inject a few more questions on what skills the company looks for in a Pharmaceutical Sales Representative. Ask and write down the person's name, title, address, fax, phone, voicemail and email address if they will give it to you. Close by thanking them for their time and requesting a face-to-face interview when available. When you complete this phase, send a follow-up letter, overnight mail. Emphasize your desire for the opportunity to demonstrate why you believe you will be a successful sales representative for the company.

JOB FAIRS

However, I am not a large fan of Job fairs, simply due to the large amount of candidates involved, they can be similar to screening interviews in that they are designed to eliminate lesser-qualified candidates. The interviewers are more likely to be Human Resource personnel, Sales Trainers and Representatives from other geographic areas. These individuals are not empowered to hire you, but can make a good case either for or against you. Approach and follow up with them as you would any sales manager.

One advantage of the job fair is that you are face to face immediately with the company personnel. Take the opportunity to set yourself apart. If anything, they are excellent practice for you. The questions they ask will most likely be standard for each candidate that allows the interviewer to use a scoring system and classification of candidates. Again, close the interviewer on getting to the next step. Collect as many business cards as there are people from the company—meet everybody, and follow up with each person.

INITIAL OR FIRST INTERVIEW (This is want we want!)

This is the real thing. Congratulations! You are probably one of five or ten candidates invited for a full interview. This is your first meeting with the District Manager, and it is the opportunity for you to become the top candidate. You will be asked specific questions by the interviewer, and you must be able to ask your own questions. Volunteer as much information about yourself as you can, and always include successful scenarios.

Most companies will allow one hour for the initial interview. Be prepared to go longer—this will be a good sign that you are a serious candidate. Otherwise, the manager would not spend the extra time with you. Some companies will arrange for more than one interview at this stage. You may interview with more than one District Manager, Sales Trainer, Regional Field Trainer, or Regional Manager if they are trying to move quickly to fill the position or hiring numerous candidates.

Always conduct yourself professionally with every individual you meet during this process. Be relaxed and confident. If interacting with other office Administrative Assistants, converse briefly with them if you are given the opportunity, asking them topical questions such as who they are and what they do.

Have your own questions to ask the interviewer, but do not ever ask about compensation or benefits at the initial interview. There is more on this topic, including questions for you to ask, in Chapter 7.

SECOND INTERVIEW

Returning for a second interview means that you are considered a serious candidate. The questions asked will be more specific. There may be additional people involved, such as another District Manager or the Regional Manager. However, the second interview may be with the same District Manager. District Manager's will not hire or advance a candidate to the final step unless they usually see that candidate more than once. This allows the District Manager to confirm or challenge their conclusions made in the first interview.

FINAL INTERVIEWS

Sometimes a third interview is necessary to answer a few remaining questions or to have someone else in the company meet you. You can be confident at this point that there are only about two candidates left. Sometimes this step takes place in a different setting, such as a restaurant, or hotel lobby. This allows the Manager to see how you conduct yourself in a less formal and controlled setting where you both can let your guard down. It permits them to see more of your personality, and you, to see more of theirs. This is where chemistry is important. So, be relaxed and confident. Be conversational but avoid controversial topics and chitchat. Be thoughtful, polite and positive in your comments at all times.

Always ask for the position. Review what has been agreed upon in your interviews to date, in terms of your qualifications. Ask if there is anything missing or still needed in order for the District Manager to reach their decision. If so, provide it. Either way, close for the job clearly and with determination. You must demonstrate your aptitude for sales! A sale is about closing the deal.

Your preparation for the interview includes the networking and research strategies outlined in Chapters 4 and 5. In this chapter, I will provide you the most common interview questions, and offer suggestions and examples of how you might answer each one. Give the finest response to every question based on *your* education, background, Preceptorships, work experience, and the recommendations in this book.

Learn the questions from this chapter backward and forward, because undoubtedly you will be asked some. Prepare your answers ahead of time and practice your responses until you are comfortable with every one. Remember, the more prepared you are, the more relaxed and confident you will be during the interview.

TIP: An excellent strategy is to utilize the enclosed two Audio CD's. Upload to a MP3 player, Ipod etc. Also utilize a video recorder. Listen to a question, pause the player and give your response. Play back until you have reached perfection. You will have these things memorized in your words in no time and better here than your interview! Be your own critic! On a video tape, note your non-verbal behavior—such as your posture, tone and the projection of voice. Do you look and sound confident? Dress the part, do you appear comfortable? These practice sessions will give you a profound advantage over other candidates. Or, you can always ask a spouse or friend to ask you the questions.

As discussed in earlier chapters know as much as you can about the company and determine how you see yourself adding value in their environment. Walk slowly and stand up straight when entering the room. When greeting the District Manager, give a brief "raise of the head" accompanied by a warm smile. Begin by telling the District Manager that you have researched XYZ Pharmaceuticals, the industry, and the job of a Pharmaceutical Sales Representative. State early, you are extremely interested in this position. The District Manager, upon hearing such an aggressive opening, will often get right down to business. This is what you want, and now puts you on a more level playing field.

Sometimes you will discover that the interviewer is not exactly what you expected, or were looking for in a District Manager. I call it the "No Love Connection" interview, and it happens. Occasionally the interviewer is not as well prepared for the process as you are. When this is the case, you need to volunteer the answers you have prepared, even without being asked. Do this by weaving your accomplishments and strong points throughout the interview. Your confidence will show, and your skills and preparation shall be rewarded. If this persist with the same DM, possibly this is not someone to work for?

The interviewer is looking for initiative. Showing the strategy you used to network, research, and prepare yourself for this process is, in itself, evidence that you have initiative and are going to succeed. Make the conclusion for the interviewer to see that you will apply the same skills and abilities that you brought to the interview process to your new career. I suggest keeping your utilization and readership of *Insight* out of the discussion, take credit for most is your effort.

Insight has provided you the questions you will be asked. I have also included questions that you want to ask the interviewer. Always ask questions during every single interview, show your interest, and prove that you have done your homework. The more the District Manager speaks, the better the interview. As you progress through the later stages, as in second and third interviews, ask more in depth questions. Why? Your original goal was to market yourself. You have their interest, but is this company a good match for you—ask questions. Never, during any part of an interview process, bring up the compensation or benefits. Get the offer in a letter of offering "in your hand" first!

There will be plenty of opportunity to discuss base salary, bonus, benefits and the dental plan after that.

TIP: Before leaving the interview, be certain to obtain the interviewer's business card. You will need it for completing your follow-up correspondence (see sample letter at end of this chapter).

The interview questions to follow are typical of what you should expect during an interview. The interviewer will use variations, but your responses will be appropriate and effective no matter how the questions are asked. Your preparation, including the industry and company-specific research, means you are ready for anything.

You should never be asked certain questions. It is illegal for employers to inquire about certain areas of your life; some of these are state dependent. However, you may volunteer any information you choose and the interviewer can listen to it once you bring it up, but they cannot ask for it. These questions include information about the following.

- Marital status
- Family
- Religion
- Age
- Sexual preference
- Race or national origin
- Political affiliation
- Arrest record; the exception is Convictions
- Type of military discharge
- Health status
- Height or weight
- Provide a photo
- Children or the possibility of pregnancy
- Spouse's vocation
- Memberships in organizations, clubs, societies

An application may ask for more information. Since 1998, I have received countless emails stating, "I've been told I'm much too old for pharmaceutical sales. Companies just hire beautiful looking, young candidates." Since the 1964 Civil Rights Act, Title VII, it has been illegal to discriminate because of age. But it can still happen. When it comes to age, gender, religion, race, or even one's weight, there are biases, whether conscious or unconscious, that may come into play. You will not hear that, of course, if you are turned down for a position in any industry. You will possibly get a brief explanation, "We are going with a candidate with more experience." I assure you that this is going to be an exception if it does occur, and there is really no way to know. In reality, companies do seem to hire more sales representatives in their twenties and thirties. But this is the most common age demographic of the candidate pool—persons who have graduated, have a few years of work experience and are searching for a better career. When you network, and observe representatives working a medical building, you will notice Pharmaceutical Sales Representatives come in all ages, genders, races, sizes and shapes!

Also, I would contend that any group of high-end sales professionals, dressing their best, would look like a stylish crowd, so let us stop with the excuses and stereotypes. By following the strategies in this book and adding your dedication and hard work, you will have all the advantages to nail the job you want. During my twenty years of hiring, I hired numerous candidates in their forties and fifties because they bring a perspective to the job that younger candidate's lack. This comes from what I call having experienced "life's firsts" (marriage, children, home, job, career, etc.). If you are an older candidate, you need to turn your age and maturity into your asset. Show off your experience, dedication, knowledge of this industry, appreciation of such an enjoyable, challenging and rewarding profession. Show your determination to making this position a fantastic success for your career. Even at age 55 and older, you have many years you can offer an organization. This is probably longer than most tenure of the members in the hiring manager's current district.

THE MOST COMMON QUESTIONS FOR INTERVIEWING IN PHARMACEUTICAL SALES:

1) Why do you want to enter a career in pharmaceutical sales?

This is a fundamental question, and one you must be able to answer without hesitation. There are two parts to this question and it deserves a two-part answer. Why do you want to sell, and why in the pharmaceutical industry. State that you want and like to sell, and that you are successful at doing so. You possess the essential qualities of high energy, motivation, confidence, dedication, creativity, and organizational skills. Provide specific examples of situations that demonstrate one or more of these qualities.

Next, selling pharmaceuticals appeals to you because it is challenging and rewarding. The challenge lies in its technical environment (product knowledge), professional customer audience, and stiff competition. The rewards are based on your own individual efforts, which is just the type of environment in which you excel. Use the same examples you gave to illustrate essential sales qualities in the first part of your answer. Only this time, relate it to something you think you would do in your new position as a sales representative for XYZ Pharmaceutical Company.

TIP: This question provides an excellent opportunity for you to describe your research into the pharmaceutical industry and specifically with XYZ Pharmaceuticals. Since you have networked with many sales representatives by this point, you can use specific examples from your conversations with them and real-life situations you have had in front of physicians. Use your answer to highlight your industry exploration. This will give you credibility when you say you want the job—you know what you are getting into and it is the perfect fit for you.

2) Why do you believe that you would find pharmaceutical sales a rewarding career?

You know from your extensive research of the job and the company that you would find this profession challenging. It will be apparent to the interviewer whether you have done your homework. Answers such as "I have a friend that likes it" will not be sufficient.

You may include that you like being responsible for you own destiny. You are aggressive. You work hard. You will succeed based on your own merit. Include an example from a previous selling or business success. You may also include your knowledge of the career advancement opportunities, as described in Chapter 2. Communicate your excitement about the possibilities for personal and professional growth. State that you are willing to dedicate the time and effort to learn the business from the field sales position.

3) Why do you think you would excel at pharmaceutical sales?

This is a similar question to the two above, but by asking it, the interviewer is seeking more information. You should answer that you know what this position requires and you have those requirements. Give some specific qualities that you possess that are also critical for success in pharmaceuticals. For example, you have individual creativity—Pharmaceutical Representatives work alone and face unique challenges that require unique solutions. You possess excellent time management skills, a busy representative must plan and work efficiently. You have excellent business acumen, a skill that will help you target your most productive customers, which is efficient and productive. Again, you are indicating that you know what the position entails.

Also, be sure to include the fact that you will enjoy it. If you are doing something that brings great pleasure and confidence, you will naturally do it better. Being happy in your work is a principal indicator of success, and that makes you sure that you are pursuing the right position.

4) How long do you believe you would like to sell pharmaceuticals?

Be sure you relate to the interviewer that as long as you feel challenged and rewarded by the position, you feel your time is unconstrained. If career advancement is one of your goals, communicate that you desire to learn the industry "from the entry sales position up." You plan to use the opportunity to develop your strengths and assess your opportunities as you add value to the company, then realistically evaluate your career goals at that time.

5) Why do you want to change careers to pharmaceutical sales?

This question is looking for your conviction about what you want to do. Think about what attracted you to pharmaceuticals and why you started researching. Prepare an honest answer and convey your excitement.

The pharmaceutical industry has much to offer. You may be looking for growth. This industry has shown compelling expansion in the past and is poised to continue to do so in the future. You may want security. This industry is virtually recession proof. You may want prestige. This industry is one of the most sought-after and well-heeled industries in the world. You may be looking for a mixture of business and health care. You may desire professional, consultative relationships with your customers where you are the expert. Perhaps you are more idealistic. You may want to be part of scientific discoveries and medical advances that alleviate suffering and improve people's lives. You want to offer solutions to real-life problems that physicians and patients face every day. Whatever the reason, deliver it with conviction.

6) What experience do you have that would lend itself to pharmaceutical sales?

If you have experience selling a product or service, this is the time to sell the interviewer on how you performed. If you have no previous sales experience, describe times in the past that you have sold an idea, a project, or a new way of doing things at your work or school. Sales experience is not essential for entering the industry. If you conduct research, then network with individuals in the profession and convey your determination to be successful, you will be conclusively more desirable as a candidate than someone with sales experience who has not prepared as effectively as you have.

7) How does your education prepare you for a career in pharmaceutical sales?
Most any undergraduate college degree will easily lend itself to the industry. Business, communications, marketing, management, education, language skills, psychology, biology, chemistry, pharmacy, nursing, and others, all enhance what you bring to this company. If your education is in science or health care, you are going to have to emphasize that you can "sell." If your background is sales, emphasize that you can learn the essential technical background needed to excel in this position.
Pharmaceutical sales are a union of science and business. Prepare your answers to incorporate your education into this union.

8) Why do want to work for XYZ Pharmaceutical Company?
The interviewer wants to know if you have done your homework. What are some unique characteristics of this company? Is it relatively large, small, or medium sized? What is its product line or area of medical specialty that you like? Are you excited about the current product line and the future possibilities of products to be released? Do you know anybody who works for the company? State that you are impressed with current pharmaceutical sales representatives that you have met through your networking, and that you would have an excellent working chemistry with the team.

TIP: If you have done your research, you may even be more informed about this organization than the person on the other side of the table. See if you can surprise him with information he was not aware of, such as an experimental compound in development, or the latest quarterly profit figures. Managers will often be unaware of some details about their company because they are more involved with the day-to-day business of their district.

9) What qualifies you to be a Pharmaceutical Sales Representative?
If you have obtained a four-year degree, are interested, have completed the research, networked with individuals, understand the position and the industry, and most importantly, want to do this job, you are qualified. However, the interviewer is looking for more. Emphasize to the interviewer that you want to make a long-term commitment to this industry based upon your research. You have devoted countless hours of time and energy towards obtaining your goal, which is employment in this business. You plan to be well versed in product knowledge, selling skills, and territory organization. You want to excel and will bring value to the company.

10) Are you currently interviewing with other pharmaceutical companies at this time?
You want to work in pharmaceutical sales. It is as simple as that, so be honest. State that your goal is to gain successful employment with a dynamic pharmaceutical company, and that you will persist until you accomplish your goal. Describe your networking strategy.

Include that you are, or will be, interviewing with prospective companies as you push to uncover opportunities.
If this is your first interview, state that. However, if you are currently interviewing with other companies make it clear. Include companies by name, names of individuals, with whom you have met or interviewed, and a major product or two made by the other companies.

TIP: 90% of the candidates interviewing today cannot state what current products are being promoted by the firm they are interviewing with, much less the products of other companies. Think of the advantage you will create for yourself with this prospective employer by being versed on multiple companies in the industry.

11) What are your greatest strengths?
Make sure that you can answer this question. It was probably used on the first interview in history. You will probably be presented with this question every time you interview in your working career.
Your strengths should be qualities that are in demand by pharmaceutical companies. You want to fit the profile of the successful representative by following the strategy that is outlined, using the competencies of a successful rep, as describe earlier in *Insight*.
Self-motivated and **self-disciplined**: Your time management and organizational skills make you productive while working autonomously or with little supervision.
Creative: You are able to differentiate yourself from other pharmaceutical sales representatives. You can create ways to access your "hard to see" doctors.
Goal oriented: You do what it takes to get the job done, including making a few extra calls to physicians, hospitals, and pharmacies.
Confident: Your background, qualities, and commitment will guarantee success in this career choice.
Flexible: You are cooperative—you can take direction well, and work together as a team to reach corporate objectives.

12) What are your weaknesses? In what areas would you like to improve?
This question usually follows the one about strengths. Design your response so that ultimately your weakness is strength. Your interviewer will probably know what you are doing, but the fact that you have done the preparation to handle this difficult question will gain their respect. They are looking for your confidence under pressure. Many of your contemporaries will struggle with this question. Poor answers are ones that shift the weakness to another person, such as a previous manager, co-workers, or company policy. Be careful not to interject blame or negative comments about past employers and others. Two examples of a good answer are as follows:
Sometimes I have trouble compiling my paperwork in an enthusiastic manner. However, I do know that timeliness of reporting is important to my managers and my company, so I make sure I am always prompt with its delivery.
Sometimes I have difficulty when other individuals do not display a positive attitude towards new ideas. I make it a point to stay positive, hoping it will influence other members of the organization or team.

13) Where do you see yourself five years from now?
From your research, you know that there are many opportunities in the pharmaceutical industry for a successful field representative: Management, Marketing, Sales Training, Sales Support, Communications, and Professional Education. Reiterate that learning the field sales position and becoming a proven performer within your organization is your primary goal for at least the next three years. After learning the business from this level, you will direct your goals so that you can grow professionally and contribute to the corporations' goals.

TIP: During the initial phases of interviewing, most District Managers will delight in hearing that you are giving yourself three to five years to fully develop and demonstrate your abilities in your new territory. It is a sign of unrealistic expectations and poor knowledge of the job when a candidate places too much emphasis on upward mobility when they have not even entered the industry. Show your ambition in other ways—by researching, networking, preparing, and interviewing excellence.

14) How do you feel about your current boss?
If you do not get along with your current boss, this is not the time to voice it. State that you have been managed effectively, provided guidance, and growth in your position. Specify that you have met your objectives, but do not talk about personalities and philosophies. As long as you perform your job, and reach or surpass your objectives, you feel just great about your current boss.

15) How do you feel about your current employer?
Again, never complain about your present position. State that the position has provided you with the ability to gain knowledge and grow professionally, but you desire a personal and professional challenge. Considering your research and career planning, the ideal career for you is in the pharmaceutical industry. Talk less about your current position and more about your decision to become a pharmaceutical sales representative. Keep your answer positive and career oriented. In other words, show that you are moving towards pharmaceuticals, not moving away from some other situation that you do not like.

16) What have you done that shows initiative in your present position?
Use a recent example in your present position, if possible, to describe the details of your current position. Your pharmaceutical research also provides an excellent response.

17) What are your immediate goals?
Your immediate goals are both professional and personal. Articulate that your number one professional priority is to achieve a career with a pharmaceutical company and begin contributing as a successful representative. Add personal goals, such as physical exercise, hobbies, family, if you would like to round out this response.

18) What are your interests, hobbies?
Choose activities that show competition, determination, motivation, creativity, or team playing. These attributes are the ones that fit the profile of success, and transfer well to the job. Leave out watching television, going to the movies, reading, and other sedentary

activities. Studies have shown that executives that list sports among their extracurricular activities earn significantly more. Show you are a team player, enjoy a challenge, and are a person that is determined to succeed with various goals.

19) Describe a problem you have encountered in your current position?
The interviewer is really looking for a solution you created. Thus, you must not only describe a problem, but also describe a solution to the problem. Example: "A problem in my current position was that we were unable to reach some of the deadlines of our department. I overcame this by placing a large calendar in the break room with our deadlines marked in red. It was a clear reminder to the other office members, which in turn improved hitting our deadlines."

20) What have been some of your largest disappointments?
Describe a situation where you experienced disappointment and were able to learn and develop from it, thus turning it into a positive experience. Example: "As I began my job search in the pharmaceutical industry I found that it was taking too long to get my first interview. Since then, I have changed my approach and have become more aggressive at discovering opportunities. Therefore, I have become much more successful. I feel most disappointments can teach us something useful for the future."

21) How do you prepare your reports or paperwork in your current position?
Example: "I create my reports to communicate relevant information about my business. Not only for my manager and my company, but also for myself. I find they are more useful when I write them down as soon as I complete a sales call. I make sure that my reports are prompt, organized, and detailed, yet concise."

22) Have you ever had to deal with a difficult person at work? How did you handle this?
If you have never done so, then say that and be finished with the question. If you have described a situation in which, though you did not agree with an individual, you were able to work through the assignment or task to complete the project. It is more important to cooperate with individuals so that the work atmosphere remains productive.

23) Do you feel you are treated and compensated fairly at your present position?
Never complain about your present position, boss, company, duties, etc. The interviewer wants to know you are a positive force. Simply answer, "Yes."

24) What is your largest accomplishment in your present position?
If you have received any awards or acclamations, mention them. Bring documentation of any recognition that you have been awarded, and show it to the interviewer. Leave a copy at the end of the interview. Describe a work situation that you resolved with favorable results, or a creative solution you used with a difficult customer. Although the question may be worded specifically to address your present position, take license to expand to other jobs or to extracurricular or community accomplishments, as well.

TIP: Use your answers to lead the interviewer to other areas you would like to present about yourself. Find a way to bridge to another topic or example that you know is a positive attribute for you. If you rely on the interviewer to ask the question, it may not be asked, and you will lose an opportunity to say something important about your successes.

25) What do you dislike about your present position?
You may want to choose some minor and menial aspect of your job. It is a good idea to pick something that deters or distracts from the business. Office chatter is a good one, waiting on people who are late, or being stuck in traffic. Be sure to include what you do to deal with the problem. Paperwork is always a good thing to dislike. Just be sure to include that because you dislike it, you are still going to complete it in a timely and accurate way. Conclude by saying that you have been satisfied with your present position, but you desire to accelerate your growth in pharmaceutical sales.

26) Do you feel you have been evaluated fairly?
Again, never complain about current or past positions. The interviewer is not looking for someone who is unhappy in relationships with an employer, regardless of who is at fault. Do not complain about anything or blame anyone. A simple "yes" is appropriate.

27) Give me an example of one of your best sales.
If you are currently selling a product or service, use a sale in which you encountered objections, misunderstandings, or a lack of customer interest, and how you overcame these obstacles. If you are not currently selling a product or service, detail the way you have gone about marketing yourself through the interview process. Describe, in detail, how you have set goals, strategies, networked with individuals, and kept records. Compare the interviewing process to a sale. Express in either situation how rewarding your sales activity and accomplishing your goals were. Example: You have felt rewarded by your increased knowledge of the pharmaceutical industry and the people who work in it. You are confident you will be successful.

28) Give me an example of a sale that you missed, and how you could have handled it differently?
Failure is universal in sales. A good salesperson thrives on it. It is common for sales professionals to experience this, and the interviewer wants to know how you will respond to it when it happens again. Give an example, be honest, state what you learned in the process, and how you tried to correct the situation. If you have no sales experience, use a business or office situation in which you created a solution and benefited from a past failure. Either way, convey your excitement over challenging sales situations, customers, and the thrill of achievement.

29) How do you go about selling your product?
Describe your sales cycle and approach to the customer. Do you initially use telephone contacts, direct mail, or any type of advertising? Be competent in your description of your sales process and how you differentiate yourself from your competition. Example: You telephone all customers within two weeks of their purchases to check their

satisfaction with your product or service. This process has led to many repeat purchases of your product line, and improvements in your service.

30) Do you believe you are able to handle the pressure of sales quotas?
Yes! State that you actually find the challenge of sales quotas motivating. You enjoy being responsible for your own destiny. You work hard and want to be recognized and compensated according to what you accomplish.

31) How do you handle rejection in your sales position?
Whether in the sales position or your current career search you must often experience some rejections before success. Rejection is an opportunity to get to know your customer better. It forces you to make changes in your approach. Creating innovative solutions has provided ways that have allowed you to move closer to your customers and understand them better.

32) What things do you and your current manager disagree on?
State that you and your manager rarely have disagreed on issues, and that your relationship has been very productive within your organization.

33) How are you motivated in your position?
This question tells the interviewer what you will be like to manage. You are motivated by a job well done. Your own accomplishment and success feeds you. Besides being self-motivated, you thrive on recognition from within your company, comments from your superiors with periodic performance reviews, and financial rewards (commission, bonuses, etc.). Also, state that you gain a sense of satisfaction by achieving personal goals. Example: To be in the top 10% of your company's sales force.

34) What things detract from some of your initiatives?
With this question, make a negative a positive. For example, you may occasionally overachieve. While good for the business, it can be better to keep a balance between your work and relaxation. You find that you are more productive when you take an occasional break to refocus.

35) How have you differentiated yourself from your peers both outside and within your organization?
Embellish the successful attributes of a salesperson: ambition, determination, organization, energy, self-motivation, ability to handle rejection, targeting the correct customer base, teamwork, etc. Give an example of a situation in which you excelled. Was there a time when you went the extra mile to help a customer? Perhaps your forte is personal rapport and relationship selling, or maybe you have a unique talent that you incorporate into your sales approach, such as cooking, fishing, or athletics?

36) How were your grades in college?
If they were admirable, bring an official transcript from your college or university to present to the interviewer. Your answer should focus on the fact that you will learn product knowledge quickly, and communicate that information to your customer. If

grades were not praiseworthy, fault it on working while attending school (if appropriate), extracurricular activities (sports), or finally, youth. Move on to illustrate recent successes in your career, continuing education, seminars, or training classes.

37) What is your current salary?
Answer briefly and to the point, and then stop talking. Do not exaggerate. From your research, you know the starting salary range for a pharmaceutical sales representative. Avoid discussing what salary you may require until you have been made an offer. Likewise, avoid the temptation to ask anything about salary or compensation.

38) Can I contact your current employer, or co-workers?
"No" is an acceptable answer. You would not want to jeopardize your current standing within your present organization. Do offer references, both business and personal, and contact information for co-workers if acceptable to you.

TIP: Do not bring pre-written reference letters. They are not of value to a prospective employer and may be insulting to the interviewer, especially if they are overstated (which most of them are). If it is appropriate in your situation to provide references, bring them typewritten on a separate sheet of paper. Provide both personal and professional references; usually three of each is appropriate. Give complete names, titles, addresses, and telephone numbers. Be sure to have permission from the individuals on your list and keep them posted when you give out the list.

39) When I call your references, how will they describe you? What would your boss say about you?
List some of the qualities that you have demonstrated for your referenced individuals. For example, they would say that you are determined to enter pharmaceutical sales, are creative and motivated, have a strong work ethic, are honest, reliable, good sense of humor, great salesperson, etc. Again, be sure you contact every one of your references before you list them. Let them know about your career search.

40) How much are you willing to travel? Are you willing to relocate?
Various positions or sales territories require that you travel, especially in the pharmaceutical industry. Even if you do not have to stay overnight to work your territory, you will surely have to travel to meetings and training activities from time to time. Your foremost consideration at this stage of the game is to obtain the job offer. Once you have an offer letter, you can decide if the particulars of the position (travel, relocation, salary, benefits, commission structure, or management style) are satisfactory for you. Do not eliminate yourself from the process before receiving the offer you deserve. Always indicate that you are willing to travel and relocate for the right opportunity.

41) What do you expect to earn in the first year?
Never discuss salary until you have the "offer in your hand". If you have done your research, you know the compensation level you can expect. Again, do not eliminate yourself by quoting too high, or even too low, a figure. State that you are confident that

you shall be compensated fairly for your efforts and you are looking forward to receiving an offer.

42) Describe what you believe a typical day, as a Pharmaceutical Representative, would involve?

This is your ideal question. Because of your networking, your field Preceptorships, and other research, you are an expert at this question. Example: "Typically, an office based Pharmaceutical Representatives will start the day by stocking the trunk of the car with literature and samples. They will have a detailed plan for the day of where to go and who the contact is. A salesperson will call on 7-9 physicians to make detailed sales presentations. This may include visiting several pharmacies to gather information about prescribing habits and to check product supplies. Additionally, stopping at a hospital or clinic to reach physicians may be an alternative to their offices. The professional representative will assess how physicians are reacting to their product, present new information, leave samples, and get a commitment from the doctor for increasing prescriptions of the medication. During the office call, talking with the nurses, secretaries, and other office staff is an important part of communications. Be sure to add a real-life example: "When I was observing Maria Sanchez for a day, we went to a new physician in the area and...."

43) How many hours a week do you feel it will be necessary for you to get your job accomplished as a Pharmaceutical Representative?

No correct answer here, so again, you have to cover all the bases. Some District Sales Managers pride themselves on working nights and weekends, and leaving voice and emails throughout the weekend. Others pride themselves on their excellent planning and time management that allows them to work a smart 40 hours per week. You must mesh the two stating you plan your time effectively but as always, projects and deadline's will demand that extra effort to get the job done. Ask the District Manager what is typical in their sales district?

44) How could you target the customers (physicians) in your territory in the most efficient way and still achieve maximum sales results?

This is a very advanced question and, if asked, means you are a serious contender. The more insight you can show about the job, the better. Answers that come from your own successes and networking are best, but we have included a few examples.

"Targeting" means choosing which doctors you are going to visit to make your sales presentations. This is your customer base. These doctors make up your call plan, as discussed in Chapter 2. Obviously, you cannot see all of the specialists in your territory. Many companies use call plans that are developed by the company or by consultants using sophisticated marketing data. Your call plan is then provided to you. However, it is usually not set in stone, and you are responsible for refining it based on your own observations in the field. The following answers are applicable to this process, and to the process of developing your own call plan.

First, match the product class to the physician's specialty. Example: You would call on a gynecologist more frequently to sell an oral contraceptive agent than you would to an internal medicine or general practice physician.

Second, evaluate the physician's practice size. Is their office busy? Do they see many patients of the type that would use your product? You can determine this by the number of patients waiting to be seen, number of support staff in the office (nurses and receptionist), or how full the appointment book is for the week. You would increase the number of calls to these physicians to promote their prescribing. This is "call frequency" and it is dependent upon the number of times you would normally call on that customer in a given period, referred to as "call cycle." Call cycle is the length of time you spend covering all locations in your territory one time. The company usually sets the call cycle. It can range from two weeks to two months, depending on territory size and sales strategy.

TIP: Familiarize yourself with the terms such as targeting, call plan, call frequency, and call cycle. Review Chapter 2 for more information.
For efficiency, plan your appointments by geography in your territory, and for the best times to see doctors without having to wait too long. Avoid walking in at busy times of the day. You will get to know this as you work a territory, and become more efficient as you learn about each customer and how the office runs.

45) What aspects of pharmaceutical sales do you feel are most vital to success in this field?
You can take your pick of the following suggestions or build your own list. The more relevant to your experience from discussions with your networking contacts, the better you will be. Examples: building customer relationships, being an expert on your products and the competition, listening for what the physician wants in a product and positioning your product accordingly, prompt follow-up, self-motivation, organization, creativity, determination, product knowledge, professionalism, targeting, and above all attitude.

46) What is the worst thing you have heard during your networking about XYZ Pharmaceuticals?
From current representatives and competitors of XYZ I have heard that you are very well respected and a difficult company to obtain a sales position, due to your thorough interview process, which I admire.

47) Tell me a story?
First, ask what would the interviewer like to hear a story about, your professional or personal life?
Always leave out the forbidden areas of interviewing (marriage, religion, age, etc.). This shows the interviewer that you are thinking through the question and your answer. If about your personal life, reference a time when you demonstrated qualities such as your tenacity, or dependability. If your choice is personal, chose some qualities such as your ability to take direction (from management) and willingness to go the "extra mile" to complete the job.

48) On a scale of one to ten, where do you rate yourself?
Go with an eight to nine, noting that one should always be striving to increase their competencies, skills, and education.

49) What was the last book your read?
Most important here, is that you actual read the book, because the follow up question could kill the interview if you have not. Arrive at a response that will differentiate you from the mass of other candidates (in other words, stay off the bestseller list). Choose a book that strives for self-improvement, and again, do not mention *Insight*.

50) Let us pretend your product is a pen. Sell it to me.
Begin by probing the interviewer for requirements he or she is looking for in a pen. For example, "Why are you looking for a pen?" or "What are you looking for in a pen?" Listen and clarify the answer, then provide features and benefits of the pen that satisfy the stated need. **Close the sale by asking for the business.**

Feature	Benefit
Round	Easy to hold
Shirt Clip	Easy to find during daily activities
Retractable point	Will not leave marks on clothing
Refillable Cartridge	Will provide years of service

Explore any reason that he or she would not want to use this pen. Close with, "How many pens would you like to order today?"

51) Let us pretend your product is XYZ Aspirin. Sell it to me.
Again, be certain to investigate what the customer would like to see (and if they currently use) an aspirin product in their practice. Listen, clarify, provide features and benefits, check for any questions or objections, **and then close, by asking for a trail.**

Feature	Benefit
Low cost therapy	Patient has more money for other things
Pain relief in thirty minutes	Patient can quickly resume normal activities
Proven medication	Doctor can prescribe it with confidence
Low incidence of side effects	Doctor will not be bothered by telephone calls from patients about side effects

Next prompt for acceptance: "Doctor, is there any reason you would not prescribe XYZ aspirin for your next patient with mild pain?" Then close: "Will you prescribe XYZ aspirin to all of your patients today with mild pain?"
Of course, there are many ways you could finesse or alter the above selling situations. This is short and to the point. Each describes what you should explore first, listen carefully, present features and benefits, urge for acceptance, and close.

TIP: Clip and save prescription drug advertisements from magazines. Medical journals are the best source for this information. Find an advertisement for a medication manufactured by the company with which you are interviewing. Bring the article to the interview and make a sales presentation to the interviewer based on the advertised product. Use the advertisements as your sakes "visual aid", aid", and make a product presentation as if you were talking with a doctor. Be sure to practice ahead of time, and ask for coaching from an experienced pharmaceutical representative, if possible. Get commitment from "the customer" to prescribe your "product".

Note: Sometime the company will give you some sales aids to help with your presentation, but if the product is a significant product, go to their web site (sometimes specifically for the product, not just the company) and pull up the main features and benefits that are stressed in the promotion. Print these out for your presentation and practice. In addition, call a few pharmacies, speak to a few pharmacist, learn what the cost is for a prescription to the consumer (you can check online pharmacies with NABP certification), and ask the pharmacist who are the largest competitors in this therapeutic class of drugs.

Open your presentation by asking the interviewer (physician) what they use for treating this disease or condition. Use the *pharmaceuticalsales.com inc. sales algorithm©* (below) to assist you; take some time to practice some product presentations. Usually its one of three things, efficacy (how well it works), safety (low side effects) or price (cost to patient). After you have determined this, then focus your features of your product that reach this need. You will always come across some objection in role-play (to see how you handle them). Take your time, and ask them to explain a little further how this fits into their (the physician's) treatment decision. The more they (the interviewer) speak the better. Finally, summarize, from what features and benefits the physician desire, and how your product accomplishes this. Then close, ask them to commit to use the product on the next 5-12 patients, make sure you close.

52) What interests you least about the Pharmaceutical Sales Representative position?

Example: "I have done plenty of networking in the area of pharmaceutical sales, and I have not encountered anything I consider as negative. Some Pharmaceutical Representatives that I have networked with have commented about waiting to see physicians, or the paperwork, or parking. I understand that these are all parts of the job, and there is a positive way to manage it, such as using downtime in waiting rooms to increase my product knowledge."

53) Respond to a physician stating, "Your product is too expensive."

"Cost is a common objection in sales, and is relative to the perceived value of the product. I believe with excellent product knowledge and persuasive selling skills, I would highlight the features and benefits of the medication over competitive therapies, and increase the value of the product in the physician's eyes. The best medication at the best price—that's a bargain!"

pharmaceuticalsales.com inc sales algorithm ™

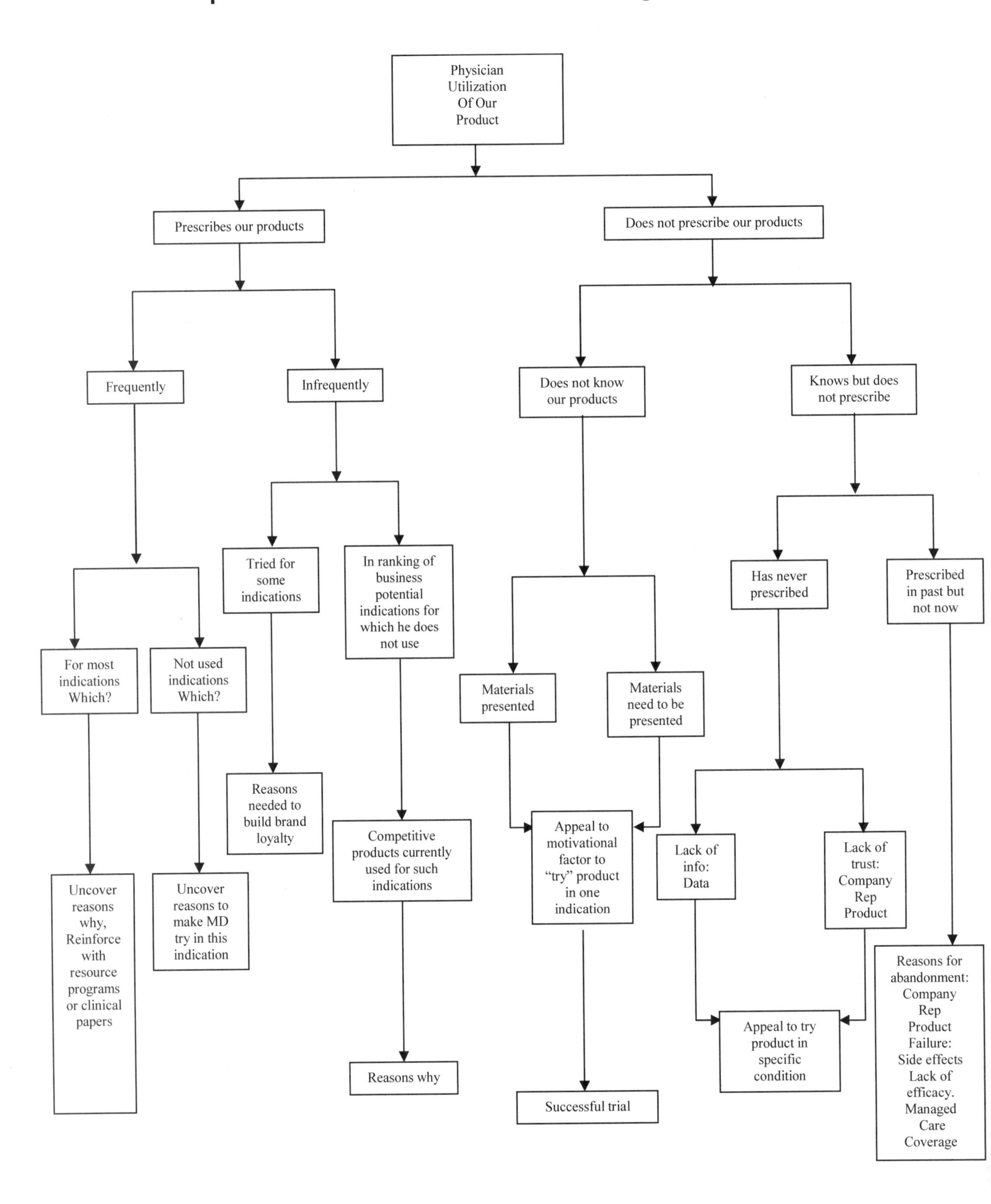

54) How do you believe you would develop your knowledge of a physician's needs in prescribing a drug therapy?
The interviewer is not looking for any one specific answer, but wants to see your poise, confidence, and sales skills. Obviously, if you have not worked in pharmaceutical sales, you will not have detailed answers. However, your industry research will give you some solid answers. Example: "Listening, as in all sales, is the tool to uncover the needs of the customer (physician). Often, the customer will volunteer information, or offer open-ended questions that help me clarify my comments to increase his knowledge. I may also assume that many needs are common to many physicians and begin by addressing one specifically."

55) How would you deal with an angry receptionist or nurse in the physician's office, who was preventing you from seeing the physician?
In this situation, it is best to exhibit empathy. If an office is busy, as is common, it may mean that you have to return at a more suitable time. State that you understand the situation and request a better time for you to call back that day or that week. Sometimes, as in all sales, a client may take out their job frustration on a sales representative. You will show great sales maturity when you can diffuse such a situation and not take it personally. You are developing a long-term relationship. The customer is always right!

56) Tell me about a time you have failed.
This question and many like it are seeking information about what may appear to be negative answers. Be aware of the concept of "balance" during an interview. If an interview is going very well and the interviewer is beginning to believe you are a qualified candidate, he or she may start looking for balance. They will do this by looking for the human side of you, and this is a step forward. Your response helps them avoid concluding that you are "too good to be true," which could create a letdown for the manager after you are hired. It is okay to be human with your answers, and provide an example of when you feel you have failed. Make it a job-related answer, not personal. Also, incorporate how you dealt with the failure and how you learned to turn it into success.

57) How would you differentiate yourself among the many sales representatives calling on the same doctor?
This question is seeking creativity and familiarity with the daily role of the sales representative. First of all, use something about yourself that already makes you stand out—sense of humor, clinical or technical expertise, an avocation that can be shared such as cooking or golf. Then choose a solid skill necessary for top performance such as product knowledge—you will set yourself apart by providing value; also mention your excellent follow through on commitments, questions, etc.

58) How do you handle change on the job?
This question is looking for a healthy attitude towards the only constant in any pharmaceutical position—change! If you do not work well with change, you are interviewing for the wrong job. To answer this question successfully, as with all your responses, include an example of when and how you were confronted with a change and the way you handled it. Common changes you will encounter in pharmaceuticals (and almost any sales role) can vary from realignments in territories, to new products or products being pulled from the market, sales teams, managers, computer systems,

sampling regulations and even company mergers. Your best attitude is that change is healthy and good; your approach is to always discern what you can and cannot control; always take a long-term view; set a good example for your colleagues by keeping them on track, too. Successful representatives stay focused on goals and opportunities. This requires flexibility and resilience; qualities that are also crucial for managers. You will be remembered for your abilities to work successfully in a constantly changing environment.

59) What would you do to get more time in front of busy doctors?
This is a good question to test your knowledge of the customer. Nine out of ten sales calls last less than two minutes. That job fact is not likely to change. You will need to follow two different directions with your answer. First, acknowledge that you know sales calls to physicians are less than two minutes and some are actually only a few seconds. This is not the end of the world, however, because doctors do everything quickly. They spend short periods multi-tasking, and are used to getting and giving information quickly and clearly. You must always be prepared to deliver your sales messages in the same manner. That takes excellent product knowledge and lots of practice. Try to extend the time of the call by presenting information the physician needs; this requires knowledge of that doctor's specific needs for their clientele, or by asking an engaging question on the disease or therapy you would like them to focus on at that time.

60) Sales representatives spend a good portion of the day behind the wheel. What would you do with that time?
This question will assess your organization and planning skills, self-motivation, and self-improvement skills. The obvious answer is listening to product or sales motivation tapes to educate you on the job, products, and selling skills. A good example would be CMR courses (Certified Medical Representative). You should include the obvious, but also set yourself apart by including this approach: efficient management of the territory to reduce windshield time. By taking time to plan each week and each day, you will know where to go and when to make best use of your own time and cut down on time spent in traffic.

61) How do you balance your work and family or non-work activities?
This question is looking for planning, setting goals, and prioritization. The pharmaceutical sales position requires 8-10 calls per day plus planning time, follow-up letters and memos, administrative reporting, etc. Your time selling is only part of the situation. For many representatives, this means working at home in the evenings at the expense of family or personal time. You will probably already have your own strategies for managing your off time. In addition, make the point that you prioritize what you need to do versus less critical activities. Though selling time is top priority, you also take advantage of downtime during the day to complete tasks. You do this by bringing materials such as clinical reprints to study while waiting in offices. You use your computer at lunch to complete memos or reports. You keep current with tasks so you do not fall behind. Therefore, you are free to enjoy your family time without being burdened by unfinished work.

62) How do you develop relationships with your customers?
The best approach is understanding and trust. Personal relationships are built on these precepts just as business and customer relationships are. Learn as much as you can about your customer's business, and about them personally; this is the best way to understand and address their needs. To develop trust, you always keep commitments and you provide

objective information. That may mean including the negative aspects of your product. You do not emphasize negatives, but fair balance is especially important with pharmaceutical products. Your customer knows there are downsides to virtually all medications and still prescribes them. They need to know what to watch for and this will go a long way to gain their trust. In your answer, include an example of how you learn about your customers (what questions you ask, research you do, etc.) and a time when you gave fair balance about your product in a sales presentation.

63) How do you work on teams?
This question can take many forms, but the answer is always regarding how you work with others and manage team conflict. It is vital for Pharmaceutical Representatives to work well on teams because so many products are co-promoted by other representatives, divisions within your company, or even by other companies. This requires excellent communication and coordination. Your answer must include an example of how you demonstrated team skills:

- Respecting the differences in others
- Knowing that not everyone approaches the job the same way
- Discovering each person's professional goals on a team
- Knowing each person's family history, brothers, sisters, parents' occupation, etc.
- Recognizing their goals is often not the same, and may even conflict, with the job.
- State how you develop a common team goal on which to focus
- Recognizing individual goals including establishing dialog and agreed upon methods of communication such as meetings, email, voice mail, time line's and conference calls
- Your ability to resolve conflict

Always try to use very specific examples with your answers than generalities.

64) What do you think is the most important factor for success as a Pharmaceutical Representative?
This question is looking for your level of knowledge and understanding of the position of pharmaceutical sales. As a side note, people generally answer this with an aspect of the job that they themselves do well. This is not necessarily a conscious process, and most managers are not aware of this connection. For the manager in the know, however, this question can be a way to identify what you consider your strength to be. There is no silver bullet answer for this one. Safe answers would be any of the core competencies listed in this guide. For example, "focus on results," or "positive attitude," or "knowledge of your products and customers" would be fine. As you give your answer, preempt the next logical question by also explaining why you chose that factor as the most important. Give an example of how you demonstrated that behavior in a current or previous job.

65) What do you expect the hardest part of being a Pharmaceutical Representative will be?
This question is looking for your job knowledge first, and whether you know enough about the job to imagine what the biggest challenge would be. It also gives an indication of where you might have a developmental requirement that the manager will want to address in the future. This is not necessarily a negative—just more information the manager needs for the decision. Everyone has strengths and weaknesses and the manager

seeks to indenify these in the serious candidates. The safe answers are, "access to the doctor", but follow your answer with ideas or what you would do to gain that access. *Insight* has previously provided answers to this topic.

66) If a competitor moves your samples, what should you do?
Consult the nurse or office manager, whoever is in charge of the drug sample closet. State that your samples have been moved and ask for their suggestions as to what to do about it. Do not jump to conclusions that it was a competitor, even if you believe that is the case. Allow the office personnel to offer information since it may have been the staff or the doctor who moved your samples. Do not explicitly badmouth a competitor. This strategy will often result in the office personnel taking your side and providing a solution that will help you sell the most. It will also allow you to have more selling time; your professionalism will be highly regarded.

67) A nurse or physician gets angry with you and says they are too busy to see you. What do you do?
Because this is a long-term relationship, you should remind yourself that everyone is allowed to have a bad day at the office. In a professional tone, agree that their schedules can be hectic and offer to return at more convenient time. Although you may have already been waiting a long time, showing poise in this situation makes you very welcome in the office. Being confrontational will aggravate the customer. When offering to return, you can often end up having more time with the doctor because they will remember that they made a commitment to see you later. You should also try to set an actual appointment. Appointment or not, it will be harder for them to turn you away the next time. Of course, when you return, you would remind them that they had suggested this was the best time to come back.

TIP: You may be asked to describe what you would do in a very specific on-the-job situation for which you have no basis for an answer—because you are not yet a Pharmaceutical Rep. You can remain calm, buy time to think, and appear very professional. As a preface or introduction to your best guess answer, you will score extra points by starting off with the honest truth—that you are not sure how to answer an industry-specific question. The interviewer and you both know that you are not a Pharmaceutical Sales Representative and have no actual first-hand knowledge of the job. Therefore, you might begin the answer as follows, "As a new Representative, I may not be certain what to do in this situation. I would consult my manager or trainer if necessary before getting back to the customer with a correct response. Because you asked, here is one approach that I think would work, given the scenario you are describing." Then continue with your best response to the scenario.

68) After meeting a doctor for the first time, and introducing yourself, what do you do next?
This question is looking for customer focus and selling skills. To answer it, describe the steps you take to understand the customer and establish trust. Even before establishing product needs, what is the best way to serve that individual in the long-term relationship? Determine the personality of the physician (such as talkative and friendly versus technically oriented) and use the correct approach. Once you learn the right tactic, you

will want to know more about the physician's practice of medicine in the areas of your products. Ask a series of questions (sales probes) to see what they prescribe for the various disease states for which your products are indicated. Why do they make those choices? Answers may include efficacy, side effect profile (safety), price, managed care recommendations, etc. Only after that process will you know the best manner and which specific information to present on your products. Always state that you will add any suggestions from your trainer/manager to your selling techniques.

69) What would you do after entering a doctor's office for the first time then you are informed the physicians does not see Pharmaceutical Representatives?
The manager is looking for your thought process as you evaluate and plan in this situation. This is more important than the specific answer. Focus your answer on how you would gather information and determine a course of action.
First, you have to know why you went into that office. Based on your pre-call planning (from prescription data, notes from previous representatives, etc.), is this a valuable target? Are you prospecting a potential target just because you are in the area? Next, you should get more information from the office to better plan your strategy for this doctor. Inquire about the policy. Have they seen representatives in the past? Is this a new policy? Why did it change? Are there any suggestions they will offer in terms of how to best reach the physician? Ask about when and where the doctor makes hospital rounds. Ask how he prefers to obtain information about drug products, and how he meets his continuing medical education requirements.
Once you leave the office, decide whether this physician can have an impact on your territory and what actions are appropriate to gain access to them. You should tap into your resources—ask experienced representatives, successful representatives, and your manager for ideas and tactics they have used. This may include seeing doctors outside the office, such as at the hospital. You may decide to provide product literature, clinical reprints, studies, and samples without seeing the doctor—using creative ways to call attention to it. You may also use mailings, educational programs, and entertainment events. On the other hand, you may discover that this physician has a very low potential for your products and remove them from your call list. Either way, research and due diligence are required on your part.

70) During your first month on the job, you meet with a doctor who just recently switched to a competitor's product. How do you persuade them to come back to your product?
This is simple! Go back to the basics. Approach this doctor as you would any new customer and understand why the physician switched. Was it efficacy, safety, price, MCO recommendations? It may be as straightforward as the lack of a sales representative calling on them to provide needed services such as starter samples and updated information on the product. You will have to gain the physician's trust that you will take good care of your new client.

71) When presented with a last minute, unavoidable change to your itinerary, such as preparing for a new product launch, what planning, and coordination would you undertake?
This comes down to solid time management to make sure that you meet your commitments. You may have to work extra hard for a week making extra calls to cover your territory and keep up with new responsibilities. State that you are willing to make

these calls in the early morning or evening if appropriate. Use time in the car and during one or two evenings or weekends to study. You may possibly even see some physicians on a Saturday morning. The interviewer wants to know how you can handle a little work pressure, so show them that it would not faze you, that you have the commitment to your territory, and product knowledge to be a top performer. You would also talk it over with your manager and other team members to assist in setting appropriate goals and priorities.

72) You go to one of your regular physician's office and are introduced to a new physician in the practice. How do you approach the new doctor?
Introduce yourself with a handshake and present your card. Then use the same approach as any new customer—probe to develop an understanding of the doctor's preferences in how you can best be of service to her with her specific interests, personality, or behavioral style in mind. Understanding the doctor may include researching information regarding her background, when and how she prefers to see reps, and her attitude towards your products. Then go into a sales presentation that describes features and benefits, and reply to her concerns or objections, and when ready, close the sale.

73) A doctor tells you he will not prescribe your product because its cost is $40 more than your competitor's product. What do you do?
The obvious answer to the cost objection is to clarify misunderstandings the customer may have on this issue including managed care formulary and reimbursement data. If the doctor has this information correct and you are dealing with a true cost objection, the next step is to outweigh it using patient and physician benefits of the product as well as with the service you provide. The cost of a product is relative to its perceived value. Highlight the features and benefits of this product as compared to the competition to demonstrate that while your product may cost more in the short term, it is ultimately a more cost effective way of treating patients overall.

74) It is your first week on the job. How do you get to see the doctors who are a priority?
At this point, the list of priority doctors is based on a territory analysis list. First, plan your day to have all the tools and supplies necessary to be effective. Next, map out the most efficient route to make the best use of your time. Consult your counterparts and manager for any advice as to the office protocol of these priority doctors. Once at an office, introduce yourself to the nurse or receptionist presenting them with your card and the name of your products. Probe for office protocol and any other information that would be important, and then ask specifically to meet the doctor. If it is not possible to see the doctor at that time, arrange the best time to return and follow through exactly as agreed upon.

75) You are on a team with four other sales representatives. For the past few weeks, you have done all the planning of lunch meetings with the doctors. In your opinion, your teammates are not doing their share of the work. What do you do?
This common question is similar to "How well do you work on teams?" First, bring it to the attention of your teammates and get their perception of the situation as you work out a solution. It may be a simple matter of asking for more help from them. If that does not bring about a resolution, the next step would be to take it to the attention of your manager for advice. There may be something going on that you are not aware of which is preventing the others on your team from assisting you with lunch meetings.

Realize that you may have set a higher standard of expectations for yourself. Lead by example.

76) Why are you thinking of leaving your current position?
This question is looking for what motivates you and your level of knowledge about the Pharmaceutical Rep position. Include positive statements that indicate your desire for challenge, increased responsibility, achievement, professional and personal growth, compensation for your effort, etc. Your answer should convey that you have done extensive research and discovered that the job of pharmaceutical sales is the ideal fit for you. For example, "Though there are many aspects of my current position that I enjoy, I have found that my skills and abilities are best suited to pharmaceutical sales. I desire the challenge for professional and personal growth within the industry and particularly with XYZ Pharmaceuticals."

77) Are you working at the last organization listed on your resume?
This is easy if the answer is, "Yes." If not, answer the question honestly, with confidence and in a matter-of-fact tone. Today's economy has brought about many job changes. Being "between jobs" does not carry the stigma it once did now that we operate in a constantly changing business environment. An example of an answer could be, "I was one of nine individuals not retained with the organization. Our profits did not meet expectations. There were many cutbacks within all departments. Due to my tenure, I was not retained." Then stop and allow the interview to move forward from there.

78) Will you have a tough time becoming acquainted with a new industry after being with the same organization for a while?
Not at all, I have worked for several different managers and interacted with numerous departments during my time with ABC Incorporated. I am very flexible and learn quickly. I know I can contribute to your sales team from the start."

79) You have had numerous positions over the past four years. How do I know that you will stay at XYZ Pharmaceutical Company?
Job changes are always good if they involve and increase in challenge, responsibility, or compensation. Show the benefit and progress of your career moves. Some factors may have been out of your control. Examples are acquisitions, mergers, layoffs, relocation, etc. Be confident, direct, and honest in your reply. For example: "With each new position, I have progressed in achieving my career goals. Over the past several months, I have redefined these goals due to extensive research, networking, completing pharmaceutical Preceptorships, etc. I know that pharmaceutical sales are exactly where I want to achieve these goals and XYZ Pharmaceutical Company is the company in which I will excel."

80) How long have you been looking for a pharmaceutical sales position?
Here is an opportunity for you to describe your research and extensive knowledge of this industry. If you are interviewing with another pharmaceutical company, disclose where you are in the interview process (second, third, final interview, or offer stage). This response will evoke the competitive nature in the interviewer. Keep the time you have been looking as short as possible because managers may feel that you may have been passed over for a particular reason.

81) You seem like a great candidate, why haven't you secured an offer in the industry to date?
This is a hardball question. It is meant to see if you can be thrown off your game. There is no right or wrong answer. Remain confident. Display your knowledge of the industry and companies with whom you have interviewed. Include offers if you have had any. For example, "I have had an offer with ABC Pharma, but the geography and the timing were not right for me. The position you have available is perfect, and I am ready to make a commitment to your organization."

82) How did you do on your last performance review? What strengths and areas of improvement did you manager observe?
This is a repeat of "tell me your weaknesses." Choose and explain the steps you took to improve yourself. Examples may be that you are impatient with the others in your department, or you tend to take on too much. You have remedied this by gaining a better understanding of other people's work habits, developing time lines and new tactics of time management. If you have copies of excellent past performance reviews, show them, and leave a copy at the conclusion of your interview.

83) Tell me about the best manager you have ever had?
This is time to give the most praise, because a hiring manager wants to see that you can interact well with management. Explain your position, how you followed your manager's direction, how management monitored your progress, and gave the appropriate praise and comments.

84) Tell me about the worst manager you have ever had?
Using the same strategies in discussing your weaknesses, avoid stating that you have ever had a bad manager. "I have learned from all of the managers I have had in my professional career. If I had to pick a particular competency in a manager that could have been demonstrated better, it may have been enthusiasm and keeping our team motivated."

85) Describe in one word what selling means to you?
Many different words can be used, but stick to the request for one word. Suggestions are value, challenge, satisfaction, integrity, relationship, or success.

86) How is your driving record?
This question is a practical matter for the company to determine eligibility for hire. It is asked in the screening interview and is always a question on the employment application. Your driving record will always be part of the background checks. Some companies will run the background check before making an offer, while others will make the offer first, contingent on the background checks. Since driving is a requirement of the job, and you will drive the company car, the insurance requirements demand that you have a good record. Moving violations are usually no problem unless you have a license suspension or revocation on your record. However, DWI and DUI's in the past three to four years may eliminate you from consideration for many companies. The best way to answer this question is to know what is and is not on your record. Include in your answer only felony or misdemeanor convictions, which is normally all that is requested. Citations such as moving violations can be requested. If you do not know what your record shows and you suspect there may be something there, find out.

Know what your record states and the state's laws in terms of how long infractions remain on your record, and always be straightforward. When required, admit your mistake, what you have learned from it, and that your record since then has been impeccable.

87) Have you ever had any financial difficulties?
When you fill an application, usually you sign a release for an employer to check your credit history. One must under the 1972 Fair Credit and Reporting Act. So, do not try to avoid this one, be up, with no lengthy details. "Filing bankruptcy is something that was not a pleasant experience, but I have learned much through the process and I am well on track to an excellent credit rating.

88) Your product and price is very similar as a competitor. How would you sell your product?
This is when it comes down to relationships. A person buying from people applies in pharmaceuticals just as any other sales venture (relationships). Give examples of how you develop rapport, provide excellent service, follow-up, call frequency to establish physician habits, the value you add, and that you close for the business. Often, this business goes to the sales representative who both earns the right to ask for it and does ask for it.

89) A doctor says that she is going to stop writing prescriptions for your drug and is switching to the competition. What do you do?
This question, like many of this type, is looking for your selling skills. While this is at first, a bad situation to encounter with a customer there is a positive aspect. Because the physician bothered to let you know she is switching products, it indicates a trusting relationship and is an invitation to talk about it. The doctor has probably heard something negative about your product, and now needs reassurance to rebuild confidence in you and your product. You will no doubt have a detailed discussion beginning with asking all the questions and listening well. Collect all the concerns, objections and misunderstandings the doctor may have before going off on a tangent. Use your best listening and probing skills with non-defensive posture and verbal tone. Once you have all the information, you can address it.

90) What do you expect is the most difficult or challenging part of being a Pharmaceutical Representative?
This question is seeking your knowledge of the Pharmaceutical Sales position and if you have the skills and confidence to be successful. There is no right or wrong answer here, but "physician access" or "time with the physician" is a solid answer. Do not wait for the next question, "What would you do about it?" Answer that question at the same time.

91) What would you do to gain access to "no see" physicians and spend more time key physicians?
This will be a common question since it is the biggest challenge you will face. Practice your answers before you interview. Some of the obvious responses are:

- Contact the doctor at hospital displays
- Invite him to educational programs
- Discover how they spend their free time
- Offer to entertain the doctor and a spouse or guest (within company guidelines)

- Always provide new information and value on your calls
- Have other "hard-to-see" doctors give you a recommendation
- Call on the doctor with increased frequency to better your chances of getting in
- Develop rapport with the staff and make a "friend" who will give you the inside track
- Acknowledge this challenge will be met with creativity, persistence, and patience

There are no "magic answers," every doctor is different. State that you would take a long-term view of this situation to develop a specific plan of action for the less available physicians in your territory. You know that even doctors with a "no see" policy will see certain sales representatives who offer them value, and whom they respect. You may consider writing to the doctor and asking for a one-time meeting that will take no more than five minutes of their time. Promise that if you do not provide value to his expectations you will not ask him again. When you do get access, always request permission for the next meeting before you leave. Finally, know that your relationship skills are critical and you must show genuine concern and interest in the physician. Show confidence and believe in your ability to influence that customer.

92) A doctor is resistant to trying your product. What would you do?
Physicians "buy" like any other group of individuals. Some will respond quickly and try whatever is new. These "early adopters" are mostly focused on effectiveness of the product. Others are cautious and wait for information from those who did try it first. These "late adopters" are more focused on safety (side effects). The majority of physicians are in between these two extremes. Once you know you are dealing with a late adopter, you can approach him or her accordingly, in addition to rapport building, probing, and listening.

93) Your counterpart is having problems with his day-to-day responsibilities. His sales results are showing it and affecting your share as well. What do you do?
If you are an experienced sales representative, you should offer your assistance in a positive manner. Maybe something you know, or a way you approach your position, can help this individual. This shows your competencies around "teamwork." If this has failed and you feel that the individual is harming your district sales, then it is a concern that you will want to address with your manager in an appropriate manner.

94) You have spent all of your month's expenses on a luncheon with three doctors and their staff. Just before the lunch, one of the staff members says that two of the doctors will not be there. What do you do?
You have to be flexible and creative in this situation. Obviously, you are going to follow through on your commitment. On the bright side, you will have more time with the doctor who is there. Next, you can leverage the situation with that doctor and the staff by asking what they would suggest could be done about meeting with those who did not join your group. Never simply excuse it. Create urgency or mild tension by reacting in a serious manner. Let them know you are out on a limb financially to provide this lunch. This will put them in the position of trying to help you out. They may offer to schedule appointments with the missing doctors to make up for it. If not, ask for an appointment or another way of accessing those doctors when they return.

95) Why should I hire you?

This is a typical "tough" question, but it is a great opportunity when you get it. Being prepared with more information will help you answer this by asking for the job. By this point in the interview, you may have already asked the manager what he or she is looking for in an ideal candidate. If not, this is the time to ask. You will show confidence in your demeanor by looking right back at the interviewer and asking, "To help me focus my answer, what are you looking for in the ideal candidate?" Then tailor your full response to his or her "hot buttons." In general, you will hit the core competencies for the job. For example, "I have demonstrated the drive to achieve (as evidenced by previous sales success); I have shown you that I am creative, persistent, self-motivated, and a fast learner. I have thoroughly researched the industry and this company and know what the position requires. I am excited about the challenges ahead and am confident that I will be a successful member of your team. I want the job! Is there anything else you need to know in order to make me the offer? Great!"

96) Describe yourself in one word.

This question is not as important as it sounds. The intention is to see how you think on your feet. As long as you maintain composure and deliver a one-word answer, you have succeeded. Keep a word in mind so you can deliver it without hesitation. Pick something you can back up with specific examples of when you demonstrated that aspect or behavior.

Here are some ideas:

- Creative
- Persistent
- Consistent
- Sincere
- Determined
- Competitive
- Motivated
- Energetic
- Tenacious

97) Since you do not have sales experience what makes you believe you will be successful in pharmaceutical sales?

Your answer should begin by stating the only indicator of future success is past performance. Then make the case for success in sales by demonstrating that you have succeeded in professional and personal endeavors that translate into sales. Many roles and responsibilities will transition well—anytime you had to convince another person on a course or action, way of thinking, for example. Or anytime you have taught something, made a presentation, worked in groups or on teams, debated a point successfully, completed a project, you have developed the competencies for success in sales.

98) Do you know the name of the CEO of our company?

Make a note of before each interview by visiting the appendix and double checking the company website.

99) We are a rather small pharmaceutical company here at TDB Pharma, with only one product, and a couple in research and development, versus some of the big Pharma companies with 3-5 products selling over a billion dollars a year, and hundreds in development. Why would you want to work for TDB Pharma?

I have always enjoyed a challenge, and the ability to be unique in the marketplace. With TDB though many physicians are not yet aware of the company and its products, I see that as a benefit, for they are interested in something new.

In addition, I enjoy the fact that the salesforce is small and there is not two to three other representatives calling on the same physicians and having the same territory. The territory is mine, my challenge, and therefore, will be my success.

100) How comfortable will you be with co-marketing XYZ's new product CuraFlu with ABC Pharma (for example)?
Many times different companies will be selling the same drug. However, only one company has developed the product and received FDA approval, but the product may need more "sales power" than some companies have (headcount). Looking through the Appendix, and you will see numerous examples where a listed drug and in parentheses, another company is mentioned (co-marketing agreement). State that with most sales efforts, the more "voice" that is available for the marketing, the more success the product will have. An additional 300-500 representative can often make or break a product upon launch (with the first six months being critical).

101) There are numerous candidates for this opening with pharmaceutical sales experience, why should I hire you for the position?
State that you have the core competencies by which to succeed in this position (refer again back to the core competencies earlier in the book). You have a demonstrated record of accomplishment in your education, prior employment. You have the advantage of training me at the level that XYZ pharmaceutical wants their representatives to obtain. I have not acquired any bad habits, or dissatisfaction in the industry that needs to be changed.

102) How does a Pharmaceutical Representative differentiate between a sales call and a sample drop?
Often when the physician is in need of your samples for their patients and having an extremely busy day, the nurse or receptionist will suggest that they just have time to sign your form (or computer). In this case, you actually just leave samples (sample drop), and witness the signature versus when you spend a few minutes talking to the physician about your product, features, benefits, indications, dosage, side effects, etc., (this is a sales call). Respect the physicians/nurse/receptionist request, show you are a professional, smile, and suggest gaining more time on your next visit.

103) With your education and prior positions, do you have any examples where you have had to learn technical information?
Most of us have had some science, statistics, and math courses in our education, develop this for your answer. State that you enjoyed this type of coursework and this is one strong attraction of pharmaceutical sales. If you have been in a position where you have learned technical features and benefits of your product, you may use that.

104) During your sales presentation, what do you feel is most important, the opening or the close?
While it is always vital to gain a physicians interest during a sales call in "the opening", there are many other aspects that are just as vital. Understanding misconceptions, answering objections, presenting clinical data, therapeutic and price comparisons, etc.

After covering these issues with proficiency, then a Pharmaceutical Representative can ask a physician for their commitment to use your product, (close the sale). Closing the sale is always the most important factor in sales, great openings mean nothing if a Pharmaceutical Representative never asks for a commitment (the close). Just as your interview, your final "close" (asking for the position) is far more important than your initial comments (though vital, not too many candidates are been hired for a great greeting).

105) How do you respond to me if I told you, your sales presentation today was terrible?
First, ask the interviewer to expand on their statement. They did say "if", correct? Do not loose your composure, then state, "I would have to ask what areas of my sales presentation was there a problem?" This is something that you are going to face in the field with your manager quite often. After a sales call (and we hope they state it more tactfully) a District Managers job is to analyze your performance, coach you, and improve your selling skills. If this is a valid concern, it gives you a chance to revisit your presentation, and address any misconceptions they may have about your statements. Often, this is just a ploy to test your nerves, hang in there.

106) How would you rate me as an interviewer?
If the interview has gone well in your eyes, state though it has been slightly stressful I feel excellent, I feel I have been able to demonstrate to you my competencies that are required in pharmaceutical sales. If the interview has not gone well, now is your time to revisit the area where you may have felt that you were not at your best. State, "Very well, but I would like to revisit the topic of …" If the District Sales Manager was poor, keep it to yourself.

A NOTE ON THE PSYCHOLOGICAL TEST

Though not very common in pharmaceutical interviews, I have heard of some organizations using a third party (to screen candidates) using some of the many available psychological tests. The tests usually are written tests, sometimes over the phone, and other times, face-to- face. Be ready for the common statement, "There is no wrong answer, and just answer the questions how you feel." When you take a test such as this, put yourself in "interview best" mode. The "corporate way" is the answers you want to give, not your "personal feelings or preferences". I am not telling you to be dishonest, but picture yourself as the #1 pharmaceutical representative in the company (which you want to be), and answer the questions from that viewpoint. Ask yourself, "what has my networking, research, Preceptorships, and education taught me? What is the most professional way I would act or select in this situation? What would you like to see in response to the question if you were the employer?" Approaching these tests with this in mind will get you through this requirement successfully.

PROFESSIONAL ATTIRE

Your efforts in networking, research, and resumes have met with success. You have just been called for an initial interview with the District Manager of XYZ Pharmaceutical Company. You scrutinize your wardrobe for the perfect look, one that says, "I am the qualified individual for this position." Why are your attire and appearance more important than your attributes, skills, and abilities?

Because that one hurdle that you must cross with every new encounter the critical first impression. Sociologists use the term "halo effect" to describe the first 30 seconds of a meeting. In those first 30 seconds, people generally make up their minds about you. They succeed whether they have just met someone who is competent, genuine, and "on top of it" or not. Your dress is a nonverbal communication as to what you think about yourself, your attitude toward business, your goals, and how well your regard the other individuals with whom you are meeting. Right or wrong, decisions about your ability and character are based upon the interviewer's response to your appearance. It is assumed that anyone who can handle personal details well will be just as meticulous with the details of the job. Thus, your goal is to create the "halo effect" for yourself. Professional attire, an engaging manner, a firm handshake, and an air of energy and vitality will set the stage on which you will perform to your highest level.

Beyond first impressions, the way you dress indicates your sense of professional judgments and establishes your credibility. While you are selling yourself orally during your interview, nonverbal communication, including attire, will either reinforce what you are saying or undermine your own words.

Recent college graduates may not yet own expensive business attire. Shop for deals on wool fabric suits, but spend the extra money to get it tailored to fit correctly. You can get away with a lesser quality suit by wearing higher quality accessories, such as shoes and ties. The hiring process for pharmaceutical sales may require two or three interviews. Be prepared with two interview suits, if possible. If not, accessorize with ties, shirt styles (men keep it all white), and shoes for a slightly different look. Finally, make sure your suit is clean and freshly pressed.

Putting time, energy, and expense into your professional appearance will always pay you back. Think of it as an investment in yourself and your career. You will command authority and assume credibility beyond that which you currently possess. "Looking the part" is critical during the interview process. The interviewer will begin to visualize you in the job instead of just another interviewing candidate. Never underestimate the power of the first impression.

Every recruiter (most who have not worked in the industry as a field representative and even rarer a hiring manager) will tell you to construct your "brag book", a binder or portfolio that contains your resume, performance reviews, and letters of recommendation and just about anything positive that has happened in your lifetime. This is also contained in some follow up books and guides to *Insight* over the past ten years. Though I agree, this is something that is a must to have at any interview, please do not consume and control your interview by paging through one of these brag books. Yes, have one for a reference is fantastic, but let the interviewer control the interview and ask the questions. I cannot tell you how many "brag books" I have had the pleasure of being put through in 20 years of management as a DM and RD. It is a similar experience to watching someone's home movies. The interviewer already knows that everything is going to be a glowing report. Often by the time the candidate was done, I was finished also, never conducting the interview, they had used all the allotted time (20-30 minutes) for their appointment for the brag book. That was it, which was all we could cover. I did not even start the process of the interview and it was time for e next candidate. There was nothing to compare at the end of the day, for the interviewee decided on what was going to be presented and would keep turning page after page. Always, let the interviewer conduct the interview.

Finally, remember to always be early at the place of the interview. Even if that means waiting in the parking lot or the lobby for 30 minutes (in which you will often see the "look" of the previous candidate)

If in doubt on the location, drive it the evening before. Besides being prompt, this will give you 10-15 minutes to collect yourself, organize your files, research, and relax as much as possible before the interview begins.

WOMEN'S GUIDELINES FOR INTERVIEWING DRESS

1) No outfit is more effective for an interview than the matched suited skirt.
2) Research has shown the most successful colors are black, navy, and gray, and you should pair it with a high-necked white or ivory silk blouse.
3) Shoes should be well polished, clean, and darker than the suit.
4) The interview process, practicality dictates that a woman may carry a purse as well as a briefcase (your files, research, even the "brag book"). You must manage both comfortably when shaking hands, sitting down, etc. A briefcase only is quite acceptable, as is a nice leather portfolio. A leather portfolio is good for note taking during the interview, but a new legal pad will do just fine. You will need a briefcase for your interviewing files and materials, and it should be leather and the best you can afford. Avoid company names or logos on anything.
5) Your hair should be neat and off the shoulders in a manageable style. Avoid bows and complicated styles. Your hair should draw attention to and compliment your face.
6) A touch of makeup is appropriate. Light makeup will enhance a woman's professional image. The goal is to wear makeup without looking made up.
7) Tattoo's (I never imagined I would be writing this one) should be hidden.
8) Nails should be short and rounded. The only appropriate nail colors are clear or natural; a French manicure is also acceptable and distinctive.
9) Jewelry should be simple and professional; avoid anything that will draw attention away from you. Gold or silver chains are smart. If worn, lapel pins should be elegant. Earrings lend authority and professionalism, and should be small and simple, no bigger than a quarter. Dangles or hoops are inappropriate. Nothing else should be pierced for display.
10) Wear a nice analog style watch (not digital) because analog watches project more of a traditional/ formal business appearance versus a sports/digital watch; a wedding ring, if married, with or without the engagement ring. No other rings.
11) Use a fine gold or sterling pen.
12) There should be no perfume or fragrance. Many individuals have chemical sensitivities that can be aggravated by hairspray or perfume.

MEN'S GUIDELEINES FOR INTERVIEWING DRESS

1) The two-piece wool business single-breasted suit is the foundation. Research shows that the most authoritative colors are dark blue and dark grey. These two colors look good on everyone. Use a traditional, conservative style versus a European designer one. The fit is more important than the quality of wool, so spend your money on proper tailoring. Button the top button while standing or walking, unbutton it when sitting. Be sure one's jacket pocket flaps should always remain out of the pockets.
2) Shirts should be solid white and all cotton for interviews. Use a straight collar instead of a button-down collar for the conservative, slightly more formal look. Avoid collars with snaps or ones that require collar pins. Your shirt should be professionally laundered, and starched for a crisp look. Pens go in the coat pocket, or briefcase, not the shirt pocket.
3) Wear a new, fashionable conservative silk tie. Choose a solid colored tie that complements, not matches your suit. Good colors are maroon, crimson, or navy blue. Patterned ties such as stripes, foulards, or small dots are acceptable. Avoid paisleys, prints, club ties, insignias, or depiction of any identifiable cartoon, or other characters. Skip the pocket-hand kerchief. The bottom point of the tie should line up with the middle of the belt buckle. Do not wear a tie clasp or pin of any kind.
4) Avoid wearing an overcoat; it is cumbersome to handle.
5) Avoid anything monogrammed. A plain black leather belt will compliment the navy or gray suit.
6) Shoes should be good quality and newly polished. A laced, plain-toe or wing tipped oxford is best. Tasseled loafers can project casualness. Always error on the conservative side. Black and cordovan are appropriate colors. Socks should be over-the-calf or long enough to cover your legs when sitting or if your pant leg rides up. Do not cross your legs during an interview. Use a solid colored sock in black for black shoes (preferred) and in navy for cordovan shoes. In some areas of the United States, cowboy boots are not out of place for business wear, but not for interviewing.
7) Hair should be short and neat. Beards and mustaches are a means of self-expression and identity, however, for the most professional look, be clean-shaven during your job search. You can always grow it back later.
8) Wear a nice analog (not digital) wristwatch. Do not wear rubber sport watches. Never look at a watch during an interview. The only ring should be a wedding band, if married. Avoid other rings, bracelets, lapel pins, or other jewelry. Cuff links are fine if they are simple, plain gold. Use a pen of excellent quality and keep it handy in your coat pocket.
9) Your briefcase should be professional, leather, well-polished and dark colored. A leather portfolio is especially valuable for taking notes during the interview. You will need a briefcase for the interviewing files and materials you have collected. Avoid company names or logos on anything.
10) Men's fingernails should be short and rounded, clean and buffed to shine. Trim and clean the cuticles for a detail-oriented look.
11) There should be no cologne avoid anything with a fragrance. Chemical sensitivities apply to many people.
12) No tattoos or piercing of any kind should be seen.

[SAMPLE LETTER; INTERVIEW FOLLOW-UP]

December 16, 2008

Janet Lynn Jones
1234 West Drive
Salestown, MA 41124

Mr. Patrick Vick
District Manager
XYZ Pharmaceuticals Corporation
2820 Burgess Avenue
Maplewood, MA 43128

Dear Mr. Vick,

Thank you for the opportunity to discuss the Sales Representative position with XYZ Pharmaceuticals. It was a pleasure meeting with you today.

I am excited about our conversation and I am especially impressed with the autonomy given to each sales representative and the challenge that it offers. You are looking for a determined self-starter with a successful sales background. I am looking for a company that rewards one for their individual effort, yet will always work hard with a team.

A career in pharmaceutical sales at XYZ Pharmaceuticals is an excellent match for my skills and career objectives. I want this position; for I know that I can make a significant contribution to your sales team.

Thank you again for your time and consideration. I look forward to hearing from you soon.

Sincerely,

Janet Lynn Jones

Chapter Seven
Your Questions

This chapter provides you with and questions you need to ask during the various stages of the interviewing process. Why should you be asking questions? The point to having your own questions to ask is twofold. First, you will demonstrate your preparation, awareness of the position, and communication skills. Second, you need to evaluate the person and company that you are considering joining, perhaps for your entire career.

There are two main questions. (1) Is the organization the best for you? (2) Can you work with, or for, this individual? You must answer each other's questions during the interview process to move forward and result in your employment.

This chapter offers twenty questions that are appropriate for you to ask the interviewer. The questions are in the chronological order of the interview process. Avoid asking questions that are easily answered with a little independent research, such as visiting the company websites. It should be a given that you know basic information at least, such as the product names and indications. Change the style to match your own, and "have fun with it"!

Many of the following questions are similar to those you may have already asked in your networking. If you are already aware of information from your networking phase, interlace it into your interview process. As discussed, presenting your knowledge about the company demonstrates preparedness and drive. For example, instead of asking the District Manager, "How many territories are in your district", use that piece of information as a lead-in to another question: "I understand there are twelve territories in your district (information from your networking). How does the open territory's performance compare with the other territories in the district?"

TIP: Every interviewer usually concludes by saying, "Do you have any questions for me?" Prepare five to ten important questions that you want answered It is completely acceptable to refer to your notes during the interview. Never state, " I have no questions".

SCREENING AND INITIAL INTERVIEWS

What qualifications and qualities are you looking for in the ideal candidate?
Do not wait long to ask it. The sooner you get the answer from the interviewer, the better job you can do tailoring your own statements to what the manager wants to hear. It uncovers the manager's "hot buttons", or the key characteristics in a job candidate. Ask this at the start of, or early in, the interview and repeat it for every different person with whom you interview. The answer is significant, and should guide you as you match your own qualifications and qualities to those the manager is looking for. Emphasize your attributes that respond to the stated requirements.

1) How did this position become available with your company?
The answer could be that it was opened due to a promotion, transfer expansion, or termination.

2) I have completed many hours of research on a career in the Pharmaceutical sales industry and your company. I am extremely interested in this position. When can we meet to discuss it in detail?
This is a solid close for the initial interview process. Be sure to mail a follow-up letter within 24 hours.

TIP: Often, initial screening interviews are accomplished over the telephone. Be free of interruptions. Turn off call waiting pressing #70 before the scheduled interview time. Have all information, notes, and questions in front of you.

3) What is the geography of this territory?
Examples may be rural or metropolitan, certain cities, towns, or zip codes. The interviewer's answer may give you an opportunity to state that you are familiar with some of the various areas. Example: I attended school in Bryn Mawr, PA., and am very familiar with the area.

4) What are the major accounts in this territory? Who are the key customers?
This answer will tell you who brings in the most business in the district possibilities may include an individual or a group of specialists who are considered to be "thought leaders". These are the experts in a given specialty, and are highly respected by other physicians in the area. Their importance is due to this significant influence. Pharmaceutical companies assign responsibility for calling on these "thought leaders" to their best and most experienced representatives. Other examples could be a large university-based teaching institution. That has an influence in the area, or perhaps a large retail pharmacy chain that is dominant in the district. One purpose of asking questions is to gain information. Another reason is to discover what is important to the interviewer. When you uncover something of significance in your interview with the District Manager, refer to that item in your follow-up letter. This demonstrates that you listen and comprehend what is important to your customer.

5) What type of physician specialties do you target?
Examples: family practice, internal medicine, surgery, pediatrics, dermatology, psychiatry, allergy and immunology, rheumatology, obstetrics, oncology, and urology.

6) How many territories and representatives are there in a district and where does this one currently rank?
Districts may average nine to twelve representatives. Regions may have six to nine districts. This is information you may already have from your networking contacts with a representative from this company and more insight to the performance of the geography that you are entering.

7) What are the various divisions of the sales force?
Different pharmaceutical companies are similar in some ways and vary greatly in others. One area where they differ is in the structure of the sales force and the various divisions or groups within it. This answer gives you the sales specialties and challenging directions in which your career could go. Examples include a Hospital Sales Force, Diabetes Specialists, Account Teams, Governmental Affairs, and many others.

8) How is this territory performing to budget? How does it rank in the district?
You need to know the current state of the business in what may be your new territory. Here you are digging a little deeper again and coming back to the issue if this is a problem or low performing territory. If not, a question that you can leave off your list. Is the territory operating at 10% below budget or 20% over budget? Whatever the answer, your goal is to improve upon it.

9) What is the total sales revenue of this territory? How is the performance with the promoted products written in this territory?
With these questions, you are asking how many dollars worth of sales you will be responsible for when you take over the territory. The performance is also significant because your goal will be to increase volume.

10) Describe the training program for new representatives and continuing education and development programs?
You want to uncover how committed to training and development the company is, the first part will be an easy answer, the second is where you will see the commitment of the organization to ongoing education and development.

11) Are there any products that have been submitted to the Food and Drug Administration (FDA) for marketing approval?
From your research, you may already know the answer to this question. If so, mention what you know and ask if there is any news on how the product is coming along. Asking shows that you are seeking information on the company's future over the next several years. You want to choose a company that has a full pipeline of new products in the near future. But often in today's industry, companies can acquire products more efficiently than pure research and development, so keep this in mind.

12) Which therapeutic areas or specific diseases does the company target for new product development?
Companies will specialize, much as physicians do, by concentrating their R&D efforts on a limited number of diseases. Are the targeted therapeutic areas (such as cardiac diseases, depression, or diabetes) similar to current treatments, or is the company expanding its research into other possible solutions? Do they have a focus for research? Does it match their product line? This question will uncover the general direction, or strategy of the organization.

13) Does the company co-market with another pharmaceutical company or use Contract Sales Organizations (CSO's)?
Co-marketing (also called co-promoting) is an agreement between two companies to promote the same product t the same time. Co-marketing usually involves a trade-off in which each company takes on one of the other company's products, though not necessarily at the same time. Example: XYZ Pharmaceutical Company is co-marketing a new antibiotic from Widget Pharmacia. Next year when XYZ Pharmaceutical Company introduces their new diabetes agent, Widget Pharmacia will co-promote it in return. This question can give you insight into how aggressive the company is in hitting the bottom line. Are they willing to use co-marketing arrangements to meet sales and profit objectives?
I like what I have learned about the company, and I have demonstrated that I

can contribute and will add value. I want this position. What is our next step in the process? This is a good closing question to get you to the next interview, but it is aggressive and should be used at or near the end. This helps you assess the interviewer's interest in you and moves you forward in the process. Be firm and convincing. Watch for the manager's reactions.

TIP: Always use a strong close at or near the end of each interview. It gives the interviewer confidence that you will close in a sales call, too. It will also give you immediate responses as to how you rate with the interviewer. When you close, use a question like the one above, accompanied by a confident statement that you WANT THE JOB.

SECOND, THIRD & FINAL INTERVIEWS

The following questions are appropriate for more advanced, or second and third interviews. You are now a serious contender for the offer, and you should ask more in depth questions. These hit harder and are designed to give you the information you need to make the best decision when you receive an offer. You need to know where you are in the interviewing process and what is still ahead of you. Alternatively, how many interviews does it generally take to get the job? This information helps you plan and enact your strategy.

14) May I contact the previous Pharmaceutical Sales Representative that occupied this territory?

This is a risky question. Ask why the territory is open before asking to contact the previous representative. If the territory is open due to a termination, do not bother asking if you can contact him or her. If the previous representative was promoted within the company, the district manager would probably welcome you to contact him or her. If the previous representative left the company voluntarily, the district manager could answer either way. Regardless of the answer, it is a smart question to ask and shows you are thorough about your research. You take seriously your decision to join a company with which you plan to spend a long career.

15) May I contact any representatives that report to you?

As in the previous question, you want to gain more understanding about this company and your decision to work for it. You need to be confident that this is the one for you. Contacting other representatives is a good way to gain this insight. Ask them why they work for the company, what their level of satisfaction is, and what their goals are (see networking questions in Chapter 5 for more ideas). In addition, by asking this question you will gauge the manager's self-assurance in his or her managerial style. Ask yourself if this is the right person to help you achieve a successful career.

TIP: Be sure you know as much about a company as you can before joining it. Always try to speak to the previous representative and at least one representative that currently reports to the district manager who would be hiring you. Do this before accepting a position with any organization if possible.

16) What has been your career path to reach your position in management?

This is a softball to soften the last two questions, set back and relax and learn some of your future boss's career history.

17) How would you describe your management style and that of the company?
This is an invitation for the interviewer to speak. Listen as the manager describes his or her own style and management philosophy within the organization. Is this a good fit for you?

18) How does the company measure sales representatives' performance? How is it rewarded? What percentage of the total compensation is base salary versus bonus?
This answer should provide insight into the sales tracking mechanism that is used. You will also hear about the commission plans, bonus structure, and field promotions. You want to discover how much of your total compensation is at risk depending on sales performance. Remember that your compensation is mostly a fixed base salary.

19) How long do you believe it would take your new Sales Representative to generate significant results in the territory?
This answer tells you how quickly the manager expects to see results, and how he perceives the learning curve. Never assume that the manager your meeting with may not be under extreme pressure themselves, to get their districts performance up in a hurry.

20) How do you evaluate your sales representative and how often?
This question offers insight into the manager's style of presenting feedback. Good managers will give frequent and consistent criticism or advice in addition to routine performance reviews, which are either semiannual or annual. You need to know what to expect in terms of suggestions and recommendations.

21) With excellent performance, how long should a new Sales Representative expect to gain experience in his or her territory before being eligible for promotion?
You will communicate a desire to climb the corporate ladder with this question. If you do not have that desire at this point, that is fine, but it opens the door for the manager to relay some career success stories of individuals or themselves within the organization. The answer tells you what you can expect for you or other representatives.

22) Describe some of the typical career path for your Sales Representatives?
The key to this question, as opposed to the previous one, is that you are asking about the potential advancement for the person who stays in sales throughout his or her career. As discussed in Chapter 2, field sales are a career that is challenging and rewarding. There are many opportunities for promotions and advancement other than entering sales management or a home office position. This answer will vary. You may hear about increasing levels of recognition, salary, prestigious titles, and additional district, regional, or national responsibilities.

Your most important question:

"Considering what I have learned in our interview process plus my research and networking within the industry, I know I can make a strong contribution to your district and your organization." "I want this position!" **"May I do the job for you?"** This is your final statement. The wording should match your style, but deliver it emphatically. The purpose of the close is twofold. First, you need to clearly communicate that you want the job. Second, you want to uncover any lingering objections or questions the interviewer may have. This may be your last chance to make your case. Although it has been known to happen, you will probably not get an offer or rejection on the spot. However, you should get some valuable comments. You will most likely receive a "qualified" maybe, pending an interview with another final candidate, reference checks, or simply the need for further consideration.

TIP: When you touch the door knob or cross the threshold to exit the room, turn back to the interviewer and state it one more time: ***"Thank you for your time. I want this territory and career, when can I get started?"*** *Use your own words, but say it with conviction!*

Chapter Eight
Decisions

Congratulations! You have just completed your interviewing process. You have networked, researched, studied, prepared, interviewed, and followed-up with a letter. Only few things can happen next: you will receive an offer, be turned down or asked to return for possibly another interview.

As you await the District Manager's decisions, you will probably be contemplating the following thoughts: What will he or she say? How should you respond? What will you do if the answer is no? What if you get the offer but do not want the job? What if you want a better starting salary? As these questions suggest there is still plenty of work ahead for you no matter what the decision.

THE REJECTION

First, let us examine the bad news- you are turned down for the position. It is important to remember that it is not the end of the world; it happens to everyone. If you respond to this unfortunate situation correctly, it will turn out to be a positive experience for your career. How should you reply? It is natural to be disappointed. However, it will serve you well to remain positive and courteous. Continue the same professionalism and determination that you got you to the interview in the first place. Be persistent with the interviewer until you get direct comments about your interview. Find out what you can do to improve for qualifications or interview techniques in the future. Ask the interviewer for honest advice. Ask for one or two key strengths that he or she feels you possess. What are essential areas in which you could improve and how? In other words, accept the opinion from a manager who has spent time getting to know you. If it is honest advice, it will be valuable for you.

It is rare that too much advice will ever be given, for today's legal system has reduced feedback to a minimum. One never knows though, so it is always good to ask, better yet, look like you want to improve your skills, as you would in the position (remember, your still interviewing).

Usually, the position will already have been offered and accepted before the runners-up are contacted. However, it can happen that a candidate receives multiple offers accepting employment with one company and then, within weeks or months, accepting another. Thus, the same position may be open again. Alternatively, a different territory in the same district could become available and since you have already been through the interview process, all of a sudden, you have another offer. Therefore, it is important to keep the door open for yourself. Tell the interviewer that you still want the job, and if their top-choice candidate does not work out, you are willing to make a commitment and are ready for a start date. Communicate that if any other sales territory becomes available, you would like to be considered for that job as well. The benefit to the manager is that he or she will not have to go through the entire hiring process all over again if they can call you and make an immediate offer.

TIP: Tell the Manager that you will call back in three months to check for any potential new openings. Be sure to schedule it on your calendar and call regardless of your job situation at that time.

If you already have an offer or are working with another company, explain that you just wanted to follow up on your commitment. Over years, these contacts will become the highest value of security you will have in the industry.
Even a rejection should be followed with a letter of appreciation to the interviewer. An example of a letter you might use for this purpose is at the end of the chapter.

"THE OFFER"

Next, the great news! You have an offer for the position you want. Congratulations! Now you are ready to accept, decline, or negotiate. Not so fast though, let's take a little time and see if we can earn you an additional 20-30K over the next 10 years.

Regardless of your intention, I suggest that you do not respond immediately with your decision. You have worked long and hard for this offer and your work has been rewarded. Take some time to think about it. Ask for a minimum of at least twenty-four hours or more to consider it, discuss it with your spouse or significant other. The spouse always seems to get a solid agreement.

The company has kept you waiting; it is acceptable to ask for as much time as you need to you make your decision. It is also important to request a letter of the job offer. This letter describes everything that the organization is proposing to you. Salary, commission, benefits, vacation time, company car, medical, dental, 401K, etc. You can review it and make sure that there are no misunderstandings before you make your decision. These can easily be emailed and sent overnight. This strategy gives you time to think about the details of the offer and review other offers you may have. You will also demonstrate to your potential new employer that you are mature and serious about your decision. Furthermore, you have been patiently waiting for the decision from them.

They will understand giving you time to make a thoughtful decision- and will appreciate your request. This is why I have mention this numerous times in the book, "wait until you have the offer in your hand". A letter of offering is that document that makes it binding. If the offer meets your requirements and you want the job, accept it. If you would like more money, take this opportunity to ask for it. For example, you were offered a base salary of $61,000 but may counter with, "I am looking for a base salary of $63,000. "Do you have a little flexibility in your offer?" If you are struggling with whether to ask for more, some quick calculations may motivate you. Consider that even a modest increase ($500 to $2000) in your starting salary accumulates from year to year. Over a 20 year career, compounded annually, this could easily add up to over $5,000-$40,000 over 7-10 years, ask for the addition thousand or two in base pay, for that is what you had in mind. All your future increases are based on a percentage of your current salary; all your subsequent raises will be larger. In addition to the financial motive, negotiating for more money demonstrates your desire to achieve more – an excellent trait for a sales person. This also builds your negotiating skills. Do it!

You are all set with your start date, yet there are more questions. Should you suspend your job search immediately? The logic response is yes, however, I believe that such a decision may be premature.

Consider this scenario: You are exited about accepting the offer and want to get underway with your new job. During your job search you have followed the strategy outlined in *Insight*. All of your efforts with other companies are still paying dividends. Ironically, two weeks after you accept your offer, a company with which you previously interviewed calls because of an unforeseen vacancy.

The vacancy is actually a better fit for you interests and the complete package is significantly more attractive.
It can and does happen much more often than you will believe, especially since you have made yourself such a desirable candidate. In your excitement over your new position you think that it would be unethical to continue the interviewing process, and politely inform the company who called that you are not interested. My advice is to reconsider all your options and make the best decision for you and your family for the long term.

Because of scenarios such as this one, I urge you to keep your options open as much as possible. It is not disloyal to leave a job in which there is no mutual benefit. Over time, it may be worse to stay in a job where you are not 100% committed. Integrity and professionalism are always paramount and lead to a more satisfying career. Be sure that you do not alienate yourself from the organization, sales managers, or human resources executives that you may want to work with in the future. A word to the wise: The old adage, "It's a small world," applies to the entire pharmaceutical industry.

TIP: Consider all options with professionalism and courtesy. You will always benefit.

DELAYS

Finally, another of the remaining possible outcome is that the decision has not been reached and more time is needed. This may occur for several reasons. First, the company may have decided to not fill the position after all. In all ever-changing and complex business environments such as the pharmaceutical industry, this may occur when a company is in a state of flux due to a merger, product sell-off, acquisition, product non approval letter, or a change in corporate strategy or direction. Another reason for a delay may be that the District Manager and Regional Manager are not completely satisfied that they have the best candidate and extend the search period adding interviews. If this is the case, you will probably not be told that you are still considered a viable candidate, but may have to show them your best one more time to secure the offer.

Regardless of the reason for a delay, your strategy should remain the same. Continue to be upbeat, positive, and emphatic, about your desire and commitment to the position and the company. Do whatever it takes in terms of additional interviewers or company contacts. Follow each contact or telephone call with a brief note. Offer to touch base every week for updates on the process of filling the position to assist in your career decision process. Thorough communication will demonstrate your commitment. A good manager knows keeping you excited and positive about the job until a final decision has been fully implemented benefits their corporation. The manager wants you to know that you are his or her number one choice. This is motivating for you and helps keep any candidate's energy level high.

[SAMPLE LETTER: FOLLOW- UP TO Rejection]

September 10, 2008

Janet Lynn Jones
631 Any Street
Anytown, USA

Mr. Bill Franklin
District Manager
XYZ Pharmaceutical Company
12345 Easy Drive way
Newark, NJ 01234

Dear Mr. Franklin

Again, thank you for the opportunity to interview with you and XYZ Pharmaceutical Company. Though I am disappointed in the outcome of your open position, I still want you to know that I can make a significant contribution to your team and my interest is still very strong to join XYZ Pharmaceutical Company.

If a position becomes available in the near future, please contact me. My telephone is 847-546-7669. As we agreed, I will contact you in three months to discuss future opportunities.

Sincerely,

Janet L. Jones

Chapter 9
Profiles

The following company profiles will compliment your efforts and will save you countless hours of research time. Since 1998, with my first edition of Insight into a Career in Pharmaceutical Sales, the company profiles have been something that numerous candidates email me back with positive feedback. I know of no other source for pharmaceutical representative candidates that involve this much research assembled in one book. Whether profiles have helped them get some quick information for an unexpected telephone contact, or be better prepared for networking.

Look through the profiles, though they are not here for you to make any decision about employment with one pharmaceutical organization over another, they will give you a backgrounder into the various types of companies that are now prevalent in the industry. Though it is stated there are 50 profiles, you will find less than 50 sheets. But actually there are way more than 50 companies profiled in Chapter Nine. Abbott and Johnson and Johnson have at least 6 organizations, others such as Genyme, Nycomed, Shire and Teva will have multiple divisions.

Often I am asked to rank companies on the basis of which companies are best to work for, which is impossible as an individual. Within profiles is a mixture of large, medium, small or biotech companies. No individual can predict what one's experience will be with an organization. In reality, it usually comes down to ***who*** (the human element) you work for rather than the actual organization, unless a culture permeates from the top to the bottom. Sometimes an organizations products or pipeline helps, but not to the degree one from the outside believes it does. As a field sales representative, your District Manager is most likely going to be a great Manager, somewhere in between, or someone that can make your position far less enjoyable than it should be. Never fear though, Managers, Sales Districts, Territories are always changing within any company. If your desire is to work within a certain therapeutic area, where you have special expertise, education and interest that is surely understood. Many individuals find much more enjoyable experience with a CSO over a biotech organization. Some may find a large pharmaceutical company more enjoyable. Others may find a small emerging biotech company the best fit for them.

An often misunderstanding is that larger companies pay higher compensation then the smaller ones. Pharmaceutical companies continually benchmark themselves within the industry to be competitive with consultant groups (i.e. the Hay Group for competitive compensation analysis). Companies want to keep that 10-15% turnover as low as possible, for that is more a cost driver than compensation. At one point in one's career versus co-workers in the industry, one may be paid on the low side, then, within ten to eighteen months, you may be the highest. Never let a few thousand dollars sway your decisions over where you believe you will enjoy your career, for it is there you will have more success. The culture, people, and individuals you report to and those you work with will for out weigh $5-10 thousand dollars of income over time. Putting a price on enjoying your place of employment is difficult, but something you probably will face in your career.

The listing includes large pharmaceutical/biotech companies (sales over $10 billion), medium size (sales over $3 billon) and small (sales below $3 billion). This is no standard, just a guideline from *Insight*.

Besides the several organizations or divisions (companies) within one parent, there is another approximately 70-200 other pharmaceutical and biotech companies out there that can offer you just as rewarding careers. These 50 companies have been chosen due to at the time of writing, their size, growth, or recent entry into the marketplace. Quite frankly, they were thought to be the companies that most likely may have an opening in your area taking these issues into account.

Even though some may have had recent reductions, with that average turnover rate of 12%, they still produce openings. If one is open to relocation, the number is staggering nationwide of openings there are each year.

The profiles listed within *Insight* are out of date the day after written, for in this book form, taking into account writing, printing, shelf life, it is impossible for a profile to be up to date. Within the ten years of writing *Insight*, it is not uncommon that 1-2 of the companies listed within the book have merged, or a drug has been approved, before the book is returned from the printer and ready to distribute. So the profile is only your template, it is not prescribing information; it is only your starting point for the organization, surely not your complete research. It will still have you better prepared than 97% of the other candidates though and that is its value. With the immense amount of material available online, you can easily update a company's research within several hours, reading the financials, annual reports, recent press releases, viewing webcast, sign up for news feeds, press alerts, webcast, email alerts, etc.

Whether a new candidate or 10 year industry veteran, keep yourself abreast of your industry until retirement (if stock options were ever involved, longer). Keep an electronic file on each company, use it for your career, print out and bring material on the company to your networking and interviews (again, differentiate yourself to a higher standard).

ABBOTT LABORATORIES
100 ABBOTT PARK ROAD
ABBOTT PARK, IL 60064
Abbottt.com
847.937.6100

Summary: Abbott is broad-based health care company devoted to the discovery, development, manufacture and marketing of pharmaceuticals and medical products, including nutritionals, devices and diagnostics. The pharmaceutical division focuses on immunology, oncology, neuroscience, pain management, infectious, diabetes and metabolic disease states. In 2004, Abbott created an independent company; Hospira, one of the world's largest hospital supplier. 2005 brought the launching of Abbott Nutritional International. In 2007, Abbott Laboratories agreed to sell its in vitro diagnostics and diagnostics divisions to General Electric for more than $8 billion.

History: Wallace Abbott a medical doctor established the Abbott Alkaloidal Company in a Chicago in 1888. The company went public in 1929 and by the mid 1930's opened branches in South America, Mexico and Britain. The 1960's brought Selsun Blue, Murine, and numerous infant formulas (Ross Laboratories). The nineties brought Norvil, Gabitrol, and Zemplar. 2000 brought Biaxin XL, Depakote ER. Abbott acquired Knoll from BASF in 2000. 2004 bought a new formulation of TriCor and Zemplar Injection for children. In 2006, Abbott purchased Kos Pharmaceuticals for $3.7 billion, with products focus on lipid management. Abbott and AstraZeneca announce co-promotion of Crestor.

Approximate annual healthcare revenue: $26 billion

CEO: Miles D. White

Approximate Salesforce: 4,500

Major Brands: *Depakote ER* >$ 1 billion, antiepileptic, mania, *Ensure*, *Ensure Healthy Mom*, *Glucerna*, *Enfamil*, *Pedialyte* and *Similac* infant formula's, *Zone Perfect*, *EAS*, nutritional supplement's, *Humira*, *Humira Pen* >$3 billion, rheumatoid arthritis, Crohn's disease, ankolosing spondylitis and JPA, *Kaletra* >$1billion HIV/AIDS, *Synthroid* thyroid hormone, *TriCor*, *Simcor*, *Niaspan* cholesterol>$1billion, *Ultane* anesthetic, *Zemplar* hyperparathyroidism.

Pipeline: *Humira* numerous indications, *Vicoden CR* pain, *Niaspan/Zocor, Crestor/Trilipix* dyslipidemia and numerous other agents in various phases of development.

ALCON LABORATORIES INCORPORATED
6201 SOUTH FREEWAY
FORT WORTH, TEXAS 76134
800.757.9195
alconlabs.com

Summary: Alcon is the world's leading eye care company. Alcon has been dedicated to the ophthalmic industry for more than 50 years. Alcon develops pharmaceuticals; surgical equipment, devices, contact lens care solutions and other vision care products that treat disorders, diseases, and conditions of the eye. Pharmaceuticals generate approximately 50% of revenue. Nestle S.A is the majority owner with 52% stock.

History: Alcon began in 1945 when two pharmacists joined to open a small pharmacy in Fort Worth Texas, Robert Alexander and William C. Conner. Taking parts of their two last names to form the company name Al-Con. Alcon entered a research alliance with ChiroScience Group PLC. Loceryl was acquired in early 1999 from Hoffmann-La Roche. Travatan obtained FDA approval in 2001. Travatan Z was approved in late 2006. In 2008, Patanase nasal spray is approved and Novartis purchased nearly 25% of Alcon stock from Nestle S.A.

Approximate Annual Healthcare Revenue: $2.3 billion

CEO: Cary Rayment

Approximate Salesforce: 300

Major Brands: *Azopt Timolol* GFS glaucoma, *DuoTrav, Travatan, Travantan Z* intraocular pressure, *Ciprodex* ear antibiotic, *Patanol, Pataday* allergic conjunctivitis, *Patanaze* nasal spray *Nevanac* cataract surgery agent, *TobraDex* sterile ophthalmic suspension, *Vigamox* eye anti-invectives.

Pipeline: *Retanne* AMD risk reduction, *Moxifloxacin* new formulation and various agents in different phases of development.

ALLERGAN INCORPORATED
P.O. BOX 19534
IRVINE, CALIFORNIA 92623
714.246.4500
allergan .com

Summary. Allergan, Inc. headquartered in Irvine, California, is a technology-driven, global health care concern provides specialty pharmaceutical products. Allergan areas are eye care, neurosciences, obesity intervention, medical aesthetics, dermatology and urologics.

History: Founded in 1950, Allergan became a public company and in 1970, merged with SmithKline Beckman in 1980, and re-established as an independent company again in 1989. Products include eye and skin pharmaceuticals, ophthalmic surgical equipment, contact lens cleaners, and intraocular lenses. The company's skin care products include acne and psoriasis treatments. 1989 brought the approval of Botox. 1996 brought the approval of Alphagan. In 1998, Allergan added 225 scientists to its global research and development team to bring to market its specialty products. Alocril was launched in 2000. New indications for Botox and approval for Lumigan were gained in 2001. In 2002 Botox Cosmetic gained approved. In 2003, Restasis, Zymar and Acular LS obtained FDA approval and Allergan entered co-marketing agreements for Finacea and Elestat. In 2004, Tazorac began promotion and 2005 brought the launch of Prevage-TM. Approval for Combigan was gained in 2007 and the acquisition of Endart SA, a Swiss researcher. Sanctura XR, Trivaris was launched in 2008.

Annual Healthcare Revenue: $1.75 billion

CEO: David E. I. Pyott

Approximate Salesforce: 1300

Major Brands: *Acular LS* ocular pain, *Avage* psoriasis, *Alocril* allergic eye symptoms, *Alphagan*, *Alphagan P*, *Lumigan, Combigan* intraocular pressure, *Botox*, *Botox Cosmetic* >$1billion, neuromuscular disorders, skin wrinkles, cervical dystonia and underarm sweating, *Sanctura XR* overactive bladder, *Tazorac* for acne psoriasis, *Trivaris* ocular inflammation, *Tazorac Gel/Cream* acne/plaque psoriasis, *Restasis* chronic eye disease's, *Zymar* anti-infective..

Pipeline: *Acular X* inflammation, *bimatopost* eyelash growth, *Botox* migraines, bladder control, *Brimonidine X* glaucoma, ocular hypertension, *Zymar X* anti-infective agent, *Lumigan X* additional formulation, *Trivaris* diabetic retinopathy and numerous other agents in various phases of development

AMGEN INCORPORATED
ONE AMGEN CENTER DRIVE
THOUSAND OAKS, CALIFORNIA 91320
805.447.4587
amgen.com

Summary: Currently Amgen is the world's largest biotechnology concern. Amgen develops and markets therapeutic products in four medical areas: hematopoiesis (blood cell production), inflammation and auto-immunity, neurobiology, and soft tissue repair and regeneration. Over 25% of the company's revenues are devoted towards research and development. Epogen and Neupogen, currently account for most of the company's revenue. Amgen has nearly a dozen new products under development. In addition to its own product portfolio, Amgen licenses products and technologies from and to other companies.

History: A group of devoted scientists to develop health care products based on molecular biological technology formed Amgen (as Applied Molecular Genetics) in 1980. In 1983, Amgen cloned the human protein erythropoietin (EPO), which stimulates red blood production in the body. Amgen established a marketing arrangement with Johnson & Johnson in 1985. In 1989, the FDA granted Amgen a license to produce Epogen (brand name of EPO) and Neupogen (brand name of G-CSF). In 2000, Amgen received approval for Neupogen SingleJect. In 2001, Aranesp gained approval. In 2002, Amgen completed the acquisition of Immunex for $16 billion, and leading product Enbrel and Neulasta was launched. 2003 brought approval of Enbrel in a once weekly dose. 2004 brought the approval of Kepivance. 2006 brought Vectibix and acquisition of Avidia a private biotech concern. In 2007 Amgen acquired Alantos Pharmaceuticals, a biotechnology company. 2008 brought the approval of addition indications for Nplate.

Approximate Annual Healthcare Revenue: $8 billion

CEO: Kevin W. Sharer

Approximate Salesforce: 400

Major Brands: *Aranesp*>$3 billion, *Epogen* >$3 billion, anemia treatments, *Enbrel* >$3 billion, rheumatoid arthritis, arthritis, psoriasis, anklylosing spondylitis, *Kinerat* rheumatoid arthritis, *Neupogen*, *Neulasta* >$3 billion, recombinant human granulocyte colony-stimulating factor, adjunct to chemotherapy, *Nplate* platelet count raising, sustention, ITP, *Sensipar* hyperparathyroidism, *Vectibix* colorectal cancer.

Pipeline: *Cinacalcet* metabolic disorders, *Sensipar* secondary hyperparathyroidism, *Motesanib* thyroid cancer, *Denosumab*, *Rhomiplostim, Panitumumab* anti-cancer agents and numerous other agents in various phases of development.

ASTELLAS PHARMA INCORPORATED
THREE PARKWAY NORTH
DEERFIELD, ILLINOIS
800.695.4321
astellas.com

Summary: Fujisawa and Yamanouchi announced their completed merger in the second quarter of 2005 with the new company name of Astellas Pharma Incorporated. This will create the second largest pharmaceutical company in Japan and the fifteenth largest pharmaceutical company in the world. Astellas world wide headquarters is located in Tokyo.

History: Founded in Osaka, Japan in 1894, Fujisawa Company has offices, plants, and research facilities spanning Japan, North America, Europe and Asia, employing over 7500 individuals. Consumer Products include OTC drugs including cough and cold, gastrointestinal, analgesic and anti-inflammatory agents. Currently the Ethical Pharmaceuticals division accounts for nearly 90% of total revenue. Yamanouchi founded in 1923. Yamanouchi launched Flummox in 1997. In 2005 Yamanouchi Pharmaceutical Company and Fujisawa Pharmaceutical Company officially combined their operations under the name of Astellas Pharma US. Maycamine was launched also in 2005. Prograf, 2006 Astellas purchased Amevive from Biogen Idec, 2007 brought Vaprisol, 2008 brought approvals of Kyapid,

Approximate Annual Healthcare Revenue: $3.5 billion

CEO: Toichi Takenaka, Ph.D.

Approximate Salesforce: 800

Major Brands: *AmBisome, Maycamine* fungal infections, *Amevive* psoriasis, *Adeocard* tachycardia, *Adenoscan, Lexiscan* cardiac imaging agents, *Cefzon* antibiotic, *Flomax* benign prostatic hyperplasia, *Prograf* >$2 billion, organ rejection prophylaxis, *Protopic Ointment* atopic dermatitis, *Rescula* glaucoma, *VESIcare* for incontinence, *Vaprisol* for hyponatremia.

Pipeline: *Atrisone* acne, *Kyapid* for atrial fibrillation, *Micafungin* fungal infections, *Prograf* additional indications, *Protopic* atopic dermatitis, *Vesicare* incontinence, *conivaptan* hyponatremia and numerous other agents in various phases of development.

ASTRA ZENECA
1800 CONCORD PIKE
P.O. Box 15437
WILMINGTON, DELEWARE 19850
302.886.3000
astrazeneca.com

Summary: AstraZeneca was formed through the merger of Astra AB of Sweden and Zeneca Group PLC. Of the United Kingdom in 1999. AstraZeneca has leading therapies in six areas health, including gastrointestinal, anesthesia, oncology, respiratory, neuroscience and cardiovascular medicines. In 2007 AstraZeneca purchased biotech MedImmune and established it as a biotech business unit.

History: Astra began in 1913 when a group of physicians and pharmacist formed the company and became its inaugural stockholders. Among this initial group of individuals was Hans Von Euler, who won the 1929 Nobel Prize in chemistry. During the 1930's research and development became the primary focus of the corporation. In 1949, the company began marketing Xylocaine (lidocaine). Xylocaine sales soared in the fifties and Astra broadened production and licensing globally. Astra continued expansion through the seventies. Astra paid $820 million in 1994 for a 50% interest in a joint venture with Merck to market Astra products in the United States. Prilosec became the world's largest selling drug in the 1990's. In 1998, Astra Merck was combined with Astra's wholly owned subsidiary Astra USA, Inc. to form Astra Pharmaceuticals L.P. Zeneca was formed by Imperial Chemical Industries which was founded in 1926. As of recent years, in 2006, AstraZeneca launched Abraxane. 2007 brought the approval of Seroquel XR and the acquisition of biotech concern, MedImmune with such products as Synagis, FluMist and Ethyol. In addition, AstraZeneca acquired Arrow Therapeutics a private U.K. biotech firm. August brought the co promotion of Crestor with Abbott in preparation for new combination agent for lipids.

Approximate Annual Healthcare Revenue: $28 billion

CEO: David R. Brennan

Approximate Salesforce: 5,700

Major Brands: *Atacand, Plendil, Toprol-XL* >$1billion hypertension, *Crestor* >$1billion cholesterol, atherosclerosis, *FluMist* influenza, *Nexium* >$5 billion, *Prilosec* >$1 billion anti-ulcer agents, *Pulmicort* >$1 billion, *Symbicort* >$1billion asthma, *Rhinocort* allergic rhinitis, *Seroquel XR* >$2 billion antipsychotic, anti-schizophrenic, *Accolate* asthma, *Abraxane*, *Arimidex* >$1 billion, *Casodex* >$1billion, *Ethyol*, *Faslodex, Iressa, Zoladex* >$1 billion oncology agents, *Merrem* infections, *Synagis* >$1 billion, respiratory syncytial virus (rsv), *Zoladex* >$1billion prostate cancer, *Zomig* migraines.

Pipeline: *Atacand* chronic heart failure, *Cerovive* stroke, *Exanta* anticoagulant, *motavizumab RSV, Onglyza* type 2 diabetes, *Recentin* anti-cancer agent, *Symbicort Toprol-XL* additional indications, *Zactima* lung cancer and numerous other agents in various phases of development.

BAYER HEALTHCARE PHARMACEUTICALS
6 WEST BELT
WAYNE, NEW JERSEY 07470
973-305-5000
bayerus.com

Summary: Bayer Corporation operates various segments producing varied products in areas of Material Science, CropScience and their largest segment, HealthCare. The Bayer HealthCare Pharmaceutical contributes approximately 50% of all revenue. The U.S. division is the second largest contributor to the segment with the first being Europe.

History: Friedrich Bayer established the organization in 1863. Breakthrough compounds such as Bayer Aspirin (1897) and synthetic rubber in (1915) were introduced. During World War I, the United States seized Bayer's American operations and trademark rights, offering them to Sterling Drug. After W.W.II Bayer promptly began rebuilding entering a joint venture with Monsanto Chemical Company, forming Mobay in 1954. In 1967, Bayer purchased Monsanto's share in the organization. Various acquisitions over the next 30 years including Miles Laboratories (Alka-Seltzer, One-A-Day Vitamins). Bayer regained American rights to the Bayer brand (known for its Aspirin trademark) and the Bayer logo in 1994 when it purchased the North American business Sterling Winthrop from SmithKline Beecham. The company returned to its original name, Bayer Corporation. Sales of antibiotic Cipro had reached over the $1 billion mark by 2000. Yaz gained approval in 2006. 2007 brings Nexavar. The organization is newly named Bayer HealthCare Pharmaceuticals in the United States with the purchase of Berlex (Schering AG) in 2006. Late 2008 Bayer announced plans to acquire Direvo Biotech for approximately $300 million, increasing Bayer's breadth in biologic agents.

Annual Healthcare Revenue: $10 billion

CEO: Werner Wenning

Approximate Salesforce: 3000

Major Brands: *Betapace* atrial arrhythmias, *Betaseron* for multiple sclerosis, *Campath* and *Fludara* leukemia, *Elmiron* painful bladder syndrome, *Leukine* fungal infections, , *Nexavar* liver cancer, *Refludan* heparin induced thrombocytopenia, *Gamimune N* immunodeficiency, *Levitra* erectile dysfunction, *Kogenate* hemophilia A, *Viadur* prostate cancer, *Angelia* hormone therapy, *Climara, Climara Pro* transdermal estrogen replacement, *Yaz*, *Yasmin* and *Viadur* pregnancy prevention.

Pipeline: *Rivaroxaban, Trasylol* anti-blood clotting agents, *Betaseron, Nexavar* additional anti-cancer indications, *Yaz* for additional indications, *Xarelto* stroke and cardiovascular events and numerous other agents in various phases of development.

BIOGEN IDEC
14 CAMBRIDGE CENTER
CAMBRIDGE, MASSACHUCETS 02142
617.679.2000
Biogenidec.com

Summary: Biogen Idec's products focus on the therapeutic areas of oncology, immunology, neurology, dermatology and rheumatology. The company focus is on developing treatments for cancer, autoimmune and inflammatory diseases.

History: In November 2003, Biogen Idec Inc. was formed from the merger of two of the world's leading biotechnology companies, Biogen, Inc. and IDEC Pharmaceuticals Corporation. This combination has resulted in a combination of biotech strengths in various therapeutic areas, research and development capabilities, and manufacturing capabilities. Biogen Idec intends to continue its growth through discovery, development and commercialization of its own innovative products and through strategic alliances. 1996 brought Avonex. 2002, Zevalin was launched. Tysabri was approved and launched with partner Elan in 2004. 2006 Conforma Therapeutics was acquired with an oncology focus. In 2007 Biogen acquires Syntonix Pharmaceuticals. 2008, Tysabri gains approval for Crohn's disease.

Approximate Annual Sales: $2.5 billion

CEO: James C. Mullen

Approximate Salesforce: 400

Major Brands: *Avonex, Tysabri* >$1 billion, multiple sclerosis, *Rituxan* >$1 billion non-Hodgkin's lymphomas and severe rheumatoid arthritis.

Pipeline: *Amevive* additional indications, *daclizumab* multiple sclerosis, *lixivaptan* acute and chronic heart failure, *Tysabri* multiple myeloma, multiple sclerosis monotherapy, *Rituxan* leukemia, lupus, and numerous other agents in various phases of development.

BOEHRINGER INGELHEIM CORPORATION
900 OLD RIDGEBURY ROAD
RIDGEFIELD, CT 06877
203.798.9988
us.boehringer-ingelheim.com

Summary: This Ingelheim, Germany concern obtains about 96% of its net sales from prescription pharmaceuticals. The business units include prescription pharmaceuticals, biopharmaceuticals, consumer health products, and animal health and pharma chemicals.

History: Boehringer Ingelheim was founded in Ingelheim Rhein in 1885 where world headquarters is still located today. The chemical business segment is the oldest of the companies units. In the fifties Boehringer Ingelheim began work in the animal health area. Products in this area focus on antibiotics and vaccines. Boehringer established itself in the United States in 1971, expanded and purchased Roxane Laboratories in 1978 and Ben Venue Laboratories to enter the hospital segment. In 1997, the company launched Mobic, Flomax, Viramune and Combivent. In 2001, Boehringer signed an agreement to co-market Spiriva with Pfizer. 2001 brought Micardis HCT. Atrovent and Spiriva were approved in 2004 along with the indication of rheumatoid arthritis for Mobic. Flomax was launched in late 2005. 2006 brought approval for Miarpex for RLS. In 2007 Boehringer announced excellent growth for Spiriva, Micardis and Flomax and the approval of Aptivus capsules.

Annual Healthcare Revenue: $8.3 billion

CEO: Rolf Krebs

Approximate Salesforce: 1250

Major Brands: *Aptivus, Viramune* HIV infections, *Actilyse* myocardial infarction, stroke, *Atrovent*, *Combivent*, *Spiriva* bronchospasm, *Aggrenox* stroke, *Micardis* >$1 billion hypertension, *Mirapex* Parkinson's disease, restless leg syndrome (RLS), *Flomax* >$1 billion benign prostatic hypertrophy, *Mobic* arthritis, *TNKase* acute myocardial infarction, *Spiriva* >$2 billion for COPD.

Pipeline: *Actilyse* immediate stroke treatment, *dabigatran etexilate* anticoagulant, *Epinastine* ocular allergies, *Pritor HCT* hypertension and numerous other agents in various phases of development.

BRISTOL-MYERS SQUIBB COMPANY

345 PARK AVENUE
NEW YORK, NY. 10154
212.546.4000
bms.com

Summary: This New York City pharmaceutical concern established in 1989 has products in therapeutic categories that include cardiovascular, anti-infective, anticancer, anti-AIDS, nutrition and wound care products. Bristol-Myers Squibb is the number one producer of oncology medications in the global pharmaceutical industry. Mead Johnson Nutrition Company is a wholly owned subsidiary.

History: William Bristol and John Myers founded Clinton Pharmaceutical in New York, in 1887, renamed Bristol-Myers in 1900, to sell pharmaceuticals. By the 1920's Bristol-Meyers profits topped $1 million and the company was first publicly traded in 1929. Mead Johnson was purchased in the sixties and Zimmer in the early seventies. The companies acquired several biotech concerns in eighties, Oncogen and Genetic Systems. In 1989, Bristol-Myers purchased Squibb for $12.7 billion. Fellow New Yorker Dr. Edward Squibb founded Squibb in 1850's. In the 1940's Squibb had the largest production plant of penicillin in the world. By the middle 1970's sales reached over $1 billion. 1989 brought the merger of Bristol-Myers and Squibb. BMS purchased DuPont Pharmaceutical for $7.8 billion in 2001. Abilify gained approval in 2005. Orencia gained approval in 2006, 2007 brought Ixempra. 2008 brought acquisition of Kosan Biosciences Inc for $190 million and offers of $4.5 billion and efforts for the acquiring of biotech concern ImClone.

Approximate Annual Healthcare Revenue: $19.4 billion

CEO: Peter R. Dolan

Approximate Salesforce: 4000

Major Brands: *Abilify* >$1 billion, antipsychotic, *Avapro*, *Avalide* hypertension >$1 billion, *Baraclude* hepatitis B, *Coumadin* venous thrombosis, *Emsam* antidepressant, *Ixempra*, *Erbitux* anti-cancer agents, *Plavix* >$4.8 billion cardiovascular agent, *Orencia* severe arthritis, JRA, *Atripla, Reyataz, Sustiva* >$1 billion HIV agents, *Enfamil, Lipil* infant formula's.

Pipeline: *Apixaban* throbosis, *Ipilimumab*, *Brivanib*, *Tanespimycin* anti-cancer agents, *Betlatacept* organ transplant, *Onglyza*, *Dapaglifllozin* diabetes, and numerous other agents in various phases of development.

CUBIST PHARMACEUTICALS INCORPORATED
65 HAYDEN AVENUE
LEXINGTON, MASSACHUSETTS 02421
781.860.8660
cubist.com

Summary: One of the newest companies at 1992, Cubist focus on becoming a leader in anti-infectives for use in hospitals and acute care environments. A research based biopharmaceutical organization.

History: After an initial public offering, Cubist licensed in daptomycin in the late 1990's from Eli Lilly. As a small pharmaceutical company, Cubist is rare in that they conduct their own Research and Development. The agent from Eli Lilly was transformed to with great scientific efforts to a first in class antibiotic, which has to date experienced the most successful antibiotic launch in U.S. history, on a dollar sales basis with Cubacin. Cubist believes that Cubacin may have a potential of reaching $1 billion in sales.

Approximate Annual Healthcare Revenue: $400 million

CEO: Michael W. Bonney

Approximate Salesforce: 200

Major Products: *Cubacin* 1st in class I.V. lipopetide antibiotic, *Merrem I.V.*serious infections.

Pipeline: *Cubacin* endocarditis for numerous other indications, *Ecallantide* for blood loss during surgery and several other agents in various phases of development.

DAICHI SANYKO
TWO HILTON COURT
PARSIPPANY, NJ 07054
973.359.2600
sankyopharma.com

Summary: Sankyo is Japan's second-largest pharmaceutical company (behind Takeda). Clinical, regulatory and commercial operations are based in New York, New Jersey and California. Sankyo acquired Daiichi in 2005, forming Daiichi Sankyo. The company's research and development efforts are concentrated on allergies, antibiotics, arthritis, cancer, cardiovascular disease, diabetes, neurological agents, and obesity.

History: Sankyo was established in 1899 in Japan, Daiichi Pharmaceutical Corporation was founded in 1915 as Japan's first research based pharmaceutical company. Discoveries include epinephrine and vitamin B12. The statin class was also discovered in 1971, including lovastatin and pravastatin. 2003 brought launch of blockbuster, Benicar HCT. In 2008 Daiichi Sanko offered to purchase a majority holding in Ranbaxy Laboratories, one of the largest generic manufacture's for $8.5 billion which is at this time scheduled to close in the first quarter of 2009.

Approximate Annual Healthcare Revenue: $7.5 billion

CEO: Tetsuo Takato

Approximate Salesforce: 1200

Major Brands: *Floxin* anti-infective, *Camptosar* oncology agent, *Evoxac* dry mouth with Sjögren's syndrome, cancer, *Benicar* >$2 billion, hypertension, *Gluco Watch, G2 Biographer* glucose monitoring device, *Welchol* high cholesterol.

Pipeline: *Azor* hypertension, *Prasugrel* anti-plalet agent, *Rivoglitazone* diabetes and numerous other agents in various phases of development.

EISAI INCORPORATED
GLENPOINTE CENTRE WEST
500 FRANK W. BURR BLVD.
TEANECK, NJ 07666
201.692.7710
eisai.co.jp

Summary: Eisai business segments include agrochemical products, bulk pharmaceuticals, diagnostics, vitamins, prescription pharmaceuticals, veterinary products, food additives.

History: Incorporated in 1941, Eisai was first to synthesize and commercially produce vitamin E, along with the production of various other bulk chemicals. In 1995, the prescription pharmaceutical company was established in the Unites States with headquarters in New Jersey. 1997 developed and brought approval of Aricept. Eisai and Neurogenetics Inc. announced in 2002 the extension of an agreement involving Alzheimer disease targets using human genetics. In 2003, Eisai announced the doubling of its United States salesforce. In 2004, Eisai acquired Zonegran from Elan. 2007 brought the agreement to commercialize NeuroBloc and increased indications for Aricept. 2008 brought the introduction of Hotmin and Aloxi.

Approximate Annual Healthcare Revenue: $5.5 billion

CEO: Haruo Naito

Approximate Salesforce: 450

Major Brands: *Aciphex* >$1 billion, ulcers, *Aloxi* nausea and vomiting during chemotherapy, *Aricept*, *Aricept ODT* Alzheimer's, severe Alzheimer's >$3 billion, *Hotmin* peripheral blood circulation, *NeuroBloc* cervical dystonia, *Zonegran* epilepsy.

Pipeline: *Aciphex* helicobacter pylori infection, *Aricept D* rapid disintegration tablet, Rufinamide antiepileptic, *Cleactor* pulmonary embolism, *NeuroBloc*, botulism toxin B neuromuscular disorders, skin wrinkles and underarm sweating and numerous other agents in various phases of development.

ÉLAN PHARMACEUTICALS
7475 LUSK BOULEVARD
SAN DIEGO, CA 92121
800.859.8587
elan.com

Summary: Élan of Ireland has transformed from a pharmaceutical delivery company in the early years into a current fully integrated biopharmaceutical researcher, developer and marketer.

History: Incorporated in 1969, Élan's first product was Tetrabid, marketed by Organon. In 1989, Élan produced Cardizem SR for Marion Laboratories. 1996 Élan acquired Athena Neurosciences of San Francisco. Carnrick Laboratories, Neurex Corporation, Ligand and Dura Pharmaceuticals were also acquired in subsequent years. In 2003, Elan announced the sale of its primary care business unit to King Pharmaceuticals for $750 million during a restructuring period which included the sales of Sonata, Skelaxin and Élan's primary care salesforce. In 2004 Elan received approval for Tysabri and Prialt. Mid 2007 brought the approval of Tysabri for Crohn's disease.

Annual Healthcare Revenue: $712 million

CEO: G. Kelly Martin

Approximate Salesforce: 500

Major Brands: *Tysabri* multiple sclerosis, Crohn's disease, *Prialt* chronic pain, *Azactam*, *Maxipime* anti-infectives.

Pipeline: *Tysabri* psoriasis, oncology, *bapineuzumab* Alzheimer's disease, Alzheimer's vaccine and numerous other agents in various phases of development.

ENDO PHARMACEUTICALS
100 ENDO DRIVE
CHADDS FORD PENNSYLAVANIA 19317
610.558.9800
endo.com

Summary: Endo Pharmaceuticals is a specialty pharmaceutical company who specializes in the research, development and sales of pharmaceuticals primarily currently used pain management and diversifying into other therapeutic segments.

History: In the 1920's Endo, a family-run business was established in Manhattan, New York. In the fifties Percodan is developed. In 1969, DuPont acquired Endo Pharmaceuticals. The seventies brought Percocet, DuPont and Merck formed and independent joint venture, known as the Dupont Merck Pharmaceuticals Company in 1990. In 1994, DuPont Merck re-establishes Endo as a separate entity within the organization, named Endo Laboratories and serves as DuPont Merck's generic products division. Endo Pharmaceuticals Inc., once again in 1997, was established as a separate pharmaceutical company in 1997. Lidoderm Patch was launched in 1999. 2004 bought Frova and 2005 brought Opana IR and Opana ER. 2008 brought Volatren Gel, the first topical NSAID.

Approximate Healthcare Revenue: $1 billion

CEO: David Holveck

Approximate Salesforce: 750

Major Brands: *Frova* migraine, *Lidoderm Patch* neuropathic pain, *0pana ER*, moderate to severe pain, *Votaren Gel* osteoarthritis and various generic agents.

Pipeline: *EpiCept, Ketoprofen Patch* analgesics, *Frova* addition indications, *Orexo* cancer pain and numerous other agents in various phases of development.

FOREST LABORATORIES INCORPORATED
909 THIRD AVENUE
NEW YORK, NEW YORK 10022
212.421.7850
frx.com

Summary: Based in New York City with operations throughout the United States and Europe, Forest develops and manufactures and markets prescription agents. Forest Laboratories has subsidiaries in the United Kingdom and Ireland.

History: Incorporated in 1956 Forest products are marketed principally in the United States and western and Eastern Europe. In the mid-eighties, Aerobid was approved. 1996 Forest introduced Tiazac for hypertension. In 1998, Forest Laboratories launched Celexa, a novel antidepressant. In 2002, the FDA approved Lexapro. Namenda was approved in 2003. Campral was approved in 2004. Nameda receives approval as the first agent for moderate to severe Alzheimer's in 2005. In 2006 Forest announced the acquisition of Cerexa, a biotech concern. Combunex was approved in 2005 and in 2007 Azor was launched. 2008 brought the launch of Bystolic for hypertension.

Approximate Annual Healthcare Revenue: $2.6 billion

CEO: Howard Solomon

Approximate Salesforce: 2600

Major Brands: *Aerobid* asthma, *Azor, Bystolic* hypertension, *Tiazac* hypertension, *Campral* alcohol addiction, *Celexa, Lexapro* >$2 billion depression and anxiety *Combunox* pain *Levothroid* thyroid disease, *Namenda* Alzheimer's disease, *Infasurf* infant respiratory distress.

Pipeline: *Lexapro* additional indications, *Licofelone* osteoarthritis, *Lercanidipine* hypertension, *Milnaciparan* fibromylagia syndrome, *Namenda* once a day, and numerous other agents in various phases of development.

GALDERMA LABORATORIES INC.
14501 NORTH FREEWAY
FORT WORTH, TEXAS 76177
817.961.5000
galderma.com

Summary: Galderma is a joint venture formed by Nestle and L'Oreal group. Galderma is a company with a single focus, dermatology. Galderma has more than 300 scientist committed to research and development. Galderma's parent company is in Switzerland, with Corporate Services in Paris, France. Galderma employs 2300 people in 33 fully owned subsidiaries worldwide. Sales divisions consist of Galderma, Cutiscience and Theracutix.

History: Galderma started as Owen Laboratories in 1961, since the creation of Galderma it has become a multi-national company with a worldwide presence in the dermatology in over 70 countries. Research and Development facilities are located in France, Japan, and New Jersey. One of Galderma's major discoveries was Differin in 1996. Metrogel is the worlds leading prescribed rosacea therapy. In 2004 Galderma announced a new R&D facility to open in 2007 in France which will be the world's largest facility focused on dermatology with over 300 scientists. 2005 brought Metrogel. 2007 also brought FDA approval of Differin Gel. Pliaglis was approved in 2007. CollaGenex a global dermatology concerned was acquired in 2008.

Approximate Annual Healthcare Revenue: Division of Nestle

CEO: Nestle, Peter Brabeck-Letmathe

Approximate Salesforce: 600

Major Brands: *Capex* dermatitis, *Clobex* plaque psoriasis, *Cetaphil* skin cleansers, *Differin*, *Clindagel, Benzac AC, BenzaClin, benoyl peroxide* acne agents, *Loceryl* nail fungus, *Metrogel, Rosanil* rosacea therapy, Mistamine urticaria. *Oracea* for rosacea, *Alcortin* topical steroid, *Pliaglis* a topical anesthetic, *Tri-Luma* pigment disorder, *Melasma, Silkis* psoriasis.

Pipeline: *Matrix PDT* actinic kurtosis, basal cell carcinoma, and other agents in various phases of development.

GENENTECH
1 DNA WAY
SOUTH SAN FRANCISCO, CALIFORNIA 94080
650.225.1000
gene.com

Summary: Genentech, Inc. is the second largest biotechnology concern in the world, using human genetic information to manufacture and market pharmaceuticals. Genentech focuses a variety of medical conditions, mainly immunology, oncology and tissue growth and repair. Genetic is currently a biotech concern with a 30 year history in the market.

History: Genentech Inc. was founded in 1976 by venture capitalist Robert A. Swanson and biochemist Herbert W. Boyer. In the early 1970's Boyer and geneticist, Stanley Cohen forged a new scientific field labeled recombinant DNA technology. In 1978 Genentech cloned human insulin, which was licensed to Eli Lilly and Company and marketed in 1982. In 1979, human growth hormone was cloned and protropin human growth hormone for children was granted approval to market. 1987 brought FDA approval to market Activase. In 1990, Genentech and Roche Holding Ltd. of Switzerland completed a $2.1 billion merger where Roche currently owns 55.6% of Genentech's stock. In addition, that year the company received approval to market Actimmune. 1993 Nutropin was introduced and Nutropin AQ was released in 1996. Rituxan was approved in 1997. Herceptin gained approval in 1998. 2001 Cathlo Activase was launched. 2002 approval for Nutropin AQ Pen. 2003 brought approval of Xolair, Raptiva. 2004 brought approval for Avastin. Lucentis was launched in 2006. Partially owned by Roche, speculation of a full buy-out of Genentech surfaced during late 2008.

Approximate Annual Healthcare Revenue: $3.3 billion

CEO: Arthur D. Levinson PhD.

Approximate Salesforce: 700

Major Brands: *Avastin, Herceptin, Tarceva* >$5 billion anti-cancer, non-Hodgkin's lymphoma agents, *Nutropin* human growth hormone, *Activase, TNKase* myocardial infarction, strokes, *Catho Activase* restoration of central venous devices for blood withdraws, *Raptiva* psoriasis, rheumatoid arthritis, *Lucentis* neovascular wet age-related macular degeneration, *Xolair* asthma.

Pipeline: *Avastin* renal and numerous other anti-cancer indications, *Herceptin, Pertuzumab* breast cancer, *Lucentis* diabetic macular edema, retinal vein occlusion, *Rituxan* rheumatoid arthritis, vasculitis, lupus nephritis, *Tarceva* various lung cancer indications, *TNKase* hemodialysis catheter occlusion removal, numerous combinations of above therapies and numerous other agents in various phases of development.

GENZYME CORPORATION
500 KENDALL STREET
CAMBRIDGE, MASSACHUSETTS 02142
617.252.7500
genzyme.com

Summary: Genzyme specializes in lysomal storage disorders, renal, orthopedic, burn treatment, immune mediated diseases, adhesion prevention, cardiovascular, cancer and diagnostic product services. Genzyme has presence in over 40 countries, product availability in 90 countries, including 17 manufacturing facilities, 9 genetic testing laboratories.

History: In 1981, Genzyme founded by Henry Blair and Sherry Snyder. In 1985, Ceredase is designated an orphan drug by FDA. In 1986, Genzyme became a public company with an initial public offering. 1991 Cerezyme was approved. 1996 approval to market Seprafilm is obtained. 1997 brings a biologics license application approval for Carticel to repair cartilage in the knee, the first approval for a cell therapy product. The late nineties bring approvals for Renagel, Thyrogen, Synvisc and Thymoglobulin. In 2000, Sepramesh is launched. Fabrazyme, Aldurazyme received approval in 2003. Clolar was approved in 2004. 2007 brought approvals for Epicel for burn victims. Renvela was launched in early 2008.

Approximate Annual Healthcare Revenue: $4 billion

CEO: Henri A.Termeer

Approximate Salesforce: 400

Major Brands: *Fabrazyme* fabry's disease, *Aldurazyme* MPSI, *Carticel* knee cartilage agent, *Campath* for leukemia, *Cerezyme* >$1 billion Gauchers disease, *Clolar* leukemia, *Epicel* for severe burns, *Renagel* renal disease, *Renvela* kidney dialysis complications, *Seprafilm* adhesions barrier, *Sepramesh* biosurgical composite, *Synvisc* knee osteoarthritis, *Thyrogen* thyroid disease, cancer.

Pipeline: *Clolar* leukemia, *Mipomersen* hypercholesterolemia, Mozobil stem cell therapy and Pompe disease, *Synvisc* expanded indications, *Thyrogen* additional indications, *Thymoglobulin* organ transplant agent and numerous other agents in various phases of development.

GILEAD SCIENCES INCORPORATED
333 LAKESIDE DRIVE
FOSTER CITY, CA 94404
650.574.3000
gilead.com

Summary: Gilead Sciences is a biopharmaceutical company that discovers, develops and commercializes innovative therapeutics in areas of unmet medical need. The company's mission is to advance the care of patients suffering from life-threatening diseases worldwide with focus on antivirals, HIV, hepatitis, cardiovascular conditions (pulmonary arterial hypertension) and respiratory diseases (cystic fibrosis, influenza). Headquartered in Foster City, California, Gilead has operations in North America, Europe and Australia. Therapeutic areas include oncology, cardiovascular, HIV infections and infectious

History: Gilead was founded in 1987, with product discoveries either new class or best in class. Gilead's scientists combined three HIV drugs into one agent, which greatly improved patient's daily routines. In 2001, Vireo gain approval, next followed Helpers in 2002 and Emotive and Macugen in 2003 and 2004 respectively. The product, called Atripla, was introduced in 2006. In addition in 2006 Gilead purchased Colorado based Myogen for $2.5 billion with agent ambrisentan, Raylo Chemicals, a German based specialty chemicals concern to increase clinical development and Corus Pharma of Seattle. Letairis was introduced approved in mid-2007. 2008 brought the approval of Viread.

Approximate Annual Revenue: $5 billion

CEO: John C. Martin, Ph.D

Approximate Salesforce: 375

Products: *Emtiva*, *Truvada*, *Atripia* HIV-1 infections, >$3 billion, *Hepsera, Viread* chronic hepatitis B, *Letairis* pulmonary hypertension, *Flonan* pulmonary hypertension. Following Gilead agents are marketed by designated organizations, Tamiflu (Roche), AmBisome (Astellas), Macugen (Eyetech),

Pipeline: *Aztreonam Lysine* for cystic fibrosis, numerous other agents in various phases of development.

GLAXOSMITHKLINE
FIVE MOORE DRIVE
RESEARCH TRIANGLE PARK, NC 27709
919.483.2100
gsk.com

Summary: As the largest based European pharmaceutical concern Glaxo SmithKline In 2000, Glaxo Wellcome and SmithKline Beecham completed a merger that would create one of the world's leading research-based pharmaceutical companies.

History: In 1873, Englishman Joseph Nathen started Glaxo in New Zealand. The company went public in 1947. In the late seventies, Glaxo first establish its first United States operations. Glaxo launched Zantac in 1981. SmithKline started in 1830 as a small Philadelphia pharmacy. Tagamet became the worlds leading product. In 1995 Glaxo, purchased U.K. based Burroughs Wellcome for $14.9 billion. Burroughs was founded by Silas Burroughs and Henry Wellcome (Americans). Vesicare with was launched in 2005. Attabax, Lexiva, and Veramyst gained approval in 2006. 2007 brought the purchase of privately held Reliant pharmaceuticals and approval of Altabax and Tykerb. In 2008, Rotarix Vaccine, Requip X and Treximet gained approval, in addition the purchase of Sirtris Pharmaceuticals.

Approximate Annual Healthcare Revenue: $38 billion

CEO: Jean-Pierre Garnier PhD.

Approximate Salesforce: 8300

Major Brands: *Arixtra* anti-thrombotic, *Advair, Flovent, Ventolin* >$8 billion asthma, *Avandia* >$1 billion, type 2 diabetes, *Amoxil, Augmentin* > $1billion, antibiotics, *Bexxar, Hycamtin Capsule*, *Tykerb* anti-cancer agents, *Boniva* osteoporosis, *Cervarin* cervical cancer vaccine, *Coreg* >$1 billion hypertension/heart failure, *Imitrex, Amerge, Treximet* >$1.3 billion, migraines, *Agenerase, Combivir, Epzicom, Epivir, Lexiva, Trizivir, Retrovir* and *Ziagen* HIV infections, *Levitra* erectile dysfunction, *Lamictal* >$2 billion seizure's, bipolar disorder, *Paxil* >$1 billion, depression, *Pediarix* >$1billion, vaccine, *Requip* Parkinson's disease, *Relenza* influenza, *Rotarix Vaccine,* prevention of rotavirus, *Twinrix* >$1 billion, hepatitis vaccine, *Zovirax, Valtrex* >$2 billion, herpes, *Avodart, Vesicare* over active bladder, *Veramyst* allergies and over 25 other vaccine's.

Pipeline: *Avandamet XR, Avandia* type 2 diabetes, *Avodart* reduction prostate cancer, *Bosatria* monoclonal antibody for hypereosinophilic syndrome, *Lamactil XR* epilepsy, once daily, *rosiglitazone XR* Alzheimer's disease, *Lunivia* insomnia, *Hepatyrix* hepatitis A, *Tyverb* head and neck cancer, *Promacta* blood disorders, *Rezonic* chemotherapy induced nausea and vomiting, *Prepandrix*i influenza vaccine, *Solzira* for restless leg syndrome and numerous other oncology combination agents and vaccine's in various phases of development.

JOHNSON & JOHNSON
ONE JOHNSON AND JOHNSON PLAZA
NEW BRUNSWICK, NEW JERSEY 08993
732.524.0400
jnj.com

Summary: United States based Johnson & Johnson is the largest manufacturer of health products in the world. J&J is organized into three business segments, Pharmaceuticals, Medical Devices and Diagnostics, and Consumer Healthcare. Pharmaceutical divisions consist of Janssen Pharmaceutica, Ortho-Biotech, and Ortho-McNeil Pharmaceutical. Recent acquisitions include Scios and Guidant Corporation (cardiovascular stents). In 2008, J&J merged their Centocor and Ortho-Biotech units.

History: Brothers James and Edward Mead Johnson founded this medical company in 1885 in New Brunswick, New Jersey. In 1886, another brother, Robert, joined to make and sell the antiseptic surgical dressings he developed. A product of Robert Johnson's dressing; the Band-Aid. In 1932, Robert Johnson Jr. became Chairman and served until 1963. The 1940's brought divisions of Ortho and Ethicon. In 1959, the company acquired McNeil Labs, who launched Tylenol in 1960. A foreign acquisition included Belgium's Janssen. In the 1990's Ortho-Biotech was formed. Company acquisitions included Centocor and Alza in 2000. 2007 brought FDA approval of Omrix and in 2008 the approval of Doribax and Intelence.

Approximate Annual Healthcare Revenue: $25 billion

CEO: William C. Weldon

Approximate Salesforce: 5500

Major Brands: *Aciphex* >$1 billion, ulcers, *Concerta* >$1 billion, ADD, *Ditropan XL* bladder control, *Doribax* urinary tract infections, *Doxil* oncology agent, *Duragesic, Floxin, Levaquin* >$1 billion antibiotics, *Natrecor* congestive heart failure, *Nizoral* antifungal, *Procrit* >$4 billion, reduction of blood transfusions, *Ortho Novum, Ortho Tri-Cyclin, Ortho Evra* >$1 billion contraceptives, *Omrix* blood clotting protein, *Retin-A* acne, *ReoPro* cardiac ischemia, *Reminyl* Alzheimer's, *Remicade* >$3 billion arthritis, Crohn's disease, *Renova* epidermal photo damage therapy, *Rispordal* >$4 billion, schizophrenia, *Sporanox* antifungal, *Intelence* HIV, *Topamax* >$2 billion, epilepsy, migraine's.

Pipeline: *Doxil* breast cancer, *Doribax nosocomial pneumonia,* Intergel post surgical adhesions, *Invega* bipolar mania, *Resperdal Consta* bipolar maintenance, *Topamax* pediatric indication, *and tapentadol* moderate to severe pain, *Prizista* anti-viral, *Yondelis* relapse of ovarian cancer and numerous other agents in various phases of development.

ELI LILLY AND COMPANY

LILLY CORPORATE CENTER
INDIANAPOLIS, IN 46285
317.277.2162
lilly.com

Summary: This Indianapolis based pharmaceutical concern produces antibiotics, insulin, growth hormones, anti-ulcer, and cancer agents, cardiovascular products, sedatives, vitamins, and feed additives. Eli Lilly acquired Icos Corporation in early 2007.

History: In 1876, Colonel Eli Lilly, a pharmacist at age thirty-eight started Eli Lilly and Company. Eli Lilly died in 1898, and his son, Josiah Lilly Sr., and two grandsons ran the organization until the mid fifties. Lilly introduced insulin in 1923, and blockbusters including, Merthiolate, Seconal. Lilly's Darvon, during the 1950's, was the leading prescription analgesic in the United States. In 1979, Lilly introduced Ceclor. The eighties brought the first biotechnology product Humulin and then the first in class blockbuster's Prozac and Axid. Lilly introduced ReoPro, in 1995. The late nineties brought approvals for Humalog, Gemzar and Zyprexa. 2001 brought the introduction of Evista, Prozac Weekly, Zyprexa, and Xigris. In 2002, Eli Lilly received approval for Forteo and Strattera. Cialis was launched in 2003. Symbyax was lunched in 2004. Alimta and Cymbalta received FDA approval in 2004. In 2008 Eli Lilly purchased $64 million of SGX Pharmaceuticals stock in an agreement, which specializes in the oncology segment.

Approximate Annual Healthcare Revenue: $12.5 billion

CEO: John C. Lechleiter, Ph.D.

Approximate Salesforce: 5,600

Major Brands: *Alimta, Gemzar >$1 billion* anti-cancer agents, *Actos, Byetta, Glucagon, Humulin, Humalog* >$2 billion diabetic agents, *Cialis* erectile dysfunction, *Cymbalta* antidepressant, diabetic neuropathic pain, fibromyalgia *Evista, Forteo* osteoporosis, *Humatrope* growth failure, *Prozac* >$1 billion, antidepressants/premenstrual treatment, *ReoPro* cardiovascular agent, *Strattera* attention deficit disorder, *Symbyax* bipolar depression, *Zyprexa* >$4.2 billion, schizophrenia, *Xigris* severe sepsis.

Pipeline: *Duloxeine* for chronic pain, *Exenatide* for type 2 diabetes, *Olanzapine LAI* for schizophrenia, *Olanzapine-Fluoxetine* treatment resistant depression, *Pemetrexed disodium* non-small-cell lung cancer, *Prasugrel* atherothrombotic events, *Ruboxistaurin mesylate* diabetic retinopathy, *Teriparatide* glucocorticoid induced osteoporosis, *Teplizumab* for type 1 diabetes, *Dirucotide* multiple sclerosis, *Arzoxifene* prevention of osteoporosis and reduction of breast cancer and numerous agents in various phases of development.

KING PHARMACEUTICALS
501 FIFTH STREET
BRISTOL, TENNESSEE 37620
800.776.3637
kingpharm.com

Summary: King Pharmaceuticals, Inc. is a Bristol, Tennessee; King's products are divided into four therapeutic areas: analgesics, endocrinology, anti-infectives, and critical care.

History: John M. Gregory, a pharmacist founded King by selling injectables and vaccines in 1984 near Bristol, Tennessee. In the fall of 1993 Gregory formed King Pharmaceuticals, the name paying homage to Gregory's faith. King expanded by using its plants for generic manufacturing for various pharmaceutical concerns including SmithKline, Ciba-Geigy and Boehringer. King then pioneered a strategy of acquiring smaller branded prescription drugs that were being divested by larger pharmaceutical companies. King went public in June 1998. King's most significant deal occurred in late 1998 with the addition of Altace, which had become available after Hoechst merged with Rhône-Poulenc (Aventis). Altace possessed even great potential, so King increased the number of sales reps promoting the drug to 600 representatives. King continued to purchase smaller pharmaceutical organizations including Jones Pharma. In 2003, King purchased the primary care division of Elan Pharmaceuticals including products Skelaxin and Sonata. In 2007, King acquired Avinza from Ligand Pharmaceuticals and late in 2008 King made a bid for Alpharma, a pain management company.

Approximate Annual Healthcare Sales: $1.9 billion

CEO: Brian Markison

Approximate Salesforce: 450

Major Brands: *Altace* for hypertension congestive heart failure, *Corgard* for hypertension, *Bicillin* antibiotic, *Skelaxin* for musculoskeletal conditions, *Thrombin-JMI* bleeding during surgery, *Avinzabchronic* pain, *Sonata* for insomnia, *Levoxyl* for thyroid disorders, *Tirosint* thyroid hormone, *EpiPen* for anaphylaxis shock and *Meridian* Auto injector products.

Pipeline: *Remoxy* narcotic analgesic, *Vanquix* anti-epileptic and numerous agents in various areas of development.

MERCK AND COMPANY INCORPORATED
1 MERCK DRIVE
WHITEHOUSE STATION
NEW JERSEY 08889-01 00
908.423.1000
merck.com

Summary: This New Jersey based manufacturer is ranked as one of the largest pharmaceutical concerns in the world and frequently recognized as a technology leader among physicians in the United States. Merck markets a broad range of human and animal health care products and services. Therapeutic areas include cardiovascular and gastrointestinal diseases, infections, ophthalmic disorders, prostate disease, and osteoporosis.

History: Theodore Weicker came to the United States from Germany in 1887 to set up an American branch of E. Merck of Germany. George Merck came in 1891 and established the firm, which imported and sold drugs and chemicals from Germany. In 1903, it opened a plant in Rahway, New Jersey. Merck research did pioneering work on vitamin B12 and developed cortisone (the first steroid). Five Nobel prizes were awarded to Merck scientists in the forties and fifties. In 1952, Merck merged with pharmaceutical producer Sharp & Dome of Philadelphia. Product approvals in 2001 include Cancidas, and Fosamax. 2002 brought Zetia. 2003 brought FDA approval for Emend. The FDA approved Vytorin in 2004. Gardasil vaccine obtained approval in 2006. 2007 brought Isentress and Janumet. 2008 brought Rota Teq.

Approximate Annual Healthcare Revenue: $24 billion

CEO: Raymond V. Gilmartin

Approximate Salesforce: 7,700

Major Brands: *Aggrastat* angina, *Cancidas* antifungal, *Cozaar, Hyzaar, Vasotec* >$3 billion, and *Prinivil* >$1 billion, hypertension agents, *Crixivan*, *Isentress*, *Stocrin* HIV/AIDS, *Gardasil* >$1 billion human papillomavirus infections, *Fosamax* >$3 billion, osteoporosis, *Emend* nausea vomiting, *Janumet* type 2 diabetes, *Maxalt* migraines, *Mevacor*, *Zocor* anti-cholesterol, *Rota Teq* vaccine rotavirus, *Pepcid*, *Prilosec* ulcers, *Proscar* prostate enlargement, *Singulair* >$4 billion, asthma, *Vytorin*, *Zetia* cholesterol, *Cosopt*, *Trusopt* intraocular pressure and numerous vaccines.

Pipeline: *Gaboxadol* insomnia, *Invanz* antibiotic, *Pro Quad* chickenpox, measles, mumps, rubella vaccine, *Singulair & Claritin* allergic rhinitis/asthma *Zostavaz* anti-shingle vaccine and numerous other agents in various phases of development.

NOVARTIS
556 MORRIS AVENUE
SUMMIT, NJ 07901
908.277.5293
novartis.com

Summary: This Basel, Switzerland-based Company holds top global positions in all its core businesses: The pharmaceutical division includes products for asthma, immunology, inflammatory diseases, central nervous system disorders, cardiovascular problems, endocrine and metabolic diseases, cancer and dermatology.

History: In 1758 Johann Geigy began promotion of spices and dyes in Switzerland. Following generations of Geigy's continued for a century and synthetic dyes were invented in 1859. At the same time another Swiss company entered the marketplace, Alexander Clavel joined, forming (CIBA). In the early 1900's, Alfred Kern and Edouard Sandoz established Kern and Sandoz in 1886 in Basel also to produce dyes. Ciba, Geigy, and Sandoz were forced to compete with the Germans and the Swiss formed their own cartel, Basel AG in 1918. The cartel was dissolved in 1951. All companies continued to branch out through the 1950's. In 1996, 45 years after the breakup of Basel AG, Ciba-Geigy and Sandoz recognizing a strategic fit, reunited forming Novartis, a $27 billion merger. 2000 In 2001 Novartis AG acquired a 21.3% of Roche Holding AG. In 2002, product approvals included Ritalin LA and Elidel. Novartis increased its shareholder stake in Roche Holding AG to 32.7% and combined its 14 generic companies under one name, "Sandoz". In 2003, 2007 brought numerous approvals. Taiga and Tekturna, which received awards for its technology innovation. In 2008 Novartis purchased Speedel biotech firm for $880 million.

Approximate Annual Healthcare Revenue: $32 billion

CEO: Daniel L.Vasella M.D.

Approximate Salesforce: 6100

Major Brands: *Aredi* tumor induced hypercalcemia, *Exelon* Alzheimer's and Parkinson's disease , *Enablex* incontinence, *Exforge* hypertension, *Gleevec* >$ 5 billion, *Femara*, *Sandostatin* oncology agents, *Foradil* asthma, *Diovan*, *Diovan HCT* >$2.4 billion, heart failure and cardiovascular agent, *Elidel Cream* atopic dermatitis, *Lotrel*, *Lotensin*, cardiovascular agents, *Lescol*, *Lescol XL* cholesterol, *Lamisil* fungal infections, *Miacalcin* postmenopausal osteoporosis, *Myfortic* renal transplant rejection, *Sandostatin*, *Neoral* >$2 billion, immunosuppressant agents, *Reclast* Paget's disease, *Rescula* glaucoma, *Focalin*, *Ritalin*, *Ritalin LA*, *Ritalin SR* ADD, ADHD, *Stalevo* Parkinson's disease, *Starlix* type 2 diabetes, *Tasigna* leukemia, *Texturna HCT* hypertension, *Trileptal* epilepsy, *Visudyne* macular degeneration, *Vivelle* postmenopausal osteoporosis, *Xolair* allergic rhinitis/asthma, *Zometa* malignancy hypercalcemia.

Pipeline: *Apligraf* wounds, *Cataflam* migraines, *Certican* organ rejection, *Prexige* arthritis, acute pain, *Femara* breast cancer, *Gimatecan* cancer, *Focalin LA* ADHD, *Foradil Certihaler* asthma, *Letrozole* breast cancer, *Provigil* daytime sleepiness *Zometa* bone metastases and numerous other agents in various phases of development.

NOVO NORDISK A/S
405 LEXINGTON AVENUE
STE. 6400
NEW YORK, NY 10017
212.867.0123
novonordisk.com

Summary: This Copenhagen, Denmark-based Company is the worlds leading producer of insulin. In addition to insulin, it produces injection and monitoring systems for diabetes care. Other therapeutic segments include human growth hormones, women's hormone replacement products and hemophilia.

History: The 1989 merger of Danish insulin producer's Novo and Nordisk formed Novo Nordisk. Engineer Harald Pedersen and brother Thorvald (a pharmacist) established Novo Industri in 1925 to manufacturer insulin and designed a syringe so that patients could administer their own injections. Within a decade Novo was in 40 countries selling insulin. In 1947, it introduced penicillin, its first product manufactured by fermentation. In the 1950's products such as Heparin (for blood clots) were introduced. In 1982 Novo was the first to produce human insulin. By 1989 it was the worlds number two manufacturer of insulin and the world's largest producer of industrial enzymes. August Krogh (winner of the Nobel Prize in physiology) founded Nordisk in 1923. In 1936, the company introduced the first slow acting insulin. In 1946, the company created a new product called NPH Insulin. 1980 has brought the Nordisk Infuser, NovoPen and Insuject Pen. After the merger Novo Nordisk introduced the NovoLet. The company introduced agents for depression, epilepsy and hemophilia in the 1990's. In 1999, NovoSeven was introduced. 2000 brought Activella and Vagifem. In 2002, NovoPen Junior was approved. 2004 brought approval of NordiFlex. In 2005 Novo Nordisk became the world leader in the production of Insulin and Levemir, NovoLog and GlucaGen HypKit gained approval. 2007 came an agreement with Sciele Pharma to market Prandin upon approval. 2008 brought NovoSeven RT and PradiMet.

Appoximate Annual Revenue: $ 4 billion

CEO: Jerzy Gruhn

Appoximate Salesforce: 3000

Major Brands: *GlucaGen HypKit* severe hypoglycemic reactions, *NovoLog Mix 70/30, Novolog, NovoPen Junior* all rDNA origin insulin's injection products,, *Levemir* long acting 24 hour insulin for type 2 diabetes, *Innolet, PrandiMet (Prandin & metformin), Prandin* type 2 diabetes, *Norditropin*, *NordiFlex* growth hormones, Turner syndrome, *NovoSeven RT* >$1 billion hemophilia agent (room temperature) , *Activella* menopause hormone therapy, *Vagifem* atrophic vaginitis,

Pipeline: ***Liraglutide*** Type 2 diabetes, and numerous other agents in various phases of development within the diabetic marketplace

NYCOMED US Inc.
60 Baylis Road
Melville, New York 11747
Nycomedus.com

Summary: Nycomed Group is a privately held pharmaceutical firm that is based in Zurich Switzerland and has a presence in over 50 countries and has become the number one dermatology manufacturer in the United States. Divisions consist of the Fougera the largest, which was founded in 1849, Pharmaderm and Savage Labs.

History: With companies that have had such a long history in the dermatology arena, Nycomeds history is now well established with such prior dermatology concerns as Fougera, Doak and Kenwood all organizations under the Nycomed umbrella. Fougera, Pharmaderm and Savage Labs (emergency medicine focus). In 2006 Nycomed acquired Altana placing Nycomed within the 50 largest pharmaceutical concerns. In addition in 2008 Nycomed acquired Bradley Pharmaceuticals increasing for their focus on dermatology for $450 million. Nycomed currently has the largest United States salesfoce focused on dermatology.

Approximate Annual Healthcare Revenue: $4 billion

CEO: Paul McGarty

Approximate Salesforce: 500

Major Products: *Pantoprazole*, *Preotact*, *Crofab* for snakebites, *Digifab* for cardiac toxicity, *Alvesco* asthma inhaler, *Zoderm* for skin dryness and generic agents.

Pipeline: *Doxas* COPD, *Zorbitive* short bowel, *Veltuzumab* for rheumatoid arthritis, *Atimos* for COPD, asthma and numerous other agents in phases of development

PURDUE PHARMA L.P.
1 STAMFORD FORUM
201 TRESSER BOULEVARD
STAMFORD, CT 06901
203.588.8000
purduepharma.com

Summary: Purdue is a privately held corporation engaged in the sales of prescription, OTC medications and hospital products. Therapeutic areas include pain, chronic asthma, relief of constipation.

History: In 1892, Dr. John Purdue Gray and George Grederick Bingham start the company in New York. In 1950's Senokot and Cerumenex are introduced. In 1966, Purdue acquires Betadine the broad-spectrum microbicide. In 1995, OxyContin is launched. In 2000, Purdue's U.S. sales top $1 billion. 2002, Purdue Pharma announced the purchase the product, Colace. 2003 Spectracef was launched. In 2007, OxyContin is granted full patent protection after numerous generic challenges the past several years. 2008 brought three additional strengths to Oxycontin tablets.

Annual Healthcare Revenue: $2.5 billion

CEO: John H. Stewart

Approximate Salesforce: 600

Major Products: *MS Contin*, *OxyContin, OxyIR* >$1 billion sustained release analgesic, *Uniphyl* asthma, emphysema and chronic bronchitis. Non prescription products include *Betadine* antiseptic, *Colace* stool softeners, *Senokot* laxative, *Slow-Mag* dietary supplement.

Pipeline: Purdue's top priority is to continue to discover and develop new pain treatments, including abuse resistant formulations and with numerous agents in various phases of development

PFIZER INCORPORATED
235 EAST 42ND STREET
NEW YORK, NY 10017
212.573.2323
pfizer.com

Summary: Based in New York City Pfizer is not only the oldest American based pharmaceutical concern, but also the largest. The combined organization is established in pharmaceuticals, consumer health care, confectionery products, and animal medications.

History: Charles Pfizer started his operation in Brooklyn, New York in 1849. The company incorporated in 1900 as Chas. Pfizer & Co. Pfizer was pulled into the modern drug business when the company mass-produced penicillin during the war effort in 1941. Pfizer purchased the drug maker Roerig in 1953. Sales reached a total of $2 billion in the late seventies. Vital companies that developed ground breaking therapies now within Pfizer include Warner-Lambert, Parke-Davis, Pharmacia, Searle and Upjohn. During that period Pfizer released Zoloft, Zithromax and Norvasc, Celebrex and Viagra. Pfizer in 2002 brought Bextra, Relpax, Rebif, Geodon I.M. and Vfend. In 2004, FDA approval for Macugen, Caduet, Lyrica and Spiriva was obtained. 2006 brought Chantix, Stuent to the market. 2007 brought Selzentry and the acquisition of Encysive Pharmaceuticals and Serenex, a biotech concern.

Approximate Annual Healthcare Revenue: $45 billion

CEO: Henry A. McKinnell Jr.

Approximate Salesforce: 7,000

Major Brands: *Aricept* Alzheimer's, *Caduet* hypertension, *Cardura* hyperplasia, *Camptosar* anti-cancer, *Chantix smoking* cessation, *Detrol* >$1 billion, overactive bladder, *Geodon* bipolar mania, *Celebrex* >$2 billion, anti-arthritic, *Lipitor* >$12 billion, anti-cholesterol, *Lyrica* >$3 billion, epilepsy, neuropathic pain, *Macugen* macular degeneration, *Norvasc* >$3 billion, cardiovascular agent, *Rebif* multiple sclerosis, *Relpax* migraine, *Viagra* >$2 billion, erectile dysfunction, *Zithromax* >$2 billion antibiotic, *Zyrtec* >$1 billion antihistamine/decongestant, *Zoloft* anti-depressant, *Activella* osteoporosis, *Genotropin* growth hormone deficiency, *Selzentry* HIV-1, *Stutent* anti cancer agent, *Xalatan* >$1 billion glaucoma.

Pipeline: *Asenapine* schizophrenia, *Apixaban* deep vein thrombosis, *Capravirine* HIV, *Dynastat* pain, *Daxas* lung inflammation, *Axitinib, Sutent* anti-cancer agents, *Indiplon* insomnia, *Lasofoxifene* bone density, *Torcetrapib* cholesterol, *Viracept* HIV, *Zyvox* antibiotic and numerous other agents in various phases of development

PROCTER & GAMBLE
ONE PROCTER & GAMBLE PLAZA
CINCINNATI, OH 45202
513.983.1100
pg.com

Summary: Procter & Gamble has five main business segments, Laundry and Cleaning, Paper Products, Beauty Care, Food and Beverages, and Healthcare, the smallest of the five business segments. The pharmaceutical division concentrates on the areas of musculoskeletal, gastrointestinal and woman's health.

History: William Procter and soap maker James Gamble merged their businesses in 1837 to form Procter and Gamble. Nearly 150 years later in 1985, Procter and Gamble enters the healthcare segment with the purchase of Richardson-Vicks and Metamucil, a fiber laxative from Searle. The pharmaceutical division began in the 1980's with products Entex and Ziac. 1998 brought osteoporosis agent Actonel. 2001 Proctor & Gamble announced that its health care unit was its strongest businesses unit with sales up 14% over the previous year. In 2002, a once a week dosage form of Actonel was launched. 2004 brought a FDA priority review to PG's female testosterone patch. 2005 Actonel with calcium was approved. In 2006 P&G entered a collaborative agreement with ARYx Therapeutics to commercialize ARYx's agent for gastrointestinal disorders. 2007 brought a strategic alliance with Dong Wha Pharmaceutical of Korea for the goal of commercialization of molecules to treat osteoporosis. In 2008, a once a month dose was approved for Actonel.

Approximate Annual Healthcare Revenue: $6.9 billion

CEO: Alan G. Lafley

Approximate Salesforce: 850

Major Brands: *Actonel* >$ 1 billion, post-menopausal osteoporosis, *Asacol* ulcerative colitis, *Dantrium*, *Dantrium I.V.* spasticity, *Didronel* osteoporosis, *Enablex* reduce urinary incontinence, *Macrobid* urinary tract infections, *Macrodantin* anti-infective. Over the counter brands include Prilosec OTC, Metamucil, Pepto-Bismol and ThermaCare.

Pipeline: *Actonel* osteoarthritis, *DW 1350* for osteoporosis with Kong Wha Pharmaceutical, *AATU-7505* for gastroespophageal reflux disease (GERD) and gastroparesis with ARYx Therapeutics and various other agents in different phases of development.

ROCHE
HOFFMANN-LA ROCHE INCORPORATED

340 KINGSLAND STREET
NUTLEY, NEW JERSEY 07110
973.235.5000
rocheusa.com

Summary: This Switzerland based pharmaceutical concern is one of the worlds largest with over two-thirds of its sales attributed to prescription medications. The Roche family has retained a controlling interest in the company since its founding over 100 years ago. Therapeutic areas include central nervous system, infectious diseases, oncology, virology, cardiovascular diseases, inflammatory and autoimmune diseases, dermatology, metabolic disorders, and respiratory diseases.

History: Fritz Hoffmann-La Roche founded F. Hoffman-La Roche & Co. in 1896. Hoffmann sold Thiocal (cough medicine), Digalen (digitalis) and other products under the Roche name. Roche expanded and became the world's leading vitamin manufacturer. Roche continued to develop successful drugs such as Librium and Valium in the 1960's. Valium was the world's best selling drug in the early 1970's. Now a common practice, Roche became the first pharmaceutical concerns to co market another company's products when it agreed to co promote Glaxo's Zantac ulcer treatment in the 1980's. The company acquired the majority stake in biotech leader Genentech in 1990. In 1994, Roche purchased Syntex, solidifying its position in the North American marketplace. Pegasys obtained approval in 2002. Product launches in 2003 include Fuzeon and Xolair. 2007 brought Lialda, Micera. 2008 brought Mircera. Speculation of a full buy out of minority controlled Genentech also surfaced during late 2008 with an offer of \$43.7 billion.

Approximate Annual Healthcare Revenue: \$20 billion

CEO: Dr. Franz B. Humer

Approximate Salesforce: 1600

Major Brands: *Avastin* >\$3 billion anti-cancer agent, *NeoRecormon, Furtulon, Herceptin* >\$4 billion anti-cancer agent, *Boniva* osteoporosis, *CellCept* >\$1 billion, organ rejection, *Valcyte* viral infections with organ transplantation, *Kytril* nausea vomiting prevention, *Lialda* ulcerative colitis, *Lucentis* macular degeneration, *Mircera* kidney disease, *Pegasys* >\$1 billion, *Copegus* for hepatitis C, *Roferon-A* hepatitis B and C, *Tamiflu* >\$1 billion, for influenza, *Cytovene* HIV complications *Fortovase*, *Fuzeon, Invirase, Valcyte, Viracept* HIV agents, *Xeloda* >\$1 billion, *Xolair* asthma.

Pipeline: *Boniva* once daily, *CERA* anemia, *Invirase* new formulations, *Fuzeon* additional indications, *MRA* arthritis, *Pegasys* additional indications, *Bondronat*, *Tarceva*, *pentumomab* cancer agents with expanded indications and numerous other agents in various phases of development.

SANOFI-AVENTIS
90 PARK AVENUE
NEW YORK, NY 10016
212.551.4314
sanofi-synthelabo.com

Summary: Sanofi-Aventis was created with the 2004 merger of Sanofi-Synthelabo and Aventis merged. Sanofi-Aventis is the third largest pharmaceutical concern in the world and the number one pharmaceutical concern in Europe. The new organization specializes in four specific therapeutic area, cardiovascular, central nervous system, internal medicine and oncology. In 2008 Sanofi announced its plan to invest nearly $6 billion into the vaccine segment.

History: Aventis and Sanofi-Synthelabo both were created by a long history of mergers and acquisitions. In the mid 1800's Hoechst began operations and began producing pharmaceuticals in 1883 in Germany.
In the 1960's, Hoechst acquired majority control of Roussel Uclaf of France (pharmaceuticals, perfumes). Hoechst acquired Marion Merrel Dow of Kansas City in 1995. Aventis was created in 1999 from the merger of German company Hoechst and the French company Rhone-Poulenc-Rorer. Synthelabo was created in 1970 by a merger of two French pharmaceutical concerns, establishing itself in 1973. 1994, Sanofi entered the U.S. market by the acquisition of Sterling Winthrop. The French merger of Sanofi and Synthelabo (owned by L'Oreal) took place in 1999. In 2002, Sanofi-Synthelabo acquired full marketing and promotional responsibility for Ambien marketing partner Pharmacia (now Pfizer). 2003 brought Uroxatral. FDA approved Ketek in 2004. Menactra vaccine gained approval in 2005. 2006 Xyzal obtained approval. In 2008 Sanofi-Aventis offered a $1.92 billion bid for Czech generic manufacturer Zentiva.

Annual Healthcare Revenue: $37 billion

CEO: Tim Rothwell

Approximate Salesforce: 8000

Major Brands: *Allegra* antihistamine, *Lovenox* >$3 billion, deep vein thrombosis, *Elotaxin*, *Taxotere* >$2 billion, anti-cancer, *Ambien* >$1 billion, insomnia, *Menactra* meningococcal vaccine, *Plavix* >$3 billion cardiovascular agent, *Copaxone* >$1 billion, multiple sclerosis agent, *Actonel* osteoporosis prevention, *Avapro* >$1 billion anti-hypertension, *Amaryl*, *Lantus* >$2 billion, diabetic agents, *Ketek* antibiotic.

Pipeline: *Acomplia* obesity, smoking cessation, *Adacel* tetanus, diphtheria, and pertussis, *Apidra* diabetes, *Alvesco* asthma, *Genasense*, *tirapazamine* anti-cancer, *xaliproden* Alzheimer's disease, *osanetant* schizophrenia and numerous other agents in various phases of development.

SANTARUS INCORPORATED
3721 VALLEY CENTRE DRIVE
SAN DIEGO, CA 92130
santarus.com
858-314-5700

Summary: Santarus is a specialty pharmaceutical company focused on acquiring, developing and commercializing proprietary products that address the needs of patients treated by gastroenterologists and primary care physicians.

History: From 2001 Santarus signed an exclusive agreement with the University of Missouri for intellectual property relating to immediate release proton pump inhibitors. 2002 brought the formulation of omeprazole in which studies began. Phase III trials were completed in 2003 with the submission of approval for Zegrid.
In 2004 Santarus gained approval for Zegrid and the company became a public traded pharmaceutical organization. In 2007 with a co-promotion with Victory Pharma, Santarus began the promotion of Naprelan.

Approximate Annual Healthcare Revenue: $110 million

CEO: Gerald T. Proehl

Approximate Salesforce: 600

Major Products: *Zegrid, Zegrid Powder, Oral Suspension and Capsules* Proton Pump Inhibitor, *Naprelan* a non-steroidal anti-inflammatory agent, *Fleet Brand EZ Prep, Phospho Soda* bowel cleansing agents.

Pipeline: *Zegrid* over the counter dosage and several other agents in different phases of development.

SCHERING-PLOUGH CORPORATION
2000 GALLOPING HILL ROAD
KENILWORTH, NJ 07033
908.298.4000
sgp.com

Summary: Schering-Plough is a global leader in the areas of allergies, respiratory disorders, oncology, infectious disease, and cardiovascular disorders. The pharmaceutical division accounts for approximately 90% of the companies' sales. Schering-Plough acquired Organon Biosciences in late 2007. Investments in research and development surpassed $ 3 billion dollars.

History: Ernst Schering, a German chemist formed this company in the mid 1800's to provide raw products to pharmacists. In the mid 1900's Schering introduced Chlor-Trimeton (one of the first antihistamines), and the cold medicine Coricidin to market. In the 1960's the company introduced such novel agents as Garamycin, Tinactin, and Afrin. In 1971, Schering merged with Plough, Incorporated forming Schering-Plough. The eighties brought the acquisition of Key Pharmaceuticals. In 1993, blockbuster Claritin was introduced. In the 1990's Cedax, Uni-Dur, and Intron-A, Temodar, Tequin and Nasonex were launched. In 2002, blockbuster Clarinex, was approved and Zetia in 2003. In 2004, 2008 brought Asmanex for pediatric use, planned divestiture of its animal health business.

Approximate Yearly Sales: $8.3 billion

CEO: Fred Hassan

Approximate Salesforce: 3,000

Major Brands: *Avelox* antibiotic, *Asamnex Twisthaler* asthma, *Clarinex*, *Clariten*, *Nasonex* > $1 billion, for allergies, *Follistim* fertility treatment, *Integrilin* acute coronary syndrome, *Intron A* anti-cancer agent, hepatitis B and C, *Implanon* subdermal contraceptive, *Nuvaring* contraceptive ring, *Peg-Intron*, *Rebetol* for hepatitis C treatment, *Proventil HFA* asthma, *Temodar* brain tumors, *Vytorin* anti-cholesterol, *Zemuron* muscle relaxant, *Zetia* hypercholesterolemia.

Pipeline: *Acadesine*, Corifollitropin alfa, *Esmirtazapine* insomnia, hot flashes, *Golimumab* ulcerative colitis, *Noxafil* serious fungal infections, *Nomac/E2* contraceptive, *Vicriviroc* HIV, *Pegintron* malignant melanoma, *Temodar* I.V. formulation, metastatic melanoma, *Vytorin* aortic stenosis, renal disease and acute coronary syndrome, *Zetia* pediatric hypercholesterolemia

SEPRACOR
84 WATERFORD DRIVE
MARLBOROUGH, MA 01752
508.481.6700
sepracor.com

Summary: Seprarcor Incorporated is a research based pharmaceutical concern with a drug development portfolio focused on respiratory and central nervous system disorders.

History: Sepracor was founded in 1984. 1989 Sepracor embarked on a strategy of developing single isomers of many of the world's top drugs including Clarinex, Allegra and Xyzal. Initially focused on out-licensing discoveries to other pharmaceutical concerns with the success of Xopenex in 2000, Sepracor announced its decision to market its own novel discoveries. Lunesta and Xopenex were launched in 2005, Brovana launched in 2007, Omnaris AQ and Alvesco were acquired in January of 2008 and approval for Alvesco HFA came in September of 2008. In addition, Sepracor entered an agreement with Arrow, for utilization of Arrow's novel drug delivery technologies with existing products.

Approximate Annual Healthcare Revenue: $1.3 billion

CEO: Timothy J. Barberich

Approximate Salesforce: 980

Major Products: *Brovana*, *Xopenex*, Xopenex HFA for asthma/COPD emphysema and bronchitis, *Lunesta* insomnia, *Omnaris AQ* allergic rhinitis.

Pipeline: *eslicarbzepine* epilepsy, *Alvesco* line extensions, *Omnaris HFA* respiratory agent and numerous other agents is various phases of development.

EMD SERONO INCORPORATED
One Technology Place
Rockland, MA 02370
800.283.8088
emdserono.com

Summary: Swiss based Serono is the Europe's largest biotechnology concern and ranks as the worlds third largest. Serono's focus is in the three therapeutic areas of Reproductive Health, Multiple Sclerosis, and Growth Metabolism. Serono is the world leader in the infertility market. Serono has a presence in over 45 countries and a world leader in multiple sclerosis therapy. January of 2007 bought the purchase of Serono by Merck KG creating Merck Serono. Biotech agents consist of over sixty percent of Merck Serono's sales.

History: Serono originally established in 1906 in Rome, Italy under the name of Istituto Farmacologico Serono. During the war years, the company extracted insulin from beef pancreases. In the early 1960's, the first child to be conceived using infertility agent Pergonal was born. Expansion of the company outside Italy started in the early 1970's in the U.S. with Serono Laboratories, Inc. established to service the needs of the infertility marketplace. In the 1970's and 1980's Serono continued expansion into numerous international markets and 1989 the approval of Saizen. The 1990's brought the launch of Serostim, and Gonal-F. Ovidrel and Cetrotide were launched in 2001. Rebif and SeroJet were introduced in 2002. 2003 brought approval of Zorbtive. Gonal-f-RFF Pen and Luveris was approved in 2004. In 2006, discussions about selling the organization arose and in December of 2006, the European commission approved the sale of Serono to Merck Kga, the world's oldest pharmaceutical company dating back to the late 1600's (not associated since the early 1900's with Merck of New Jersey, U.S.). Over $50 million was invested in Billercia, MA research facility with over 200 scientists. Currently biotech sales consist of 60% of EMDSerono's sales.

Approximate Yearly Sales: $2.5 billion

CEO: Elmar Schnee

Approximate Salesforce: 410

Major Brands: *Cetrotide, Metrodin HP, Pergonal, Profasi, Luveris,* and *Ovidrel* infertility treatments, *Crin* progesterone gel, *Gonal-F, Gonal F Multi-Dose and Gonal-f-RFF Pen* ovulation disorders, *Novantrone, Ebuitux, Raptiva* for *Rebif*>$1 billion, multiple sclerosis agents, *Saizen* growth hormones, *Serostim* AID's wasting, *Serophene* ovulatory failure, *Zorbtive* short bowel syndrome, *SeroJet* needle free drug delivery systems.

Pipeline: *Anastrozole* female infertility, *Erbitix* anti-cancer treatment, *Onercept* psoriasis, endometriosis, *Raptiva* plaque psoriasis, *Ribif* new formulations, *Stimuvax* therapeutic cancer vaccine and over 28 other agents in various phases of development.

SHIRE PHARMACEUTICALS
725 CHESTERBROOK BOULEVARD
WAYNE, PENSELVANIA 19087
484.595.8800
shire.com

Summary: U.K. based Shire is a global specialty pharmaceutical company. Shire currently focuses on three therapeutic areas, Central Nervous System disorders, Gastrointestinal and Renal. Currently the third largest pharmaceutical company in the UK and one of the fastest growing specialty companies in the world.

History: Founded in 1986, Shire Pharmaceuticals Group PLC has a significant emphasis on the treatment of CNS disorders. In 1997, Shire acquired drug delivery company, Pharmavene Inc. and the specialty sales organization, Richwood Pharmaceutical Company. This followed in 1999 by the acquisition of the German, French and Italian subsidiaries of Fuisz Technologies Ltd. In addition, Shire acquired Roberts Pharmaceutical Corporation of New Jersey to enter the United States marketplace. In 2004 Shire officially established its United States corporate headquarters in Wayne, PA and received the FDA approval of Equetro. Early 2007 brought the approval of LIalda Vyvanse. In 2008 Shire purchased Jerini of Berlin for $521 million.

Approximate Yearly Sales: $1.5 billion

CEO: Matthew Emmens

Approximate Salesforce: 560

Major Brands: *Adderall XR* >$1 billion, *Adderall* and *Vyvanse* attention deficit disorder, *Agrylin* abnormal bleeding, *Carbatrol* epilepsy, *Epivir* HIV, *Equetro* bipolar disorder, *Firazyr* angiodema, *Fosrenol* renal disease, *Reminyl* Alzheimer's disease, *Pentasa* ulcerative colitis, *Proamatine* orthostatic hypotension.

Pipeline: *Methypatch* ADHD, *Fosrenol* hyperphosphataemia, and numerous other agents in various phases of development.

SOLVAY AMERICA INCORPORATED
901 SAWYER ROAD
MARIETTA, GA 30062
770.578.9000
solvaypharmaceuticals-us.com

Summary: Solvay is based in Brussels, Belgium. Solvay produces numerous plastic compounds for construction and auto industries. Solvay' customers are manufacturers and commercial businesses operating in areas of construction, consumer and capital goods and services sectors. Plastics account for more than half of the corporation's revenue. The pharmaceutical division accounts for 25% of Solvay's total revenue. In the United States, the company operates through Solvay Pharmaceuticals, Inc.

History: Ernest Solvay discovered Solvay in 1863. Solvay had developed a unique process for producing sodium carbonate (soda ash). In the late, 1800's Solvay had soda ash plants in most of Europe and became the world's leading producer. In the fifties Solvay started selling polyvinyl chloride (PVC) and in the seventies a range of polypropylene products including automobile parts, pipes and interior decoration goods. In 1980, Solvay with its experience in organic chemistry set up a separate health sector. Solvay acquired various pharmaceutical concerns including KaliChemie (Germany), Latema, and Sarbach (France) Duphar (Netherlands) and Reid-Rowell (USA) in 1986 (presently Solvay Pharmaceuticals Inc., USA). In 1999, Solvay Pharmaceuticals Inc. agreed to acquire Unimed Pharmaceuticals Inc. Solvay acquired hypertension product Aceon from Servier SA of France. Solvay markets Estratest and Prometrium with Duramed in the United States. 2000 brought AndroGel and the acquisition of Sintofarma Pharmaceuticals of Brazil. In 2001, Solvay acquired Marinol (Roxane Laboratories). Solvay agreed to sell U.S. marketing rights for Teveten and Teveten HCT in 2002 to Biovail Corporation. 2003 brought Solvay's acquisition of Cetrorelix from Zentaris, a German biopharma company. In 2004 Solvay gained approval of EstroGel and August of 2005, Aceon gained the indication to reduce risk of cardiovascular mortality in patients with coronary artery disease. 2007 brought an agreement to co-promote Simcor with Abbott Laboratories.

Approximate Annual Healthcare Revenue: $4 billion

CEO: Stephen Hill

Approximate Salesforce: 900

Major Brands: *Aceon* hypertension, stroke risk, *AndroGel* testosterone deficiency, *Creon Minicrospheres* pancreatic deficiencies, *Estratest* estrogen replacement, *Marinol* appetite stimulant, *Prometrium* oral progesterone, *Simcor* lipid therapy

Pipeline: *Aceon* additional indications, *Androgel* male adolescents with hypgonadism, *bifeprunox* antipsychotic agent, *Estratest* expanded indications, *Fluvoxamine* obsessive compulsive disorder, *Tedisamil* arrhythmia's and numerous other agents in various phases of development.

TAKEDA PHARMACEUTICALS NORTH AMERICA, INCORPORATED
MILLBROOK BUSINESS CENTER
475 HALF DAY ROAD
LINCOLNSHIRE, ILLINOIS 60069
847.383.3000
tpna.com

Summary: Takeda Chemical Industries Ltd. makes and markets pharmaceuticals, vitamins, food additives, bulk vitamins and chemical products. Headquartered in Lincolnshire, IL, TPNA is a wholly owned U.S. subsidiary established in 1998, of Takeda Pharmaceutical Company Limited, Japans largest pharmaceutical concern. Takeda Pharmaceutical Company Limited of Japan, is the largest pharmaceutical company in Japan with a history of nearly 228 years. Focus is on cardiovascular disease, central nervous system disorders, gynecological disorders, infectious disease, kidney disease, diabetes and gastroenterology.

History: Over two centuries ago in 1781, 32-year-old Chobei Takeda started a business selling traditional Japanese and Chinese medicines. In 1895, the Company established its own factory and became a pharmaceutical manufacturer. During the late forties Takeda produced antibiotics, cardiac agents, and vitamins. In the fifties Takeda steadily expanded its pharmaceutical business and even began exports to the United States, Russia and China. The sixties brought expansion into Asia, and the seventies brought expansion into Europe. In 1985, Takeda first enters the United States market by forming TAP Pharmaceuticals Inc. In the U.S. in a 50:50 joint venture with Abbott Laboratories. TAP began marketing Lupron in the same year, followed by Lupron Depot in 1989, and Prevacid in 1995. Established in 1998, Takeda Pharmaceuticals North America was created to take advantage of Takeda Chemical Industries' growing international pharmaceutical presence. Actos was launched as Takeda Pharmaceutical North America's first product. In 2008, Abbott and Takeda concluded the TAP joint venture.

Approximate Annual Healthcare Revenue: $10.2 billion

President North America: Mark Booth

Approximate Salesforce: 400

Major Brands: *Amitiza* irritable bowel syndrome, constipation, *Actos, Actosplus met* >$4 billion, Type 2 diabetes agent, *Duetact* diabetic combination agent, *Rozerem* insomnia, *Prevacid* proton pump inhibitor.

Pipeline: *Alogliptin* diabetes mellitus, *dexlansoprzole* gastroenterology, *Febuxostat* arthritis, *Medatide* chronic kidney disease and numerous other agents in various phases of development.

TEVA NEUROSCIENCE
901 EAST 104th STREET
KANSAS CITY, MISSOURI 64131
tevaneuroscience.com

Summary: Teva Neuroscience is the branded product franchise of Teva Pharmaceutical Industries Ltd., headquartered in Israel, which is among the top 20 pharmaceutical companies in the world and is the worlds leading generic pharmaceutical company. The parent company develops, manufacture's human pharmaceuticals and active pharmaceutical ingredients, as well as animal health pharmaceutical products. Over 80 percent of Teva's sales are in North America and Europe.

History: Teva is the world's largest generic pharmaceutical company based in Jerusalem. Using that revenue, they have acquired some early agents in development and brought several large biotech brands to market with Teva Neuroscience. Teva's business model is excellent, for it is one that generates the largest portion of its revenue from generics but at the same time brings innovative brand name agents to market. *Barr* become one of the first generic pharmaceutical companies in the early 1980's. In 2001, Barr purchased Duramed pharmaceuticals and their entry to branded pharmaceutical marketplace with its woman's healthcare segment. Seasonale was approved in 2003.
Teva entered the branded market, acquiring Azilect in mid 2006. Capaxone was introduced in 1996, now the world's leading treatment for MS. Teva pharmaceuticals acquired Barr for $360 million, making it's' depth in generics even larger and the addition of Barr's woman's health brand product line (Duramed Pharmaceuticals). In addition, in late 2008, Teva purchased Bentley Pharmaceuticals for approximately $360 million and CoGenesys, a smaller biotech concern.

Approximate Annual Healthcare Revenue: $14 billion (Teva and Barr)

North America CEO: Bill Marth

Approximate Salesforce: 600

Major Products: *Capaxone* >$2 billion for multiple sclerosis, *Azilect* Parkinson's disease (Teva Neuroscience), *Seasonale, PlanB* contraceptives, *Cenestin* estrogen, *ViaSapan* transplant preservation agent, *Trexall* arthritis, *Aygestin* secondary amenorrhea (Barr Laboratories, Duramed)

Pipeline: *Adenovirus* respiratory vaccine, *Cenestin* line extensions, *CyPat* prostate cancer (Barr Laboratories, Duramed), *Stemex* oncology agent (Teva Neuroscience) and numerous other agents in various phases of development.

UCB PHARMA INCORPORATED
1950 LAKE PARK DRIVE
SMYRNA, GEORGIA 30080
770.970.7500
ucbpharma.com

Summary: UCB Pharma worldwide headquarters are located in Brussels, Belgium. UCB Pharma has nearly fifty subsidiaries in Europe, North and South America, and Asia. UCB's fields of research and development are allergic/respiratory diseases, central nervous system, inflammatory disorders and oncology.

History: Established in Brussels, Belgium in 1928, UCB has developed from a chemical company to an international group active in the fields of pharmaceuticals, chemicals and films. In the 1950's, UCB has increased their focus within the pharmaceutical segment. The expansion of its own research facilities has resulted in the discovery of a variety of drugs for treating allergic diseases and disorders of the central nervous system. In 1999 UCB obtained approval for Keppra. UCB and Pfizer jointly promote Zyrtec in the USA, which reached the status of the most widely used second generation antihistamine. In 2004, UCB announced the sale of its Surface Specialties unit with the goal of transforming UCB to a pure biopharmaceutical concern and UCB acquired Celltech Group PLC for $2.7 billion. 2006 brought the launch of Xyzal. January 2007 brought the purchase of Schwarz Pharma by UCB 2008 and the approval of Cimzia, Keppra XR, Xyzal and Neupro.

Approximate Annual Healthcare Revenue: $4.6 billion

CEO: Roch Doliveux

Approximate Salesforce: 800

Major Brands: *Edex* Erectile dysfunction, *Cimzia* for Crohn's disease, *Keppra, Keppra XL* >$1 billion, epilepsy treatment, *Univasc, Uniretic* cardiovascular agents, *Dipentun* ulcerative colitis, *Elantan Long* coronary heart disease, *Lortab* pain, *Metadate CD* attention deficit disease, *Neopro* Parkinson's disease, *Zarolxolyn* congestive heart failure, hypertension, *Xyzal* seasonal allergies.

Pipeline: *Cimzia* rheumatoid arthritis, *Vimpat* anticonvulsant and other agents in various phases of development.

VALEANT PHARMACEUTICALS INTERNATIONAL
3300 HYLAND AVENUE
COSTA MESA, CA 92626
714.545.0100
valeant.com

Summary: Valeant Pharmaceuticals International has more than 4,400 employees around the world in more than 30 countries. Valeant focuses primarily in the areas of neurology, dermatology, and infectious disease.

History: Founded as ICN Pharmaceuticals in 1960. 1970's brought approval for L-dopa. In 2001 Schering-Plough markets ICN's drug Rebetol. 2003 ICN changes its name to Valeant Pharmaceuticals International. In 2004 Valeant acquires Amarin Pharmaceuticals with Permax, Zemplar. In 2005, Valeant announced the acquisition pharmaceutical concern Xcel's neurology products Diastat and Migranal. Late 2008, Valeant increased their focus on dermatology with the purchase of Coria Laboratories for $95 million.

Approximate Annual Healthcare Revenue: $900 million

CEO: J.Michael Pearson

Approximate Salesforce: 300

Major Products: *Dermatix, Efudex, Kinerase, Oxsoralen-Ultra,* dermatology agents, *Mesinon, Tasmar, Diastat* for seizures, *AcuDial, Migranal* for migraines, *Cesamet* neurology agents.

Pipeline: *Spirapril* heartfailure, *Aceclofenac* rheumatic disorders *retigabine* for epilepsy and other agents in development.

WYETH PHARMACEUTICALS
5 GIRALDA FARMS
MADISON, N.J. 07940
973.660.5000
wyeth.com

Summary: This diversified chemical maker's products include pharmaceuticals, consumer health products, veterinary products, and human vaccines. Pharmaceutical division Wyeth Pharmaceuticals focuses on woman's health, infant nutritionals, cardiovascular, neuroscience therapies, gastroenterology, anti-infectives, vaccines, oncology and musculoskeletal therapies.

History: Established in 1926, American Home Products acquired over 30 food and drug companies through the depression. John Wyeth increased its size and product line dramatically. Preparation H, actually a sunburn treatment was acquired in the 1930's as was Anacin. Canadian company Ayerst Laboratories with blockbuster Premarin was acquired in 1940's. Ayerst developed Inderal in 1960's. Acquisitions continued with A.H. Robins in the late eighties. In 1994, American Home Products purchased American Cyanamid (Lederle) for $9.6 billion. American Home Products introduced various new products in the United States, 1996 brought Effexor. 1997 brought Lodine XL and Prempro. 1999 brought Enbrel, Meningitect and Rapamune. In 2000, products launches included, Mylotarg, ReFacto, Prevnar, and Protonix. In 2001, American Home Products obtained approval of Effexor XL. In 2002 American Home Products changed the name of their organization to Wyeth, paying tribute to founder John Wyeth. 2003 brought approval of Enbrel Once Weekly and FluMist. 2004 brought approval of Protonix I.V. 2006 brought co-promotion with King Pharmaceuticals and Altace. Lybrel and Torisel gained approval in 2007. Early 2008 brought approval of Pristiq and Zyntha.

Approximate Annual Healthcare Revenue: $19 billion

CEO: Robert A. Essner

Approximante Salesforce: 4,000

Major Brands: *Cordarone I.V.* arrhythmias, *Triphasil, Lybrel* oral contraceptives, *Pristiq*, *Effexor* >$4 billion, antidepressant/anxiety agents, *Enbrel* >$2 billion rheumatoid arthritis, *Rapamune* prevention organ rejection, *Mylotarg*, *Neumega* and *Torisel* oncology agents, *Novatrone* multiple sclerosis, *Premarin*, *Prempro*, *Premphase* >$1 billion, hormonal replacement, *Prevnar* >$2 billion, pneumococcal disease vaccine, *Protonix* >$2 billion ulcers/heartburn, *Torisel* renal cancer, *Rapamune* organ rejection, *Xyntha* hemophilia A, *Zosyn* antibiotic and numerous vaccines.

Pipeline: *Alesse* acne, *Bapineuzumab* Alzheimer's disease, *Bazedoifene/CE* osteoporosis, *Bifeprumox* schizophrenia, *Tanaproget* contraceptive's, *Tygacil* antibiotic and numerous other agents in various phases of development

Contract Sales Organizations

Contract sales organizations (CSO's) have been well established in the pharmaceutical arena. Recognized as a solid business strategy, there are numerous CSO's that are within the industry. Below are the largest organizations that one will most likely encounter. The strategy is simple, a traditional pharmaceutical/biotech organization can simply plug in from 25-2500 trained and experienced pharmaceutical representatives in a matter of weeks. As tighter margins and flexibility become an ever increasing demand, this will probably be one of the largest and fastest growing segments within all of pharmaceutical sales. This will create the demand for representatives to retain and keep their staff, which in turn will lead to increased salaries and benefit packages. Below are a few reasons of a pharmaceutical/biotech company may elect to enter a contract with a CSO:

1) A traditional pharmaceutical company wants to increase their salesforce for an unexpected product approval or product purchase, yet they have downsized over the last two years and require a larger salesforce immediately.
2) A prescription drug is moving to over-the-counter (OTC) status and requires a separate sales force.
3) One of the two to three hundred pharmaceutical-biotech companies involved in research and development sees a promising molecule and decides to establish their own salesforce by using a CSO. This is reducing the start up time of field sales force recruiting and setting the infrastructure in place.
4) A mature product that provides significant revenue and profit to the organization is not receiving appropriate promotional attention and "voice" in the marketplace requiring a CSO to increase the visibility.
5) A Region of the nation has special needs, for example a Managed Care Organization that blankets the Northeaster United States had a company's product in a preferred position. The pharmaceutical/biotech company would like to capitalize on this, with additional representatives in that area during the life of the products contract with the MCO, with a CSO contract.
6) A pharmaceutical/biotech company obtains a new product, but the owner of the new product desires at least 600 representatives selling the product as the primary agent. The company does not have that "voice" or pharmaceutical representatives internally to launch the product adequately, so utilize a CSO.
7) Numerous openings, turnover, disability time is hurting companies reach their goal, so they enlist a CSO to fill various territories in the nation on a "on call" basis reducing the 10% vacancy rate in territories across the nation.
8) An emerging pharmaceutical company has not reached the size to establish Account Executives to reach long-term-care facilities. Special CSO's have groups by which to again access within 8 weeks to this market place, beer
9) An organization wants to use on a limited basis, twice the amount of representatives, to validate that a major expansion, so a CSO will do a trial in a particular geographic region to confirm the business strategy.

As with a Pharmaceutical/Biotech Sales Representative, employee's of CSO's are in everyway similar to a traditional company employed representative. Training, compensation, career opportunities are almost identical.

Surely, every contract has its nuance's, whether time, products, integration with existing salesforces, etc. Years ago, the CSO segment was one that had some compensation differences and was often looked at as one to start or gain entry to the industry with not as stringent of a hiring process. This gap has closed over the last 7 years, as mentioned earlier, with some of the "big pharma" downsizings, many representatives have chosen a CSO, and so it can very well be possible that the CSO pharmaceutical employee has more years of industry experience than the traditional pharmaceutical companies own staff. Other than the aforementioned benefit of gaining entry to the pharmaceutical industry, CSO's often offer individuals various options such as flexible schedule's, part-time work, numerous company contracts over years, with varied disease states, that meets the employee's needs or desire in a position.

As always, the client is the reason for this decision and their response's are that they often are not aware that the individual is actually employed by a CSO rather than the companies products that are being discussed. Many times, the CSO representative's business card is identical to a traditional employee; compensation and "true" employer are a matter of logistics only.

A great analogy is to compare a CSO to a Hybrid car, which is becoming very popular, where two areas of power are delivering their efforts to accomplish the same result, better power (or sales), with as much efficiency as possible and at an improved cost savings.

Below is a small sampling of the larger Contract Sales Organizations operating today:

1) Innovex

Waterview Corporate Centre
10 Waterview Boulevard
Parsippany, New Jersey 07054
973.257.4500
866.331.7803
innovex.com
Note: 20 plus year history with over 7000 representatives working in pharmaceutical and biotech organizations

2) InVentiv

Vantage Court North
200 Cottontail Lane
Somerset, JN 08873
800.416.0555
inventivhealth.com Note: 20 year history with pharmaceutical industry

3) PDI

Saddle River Executive Center
1 State Route 17
Saddle River, NJ 07458
201.258.8450
800.242.74.94
Pdi-inc.com Note: 20 plus year history with pharmaceutical industry

Chapter 10
Commitment

When writing the first edition of Insight into a Career in Pharmaceutical Sales in 1998, it was first book of its kind, to address how to obtain a position in the pharmaceutical/biotech industry. With nearly 30 years of experience, 20 of those spent interviewing, including being the candidate several times. The objective has remained; give the pharmaceutical representative candidate a specific strategy by which to reach their goal. This was by learning from my experience as a candidate, a representative, a sales manager and numerous other roles within a pharmaceutical corporation.

Too often over the years, there was the candidate that if they just tweaked their approach to the interview it was evident, that they would probably have gained an "offer". Over these past ten years the number of success stories that have been sent are numerous and just outstanding. These success stories are surely the highlight of a day, if not a week, when a candidate secured a position in the industry and this book gave them a few tips by which they felt it assisted them. It is always you that does the work though.

As you follow the strategy that you have read about, keep in mind these words of encouragement and from nearly 40 years now of personal experience:

- It is common to receive rejections during all phases of the process, from networking to any stage in the interview process.
- Not everyone will be as determined in meeting their goals as you will, stay committed to the process in every single detail with each meeting.
- Be persistent and resolute: set yourself apart from those who will become discouraged or quit the process after being turned down by two or three companies (remember, the author, without one day of sales experience, when in the day a formal letter was sent out for that "rejection", versus hearing nothing at all, or an email today, had enough of these rejection letters by which to wallpaper a bathroom.

Stressed throughout the book is always asking for the position (the job) and with that every salesperson is taught to ask for action. Here are three requests that I asked of you.

The **First** is that when you receive an offer in the industry, you have reached your goal, live up to your promises starting with the interviewers and the company. Continue to apply the thoroughness and determination you showed through the process. Distinguish yourself; begin by sending brief letters to your new District Manager and any other District Manager, Regional Manager, Field Sales Representative and Human Resource staff with whom you have had contact with during the hiring process. State that you are excited and look forward to meeting the goals of the organization. Apply yourself meticulously during the various training programs in which you will participate. Professionalism at all times is the supreme rule. In addition, please email and tell me about your experience.

Bear in mind that the superiority of your performance is essential, for you are the example of a District Managers comprehensive hiring process, make your mark by excelling in your initial training. Yes, you will hear stories of when someone's behavior was not proper and they were sent home and excused from the organization, this does take place. Perceptions even wrong one's, can become reality in corporate cultures, and so give your best.

When training is wrapping up and your back in your territory, continue your research and networking; these skills will always improve your career. Focus on getting to know other sales representatives, managers in your territory. Always be gracious and smile to the other representatives you meet, swap business cards.

I learned from so many other company representatives. Information about physicians and the atmosphere of a territory by having frequent discussions with other company representatives. There is far enough business by which you can meet your goals, surely without taking an approach of not speaking to others in the industry. Of course this does not mean that you break anti-trust laws, like having any dialogue about your specific products, plan of action, pricing. Follow and know the regulations and laws of your industry. You will encounter many opportunities to meet others, whether those long waits in physicians' office, clinics, hospitals and seminars. Use these occasions to introduce yourself and learn more about your contemporaries, not only in your district but in your territory. Establish what they are doing that can be helpful to you. In future years, this person may be a co-worker, interviewing you, reporting to you, or even managing you. After three years in the same territory a representative and I were talking on a parking lot and they mentioned an enormous practice and asked me if that was my next stop. These two physicians and their practice, I did not even know existed (they had worked out of an older residential home). They were tremendous and one must remember our call plan in those days was the yellow pages. It was soon a great increase to my business.

Continue to always network, ask, do the representatives from other companies seem content with their organization, do they complain about their work, management (in person, not anonymously on line)? This information provides you continued insight, possibly you may be telling them about an opening at your company or the opposite in the future? These are opportunities that you never want to pass up, each day in the field.

Some metropolitan areas have professional pharmaceutical representative associations and I emphasize the word ***professional***. This is a great group to meet with and in my past gave much support to those early years of a career. You will not find that on-line, at least anywhere that I have found to date. Contrary to what many outsiders's believe, this is one tough career. It is lonely; you have few co-workers with you 93% of the work days in a year. No one will complain if you do not arrive. Many individuals are not cut out for this career due to some of these factors. There is a reason for these compensation levels, this job is not easy and there is pressure. But networking will open new doors and enhance your own career as people learn who you are. This is your career, your living, take care of yourself.

Secondly, I ask that you take this career path seriously and be a true professional. This does not mean act serious, wear a smile and as stated by a long time friend and mentor that is now deceased, "Don't take it too serious try to have some fun with it".

Keep away from the rumors and pessimistic areas. I am just dismayed and uncomfortable by some the postings I see on websites postings, as well as the so called moderation of such sites. Perhaps some areas grew so fast that the moderators are just not able to keep their site in order. Remember to work smart, but remain just as smart and professional off the job about your industry and company. Your gain from doing such an action will be minimal; your loss may be very everything. Talking to someone live, whether in your company or even a professional, it will be for less costly. One rumor of a product not being released, one incident that has the stock market make a drastic turn picked up by an analyst, and then you have a posting 10 spots down, you may be departing such a great income and position that you will soon realize.

It is hard to realize how someone would place their individual industry in such an unfortunate darkness by writing these topics in the public domain. Perhaps this is an opportunity by which one can "let off some steam", that an District Manager or co-worker does not assist or listen or recognize, but please, don't issue a "press release", which in fact, you are creating. Often this will even be referenced by future web searches. Perhaps it is youth, where one has not worked in a variety of other positions.

In addition with all the negatives of aging, comes one great thing, wisdom. Surely the work is hard, but a public forum with individual's names, administrative names is tactless, not only to those written about, but to the company and the industry. I know this is probably less than 5% of the workforce, so enough said.

Be thankful for an industry that though is not perfect (and no industry is), it is an industry that has truly saved and improved millions of lives across the globe, a statement, which no other corporate industry can claim in our history.

Why not promote your own industry by which you earn your living and support your family and yourself? That does not seem out of place? Quite honestly, that is what one should be doing; help secure your potential, you and your families' wellbeing, your standard of living, and your ability to secure a high standard of education for your children. Quite frankly, the industry did all those things for me.

As I am in the twilight of my life, I enjoy hearing from you. By doing this for 10 years, with having the same email address, phone number and website, I receive about 125 spam mails each day (ironically half of those for somewhat non-ethical pharmaceutical agents) and sometimes up to 50 plus voicemails per day, which I just can not take the time to listen to, or begin to hire a staff for. It is just impossible to communicate effectively as one doing this mostly for fun. Every email will be answered though, so please, use email. It is a policy I have had since 1998 to not take on a full-time job, and being on the phone for countless hours each week is too much. I do go through every spam mail (about every three to five days) and try to make sure there are not some legitimate one's missed, but occasionally a few get by, so if you do not receive a response, write another email with a relevant topic in the subject line (such as Anne Clayton or pharmaceuticalsales, question from reader). This will really assist both of us in more efficient communication.

Finally, be a leader and keep a few others on the right course with you. From the first weeks of training until the last days of your career, you will have choices, whether to take the high road and be a true professional or not. Keep me posted and I love any success stories, by emailing me at RxSales@aol.com. I have confidence that you will take the high road and "don't take it to serious and have some fun with it"!

Best of Success

Anne Clayton

Notes

Notes